The Unpunished Vice

Forgetting Elena: A Novel
The Joy of Gay Sex (co-authored)
Nocturnes for the King of Naples: A Novel
States of Desire: Travels in Gay America
A Boy's Own Story: A Novel
Caracole: A Novel
The Darker Proof: Stories from a Crisis
The Beautiful Room Is Empty
Genet: A Biography
The Burning Library: Essays
Our Paris: Sketches from Memory
Skinned Alive: Stories
The Farewell Symphony: A Novel
Marcel Proust: A Life
The Married Man: A Novel
The Flâneur: A Stroll Through the Paradoxes of Paris
Fanny: A Fiction
Arts and Letters: Essays
My Lives: A Memoir
Chaos: A Novella and Stories
Hotel de Dream: A New York Novel
Rimbaud: The Double Life of a Rebel
City Boy: My Life in New York During the 1960s and '70s
Sacred Monsters: New Essays on Literature and Art
Jack Holmes and His Friend: A Novel
Inside a Pearl: My Years in Paris
Our Young Man: A Novel

The Unpunished Vice

Vice

A Life of Reading

Edmund White

BLOOMSBURY PUBLISHING

LONDON · OXFORD · NEW YORK · NEW DELHI · SYDNEY

BLOOMSBURY PUBLISHING
Bloomsbury Publishing Plc
50 Bedford Square, London, WC1B 3DP, UK

BLOOMSBURY, BLOOMSBURY PUBLISHING and the Diana logo are
trademarks of Bloomsbury Publishing Plc

First published in Great Britain 2018

A catalogue record for this book is available from the British Library

ISBN: HB: 978-1-4088-7025-9; TPB: 978-1-4088-7026-6; eBook: 978-1-4088-7028-0

2 4 6 8 10 9 7 5 3 1

Typeset by Westchester Publishing Services
Printed and bound in Great Britain by CPI Group (UK) Ltd, Croydon CR0 4YY

MIX
Paper from
responsible sources
FSC® C020471

To find out more about our authors and books visit www.bloomsbury.com
and sign up for our newsletters

Contents

Preface	1
Chapter 1	8
Chapter 2	17
Chapter 3	31
Chapter 4	46
Chapter 5	52
Chapter 6	71
Chapter 7	79
Chapter 8	90
Chapter 9	109
Chapter 10	125
Chapter 11	138
Chapter 12	146
Chapter 13	169
Chapter 14	175
Chapter 15	194
Chapter 16	203
Chapter 17	213
Postface	219

To Rick Whitaker

Preface

Reading is at once a lonely and an intensely sociable act. The writer becomes your ideal companion—interesting, worldly, compassionate, energetic—but only if you stick with him or her for a while, long enough to throw off the chill of isolation and to hear the intelligent voice murmuring in your ear. No wonder Victorian parents used to read out loud to the whole family (a chapter of Dickens a night by the precious light of the single candle); there's nothing lonely about laughing or crying together—or shrinking back in horror. Even if solitary, the reader's inner dialogue with the writer—questioning, concurring, wondering, objecting, pitying—fills the empty room under the lamplight with silent discourse and the expression of emotion.

Who are the most companionable novelists? Marcel Proust and George Eliot; certainly they're the most intelligent, able to see the widest implications of the simplest act, to play a straightforward theme on the mighty organs of their minds: soft/loud, quick/slow, complex/chaste, reedy/orchestral. But we also cherish Leo Tolstoy's uncanny empathy for diverse people and even animals, F. Scott Fitzgerald's lyricism, Colette's worldly wisdom, James Merrill's wit, Walt Whitman's biblical if agnostic inclusiveness, Annie Dillard's sublime nature descriptions. When I was a youngster I loved novels about the Lost Dauphin or the Scarlet Pimpernel or the Three Musketeers—adventure books enacted in the clear, shadowless light of Good and Evil.

If we are writers, we read to learn our craft. In college I can remember reading a now-forgotten writer, R. V. Cassill, whose stories showed me that a theme, once taken up, could be dropped for a few pages only to emerge later, that in this way one could weave together plot elements. That seems so obvious now, but I needed Cassill to teach me the secrets of polyphonic development. In her extremely brief notes on writing, Elizabeth Bowen taught me that you can't invent a body or face—you must base your description on a real person. Bowen also revealed how epigrams can be buried into a flowing narrative. She said that in dialogue people are either deceiving themselves or striving to deceive others and that they rarely speak the disinterested, unvarnished truth. Henry James's *The Turn of the Screw* showed me how Chinese-box narrators can destabilize the reader sufficiently to make a ghost story seem plausible.

Sometimes I read now to fill up my mind-banks with new coins— new words, new ideas, new turns of phrase. From Joyce Carol Oates I learned to alternate italicized passages of mad thought with sentences in Roman type narrating and describing in a straightforward manner. To me the first half of D. H. Lawrence's *The Rainbow* shows how far prose can go toward the poetic without falling into a sea of rose syrup.

Each classic is eccentric. Samuel Beckett is both bleak and comic. Karl Ove Knausgaard is both boring and engrossing. Proust is so long-winded he often loses the thread of an anecdote; too many interpellations can make a story nonsensical—and sublimely interesting, if the narrator possesses a sovereign intellect. V. S. Naipaul's *The Enigma of Arrival* is both confiding and absurdly discreet (he doesn't mention he's living in the country with his wife and children, for instance; nor does he tell us that his madman-proprietor is one of England's most interesting oddballs, Stephen Tennant). I suppose all these examples demonstrated to me that any excess can be rewarding if it explores the writer's unique sensibility and goes too far. The farthest reaches of fiction are marked by Mircea Cărtărescu's monumental *Blinding* and Samuel Delany's *The Mad Man* and *Compass* by Mathias Énard—and there are no books more memorable.

If I watch television, at the end of two hours I feel cheated and under-nourished (although I'm always being told of splendid new TV dramas I haven't discovered yet); at the end of two hours of reading, my mind is racing and my spirit is renewed. If the book is good . . .

I rely on other writers and experienced readers to guide me to the good books. Yiyun Li told me to read Rebecca West's *The Fountain Overflows*. I'll always be grateful to her. My husband, the writer Michael Carroll, lent me Richard Yates's *The Easter Parade* and Joy Williams's stories in *Honored Guest*. The novelist and essayist Edward Hower, Alison Lurie's husband, gave me a copy of Elizabeth Taylor's stories, reissued by the *New York Review of Books* (not *that* Elizabeth Taylor, silly). Because I lived in Paris sixteen years, I discovered many great French writers, including the contemporaries Jean Echenoz and Emmanuel Carrère and the extraordinary historical novelist Chantal Thomas, and I spoke at the memorial ceremony of the champion of the *nouveau roman*, Alain Robbe-Grillet, who was a friend. Julien Gracq is in my pantheon, along with the Irish writer John McGahern.

I've read books in many capacities—for research, as a teacher, as a judge of literary contests, and as a reviewer.

As early as *Nocturnes for the King of Naples* (a title I stole from Haydn, who also contributed the title of my novel *The Farewell Symphony*), I was researching the odd bit. In that book, I liked the Baroque confusion between sacred and sexual love, and I threaded into it references to several poets and mystics. I also disguised poems (couplets, a sonnet, a sestina); I wrote them out as prose. With my *Caracole* I drew inspiration from the life of Germaine de Staël—but also from eighteenth-century Venetian memoirs I consulted in the library of the Palazzo Barbaro, where I spent several summers. Perhaps my biggest research job was my biography of Jean Genet, though I was helped on a daily basis by the great Genet scholar Albert Dichy. We read copies of the lurid magazine *Detective*, which inspired Genet at several junctures; old copies were stored in the basement of Gallimard. I read the semi-gay Montmartre novels (such as *Jésus-la-Caille* by Francis Carco) that Genet surpassed; we consulted everything we could find in print about the Black Panthers. I found a store on lower Broadway that sold political posters and other ephemera. Since it was the first major Genet biography, we interviewed hundreds of people he'd known. And all this was before Google or the Internet. For my other two biographies (short ones on Proust and Arthur Rimbaud) I did no original research, though I had to read the enormous secondary literature on each writer; much of my work was done at the main Princeton library.

For my novel *Fanny*, about the abolitionist Frances Wright and Frances Trollope, the mother of the novelist, I was living in London and working every day in the then-new British Library at St. Pancras in 2001; I read endless books about America in the 1820s, crossing the Atlantic, slavery, Jefferson, what people wore and ate; of course I read each of my two ladies' books. I loved ordering up the day's books and waiting for them to arrive at my station. I loved passing teatime in the library cafeteria. I never got up the courage to say hello to anyone—but that, too, felt very English.

When I wrote my Stephen Crane novel, *Hotel de Dream*, I was a fellow of the Cullman Center at the Forty-Second Street library. I had millions of books at my disposal, hundreds of images of New York in the 1890s, even a complete set of menus for the period. Research librarians were at my disposal; I asked one, Warren Platt, to tell me how much a mediocre life-size marble statue would have cost in the 1890s—he studied the *Stonecutter's Manual* and auction catalogs of the day. I read newspaper accounts on microfilm of a bar raid of the first New York gay bar, the Slide on Bleecker. I read the biography of Giuseppe Piccirilli, who became a character; he was the man who'd sculpted the lions in front of the library. Even in my latest novel, I had a character who forges paintings by Salvador Dali; I had to bone up on art forgeries.

I love research, and in my next life I want to be a librarian.

I've taught creative writing (and occasionally literature courses for writers) since the mid-1970s at Yale, Johns Hopkins, Columbia, New York University, Brown, and Princeton, among other schools. Even in workshops we read published stories by celebrated living writers— Richard Ford, Ann Beattie, Joy Williams, Richard Bausch, and dozens of others, including stories by Deborah Eisenberg and Lorrie Moore, the best of the bunch. People assume that college kids are on the cutting edge of contemporary fiction, but if you want to know what's happening, ask someone thirty, not twenty. Undergrads are too busy reading about quantum physics or, if they're literary, *Ulysses* or *To the Lighthouse*.

When I taught literature courses for writers in 1990 at Brown, I tried to expose students to all kinds of international writing different from American realism. We read *A Hundred Years of Solitude*, *The Tin Drum*, *Gravity's Rainbow*, John Hawkes's *The Blood Oranges*, Yasunari Kawabata's *The Sound of the Mountain* (he'd won—and deserved—the Nobel Prize), Raymond Queneau's *The Sunday of Life*, and many others. Sometimes I felt I was the only one in the class who'd read the books. Brown, however, had a real avant-garde mission in both poetry and prose, and good writers came out of the program, such as Alden Jones, Andrew Sean Greer, and Ben Marcus, author of *The Age of Wire and String*.

I've judged many literary contests. For the Booker in 1989 (the year Kazuo Ishiguro won for *The Remains of the Day*), I had to read 130 books, but since I'd lived in France so many years I read them cynically *à la diagonal* (very rapidly, or only the first third); the other judges, being English, took the job much more seriously. I remember my fellow judge David Profumo saying of a particular title, "Wait till you read it a second time." I think Ishiguro's novel was an ideal prize candidate because it was short and very high-concept—the plot was easy to retain and summarize. I judged the PEN/Diamonstein-Spielvogel Award for the Art of the Essay. For several years I was on the prize committee of the American Academy of Arts and Letters, and for almost a decade I've been a judge for the Premio Gregor von Rezzori, an award given to the best book in any language translated into Italian that year (not the best translation, but the best book), though I read them in French or English. This job has led me to read a whole host of books written in Chinese, Arabic, German, Rumanian, and so on. Cărtărescu's *Blinding* is the best book I read for the contest.

Almost every literary gay book gets sent to me for a blurb, and I've become a true "blurb slut." It's a bit like being a loose woman; everyone mocks you for your liberality—and everyone wants at least one date with you. I like to help first-time authors (if I admire their work), but serious writers aren't supposed to be so generous with their favors. Now that I'm old I turn down most manuscripts, and I always remind publishers that I might not like their new books if I do read them. A good blurb is pithy, phrased unforgettably, at once precise and a statement that makes broad claims for the book.

Reading books by friends is a special problem. They usually want a review, not a mere blurb. If I have mixed feelings about a friend's book, I phone him or her rather than write something. In a conversation one can judge how honest the writer wants you to be. He or she will clam up right away or press for a fuller statement. Sometimes I give writers reports as I read along; most writers can't wait for a week to get a full report.

I've written hundreds of book reviews, and I always overdo it. I feel obliged to read several other books by the same author—if not the collected works. A review should summarize the subject if not the plot, give a sample of the prose, relate this book to other relevant ones, and, most important, say whether it's good or bad. Of course a long review in the *New York Review* becomes an essay. All reviews take three times more effort than one foresees—at least for an American, slow-witted and thick-tongued as we are, and so unused to having a sharp, biting opinion. I remember reading in George Bernard Shaw's youthful journals something about spending the morning at the British Library and dashing off his reviews. Reviews, plural.

Reading books for pleasure, of course, is the greatest joy. No need to underline, press on, try out mentally summarizing or evaluating phrases. One is free to read as a child reads—no duties, no goals, no responsibilities, no clock ticking: pure rapture. Proust's essay "On Reading" is a magical account of a child's absorption in a book, his regret about leaving the page for the dinner table, even the erotic aspect (he reads in the water closet and associates with it the smell of orris root). Perhaps my pleasure in reading has kept me from being a systematic reader. I never get to the bottom of anything but just step from one lily pad to another. The title of this book comes from Valery Larbaud's 1941 *This Unpunished Vice: Reading*. The French supervisor of the translation of James Joyce's *Ulysses*, Larbaud read in many languages; he had his English books bound in one color, his German books in another, and so on. He inherited wealth, but his fortune became meaningless when he succumbed to a paralysis that rendered him speechless and motionless the last twenty-two years of his life.

Until something dire happens to me, I'll continue to read (and occasionally to write). Someone said a writer should read three times more than he or she writes. I'm afraid I read much more than I set to paper. There is no greater pleasure than to lie between clean sheets, listen to music, and read under a strong light. (I write to music, too—it cuts down on the loneliness and helps a nonmusician like me to resist and to concentrate.) I suppose everyone who has gotten this far in my book has felt the secret joy of knowing that a good, suspenseful book is waiting half read beside your pillow. For me, right now it's John Boyne's *The Heart's Invisible Furies*, dedicated to John Irving, whose books have kept me awake for decades.

Chapter 1

All my life I've been a tireless if slow reader, happy no matter where I find myself if I have words to look at, content to stand in a grim line in the cold, to undergo the worst sort of medical procedure, or to endure boredom if I can only read something—until I suffered a massive heart attack at the end of 2014. After open heart surgery, I was unconscious for three days. When I came to, the painkillers made me sound childish. I couldn't walk, I had no appetite, I slept all the time. And I had no desire to read!

In my twenties I'd known champion readers such as New York poets Richard Howard and John Hollander, who'd scribble down the name of any book that sounded intriguing and immediately order it, in a day when ordering wasn't just a matter of touching a key on a computer. Later I met Susan Sontag, again an encyclopedic reader, who would buy me (and many other friends) books she thought were essential to my education. She once said to me, "When you see a book you want, buy it instantly because you may never find it again." I remember she bought me Sergey Aksakov's memoirs of his childhood among the Cossacks—a thrillingly beautiful hymn to the simple life, mare's milk, and the joyous arrival of spring on the steppes.

In the hospital I'd pick up a book, but I couldn't concentrate. The letters remained stubbornly crisp and sharp and separate, isolated, resistant to flow. They didn't resolve into words, nor words into paragraphs. I'd always been curious about things to the point of forgetting my own identity. Sometimes I thought I was preparing for the high-cultural questions God would pose as the price of admission into paradise. I wanted to know everything; until about age twenty-five, I'd guess, I'd remember most information I looked up, an arduous process before Google. I was a fierce little autodidact, to the degree that when I was eight my father warned me not to say "I know" to my elders but to temper my pronouncements by preluding them with "I may be wrong, but I think I heard somewhere that Cortés conquered the Aztecs," a wimpish disclaimer that irritated and humiliated me. I was a know-it-all then who cared more about ascertaining the truth than about appearing humble. I loved the truth and had no patience with those who said, "There are many truths" or "The truth is always relative." For me, the truth was absolute; circumstances could not modify it, nor differing cultural perspectives dilute it.

But after my heart attack? Now I took pleasure in telling tall tales, never submitting them to any sort of skepticism. I went from being a fierce absolutist to a sly imp of the perverse. Perhaps what really happened was far easier to explain: I suddenly couldn't tolerate any ambiguity, struggle, puzzle, or potential conflict because I felt too weak, too vulnerable, too simple to sustain complexity. Also I was living in a world without event except the arrival of meals (which I couldn't bring myself to touch) and the punctual measurement of my "vitals." I, who'd always swum in the muddy waters of psychological nuance (the fiction I made and read), now couldn't endure its trying suspense, its destabilizing subtlety, its openness to conflicting interpretation. If I rejected narrative as words on the page—and I didn't even watch TV!—the repressed returned in the form of elaborate, hallucinatory dreams. Someone said, "Your brain isn't getting enough oxygen. That's why your dreams are so vivid and surreal." These dreams became my new reality; I could scarcely distinguish between what I'd dreamed and what I experienced.

When I had my heart attack and first lost consciousness, the floor seemed to rush up to greet me, almost as if I'd fallen onto it headfirst. Whereas before it had been patterned and intricate, now it had simplified itself into two interlocking but huge, glossy shapes—an oily, untopographical khaki-green shape joined to a tan shape. I had fallen on these strong shapes in unpromising colors cut out of linoleum; they were disgusting colors, big and flat and shiny, a Marca-Relli for nausea.

Speaking of which, the next thing I remember is vomiting an entire chicken dinner, not knowing where to direct the stinking yellow-and-green curds, and finally finding a crystal epergne, the sort of thing on which one usually displays pastry or food. Except I made it all up. There was no vomit, no epergne.

I guess I was taken by ambulance to a hospital, "stabilized," operated on the following morning, kept sedated for three days—but I have no memory of those events. I was intubated (does that mean I was fed through a permanent tube?). My husband Michael kept talking to me and stroking my face and saying, day after day, "It's time to wake up. Come back to us"—all to no avail. He also read to me from my own books. His ex-lover (and my dear friend) Patrick Ryan also kept calling me back.

When I did finally come to, I reported to Patrick that Valentino (not the dress designer but the silent movie star) had auditioned Patrick and me. At the climactic moment we had to twirl pantless, go into splits, and leave on the floor an inked impression of our anuses. Valentino had liked my impression more than Patrick's and called me back for a second audition, which didn't go so well. I can still see Valentino in his black sombrero and sideburns hovering over us. I was sorry to disappoint him and to exclude myself from a whole new career.

I promise not to bore the reader with more dream plots, but I did have one that seems so real I still feel guilty about not claiming my merchandise. I guess I knew we were someplace in New Jersey. In my imagination it was a wealthy town, like Princeton, but it felt more like Dallas. In any event, it was rich enough to have a Sotheby's and a deluxe mall. There I was at a sparsely attended auction. The item being presented was a small silver plaque, giving all the details about a man of the fourth century A.D. reputed to be "the stupidest man of his day." The work was being presented in a small theater with a gray velvet curtain, footlights, and white plaster scrollwork on the proscenium arch. Two of Valentino's henchmen were sitting in the orchestra pit, though they kept dozing off.

Suddenly the mechanism switched on, and out of a vent by the footlights long white swan feathers unfurled with a mighty rustle and whoosh, until soon they stood several feet tall, blindingly white despite the centuries. Nestled in a bed of swansdown was the silver plaque, which bore the life dates of the stupidest man of the fourth century.

Seated behind was an aristocratic Portuguese family. The wife boasted that she was a direct descendant of the stupidest man and dearly longed to have his plaque and feathers back in her hands. She bid a thousand dollars, but I doubled the bid—and won! Suddenly I was being told how to collect my new possession and what forms of payments would be acceptable. A runner from the house even snipped off a feather ball and handed it to me as a sort of gauge.

So vivid were these dreams that to this day I feel guilty about never having claimed my plaque. I even thought of googling all the New Jersey locations of Sotheby's.

I suppose I'm saying that the narrative urge, stifled for a month of not reading and writing, had to go somewhere, and where it went was into my waking dreams. I call them waking because I was often aware of the real space I was occupying, or some weirdly distorted version of it, almost as if I were seeing it through half-closed lids. I was transferred (or was I?) to a special wing of the hospital for an MRI or something, and from the next room I could hear a conversation. I'd had a music theory professor as a freshman at the University of Michigan in 1958, a composer named Ross Lee Finney. Imagine my amazement when I discovered that the low-voiced adolescent in the next room was Finney's grandson from Puerto Rico, where the great man had retired. The kid had a Spanish accent. He was married to a much older woman—"Some kind of wife," as he said. I repeated that phrase to Joyce Carol Oates, who was visiting me. "That would be a good title for a novel: some kind of wife," she said.

I thought how touching it was that Finney's grandson was trying to carry on his legacy. The hospital treated him, his "wife," and all the other Puerto Rican relatives with great deference, and soon I found out why.

Among the hospital's treasures was a sort of metal rod on which had been recorded in the 1930s a rare composition by Finney. It was like a rod in a nuclear reactor. Improbably, it was entrusted to me for my listening pleasure, although I had to stand in a soundproof elevator halfway between two floors to audition it in optimum conditions. I explained all this to Joyce's husband, a famous neuroscientist, and he was captivated by talk of this early sonic experiment, a way of recording an exact pitch and volume and timbre without any distortion. Admittedly, being forced to stand in an elevator between two floors was not conducive to the most relaxed listening, but it was remarkable that in the 1930s a sort of Library of Congress standard of purity had already been achieved. As I stood in the padded elevator I marveled at the stereophonic clarity of the recording. It was as clear as the headache-inducing high hum of a wet finger on the rim of a cocktail glass.

Later, weeks later, I looked Finney up on Google. He'd retired to California, not Puerto Rico, and died in 1997 at age of ninety, entirely forgotten, though he left behind four symphonies, eight string quartets, and an unfinished opera, *A Computer Marriage*. He tried to reconcile the twelve-tone system with conventional harmony through a theory of complementarity. I remember he taught us Béla Bartók's string quartets in a bell tower at the University of Michigan, where powerful speakers were hung from the walls of a single large room. Although the quartets sounded like a frightful if sometimes lovely mishmash to me, he was determined to point out that each began and ended in the same home key, a uniformity lost on my untutored ear.

I suppose that like any narrative, these dreams disguised elements from my real life, even my distant past, and served them up in an aspic of fantasy. For instance, in *Forgetting Elena* I used the familiar landscape of Fire Island as a solid setting for staging an invented tale. Places, of course, can be repurposed, but they usually juggle familiar landmarks, as Thomas Hardy did in his Wessex novels; "Wessex" is his name for Dorset (and eventually Wiltshire and Somerset and several other counties). Hardy can describe roads and sites with great verisimilitude and consistency because he has real places in mind.

There is a sort of violence in novels—a contest of wills, a conflict of interest, the very motor of the plot—which suddenly felt like an assault on my vulnerable body and the deep scar in my chest that showed where I'd been split open, filleted, and glued back together. Since I couldn't eat the hospital food, I lost fifty pounds, so I also had to adjust to my loss of a Jovian body. I was so disoriented that I pointed to my mouth and asked

Michael, "Is this my original mouth?" It felt so dry and gritty that I suspected it had only recently been excavated.

Freud may be right that as babies we can't imagine anyone else or picture a world that's larger than us—a sort of preplot universe of the absolute and unique ego. Like an infant, I was cranky and couldn't bear contradiction or challenge or frustration. I wanted to return immediately to the comforts of home, and I accused Michael of being a tyrant in denying me. Nor could I banish from my mind lurid scenes from *Whatever Happened to Baby Jane?*, in which I was the helpless Joan Crawford. Michael tried to interest me again in books by reading to me from Stephen King, someone whose work I'd never looked at; but it was precisely plot that I resisted, that I found jangling and frightening. When Michael suggested that when I got well, I could start writing again, I made a face and said something sour.

Finally I was released from the hospital, and Michael hired a car to hurry me home. What bliss to see all my thousands of books. If I couldn't read them, at least, like Jorge Luis Borges, I slept best surrounded by them.

My reading fast was broken when a handsome young friend of mine who worked for Archipelago brought me one of their latest publications, *A Useless Man* by Sait Faik Abasıyanık. I remember Ronald Firbank once said, upon entering a bookshop, something like, "Do you have anything in my line, you know, something dreamy and vague?"

That was precisely what I was looking for, and here it was.

First of all, I love anything about Istanbul, where I had spent many happy summers. And then I'd written a story set in Istanbul, one of my favorites, "A Good Sport," in which I invoked an opium-smoking (and thus unreliable) narrator who recalls his real (or imagined) affair with an Ottoman dandy. Finally, my favorite "dreamy" writers wrote about Istanbul: for example, the Frenchman who wrote under the pseudonym Pierre Loti, after whom a teahouse looking down on the Golden Horn is named. Loti's novel *Les Désenchantées* (*Disenchanted*), about a sensitive French sailor's hushed encounters with three veiled Turkish women who long to escape the harem, was a favorite childhood book that I discovered in fourth grade. (I was initially attracted to it because it was bound in white calfskin with embossed gold lettering, and inside it had several murky full-page black-and-white illustrations, each protected by a gauzy, translucent tissue guard, which suggested that the pictures were more valuable than they really were.) The women, it seems, may have duped Loti; in any event they ended up in Paris as literary celebrities.

I'd always been haunted by the idea of Loti, who'd sailed the world as a navy officer, was an officer of the French Academy, wrote the forerunner of *Madame Butterfly* in his own *Madame Chrysanthème*—just as Léo Delibes's *Lakmé* was inspired by his Polynesian idyll *The Marriage of Pierre Loti*—and installed a mosque and a medieval banqueting hall inside his house in Rochefort along the Atlantic coast. He was the King of Dressing Up, much given to exotic drag, as an imam, a pharaoh, a monk, or a French monarch. His descriptions of nature and architecture were much influenced by his contemporaries the Impressionists, especially Claude Monet. Just as Monet might indicate a hand with the unarticulated sketch of a pink mitt, in the same way Loti brushes in his figures with a blur of significant vagueness. Critics always praise precision in writing, and some great writers (Joyce, Beckett, Gustave Flaubert) are masters of clarity—but one of the great (and seldom mentioned) resources of fiction is vagueness. As Paul Verlaine says in his *Ars Poetica*:

> For nuance, not Color absolute,
> Is your goal; subtle and shaded hue!
> Nuance! It alone is what lets you
> Marry dream to dream, and horn to flute!

We don't know what the furniture the ladies squabble over in Henry James's *The Spoils of Poynton* looks like. James doesn't talk Chippendale or Tudor—instead he evokes: "The shimmer of wrought substances spent itself in the brightness; the old golds and brasses, old ivories and bronzes, the fresh old tapestries and deep old damasks threw out a radiance in which the poor woman saw in solution all her old loves and patiences, all her old tricks and triumphs." The moralized vague, the unspecified, has the advantage of being incontestable. If you say "She owned a beautiful painting," no one can challenge you. If you say "She owned a Modigliani," half your readers will say "Ick." Vagueness also, in the case of Loti (the genitive of *lotus*, just as Cocteau is the plural of *cocktail*) or Sait Faik, has a strong note of imprecise melancholic charm, as lapsang tastes of smoke. Sait Faik sets scenes in nearly empty Golden Horn teahouses on a snowy night, or plays off one old man in a café against another, who's certain the stranger has stolen his valuable amber prayer beads. Or he gives us two rough workingmen who share a rented room for economy's sake: they are secretly in love with one another, though they dare not admit it. They are even more reticent than the two Pakistani workers in Colm Tóibín's "The Street," a brilliant story in his collection *The Empty Family*.

The music of the general . . . Here Sait Faik writes: "I light my cigarette. I face the window to watch the heavy snowflakes falling. And suddenly I am shrouded by bliss. Where did it come from? I just don't know. How did it arise from such a dark mood? It fits me as snugly as a shoe on a beautiful little lady's soft foot. But what can I make of it?"

There's something mystic and beautiful in the ineffable. Vladimir Nabokov in his book on Nikolai Gogol states that Gogol was the first writer ever to describe the exact color of the shadow cast by leaves. Whereas Nabokov finds beauty in precise descriptions, I want to hold out for the poetry of the vague—no rough corners, no details that snag and arrest the movement of the spirit (if we admit there is such a thing as the spirit). We learn next to nothing from Sait Faik's paragraph, and even the queer comparison with the shoe "on a beautiful little lady's soft foot" is as zany as any Gogolian metaphor. Nothing is nailed down with adjectives except in the metaphors—and they are inscrutable. A beautiful little lady's soft foot? Really? And why all the snow? We mustn't forget that Orhan Pamuk's novel about provincial Islamists in Turkey is called *Snow*, the form of precipitation that effaces detail, the very soul of vagueness; snow, which eliminates color and thickens lines, puts a sheet of billowing cloth over everything definite.

In any event, it was the Turkish book of stories from the 1950s that was gentle enough to lure me back to the written page. Soon I began writing my own pages and completed my novel, *Our Young Man*. Writing at top form—and not at all vaguely but with thousands of precise details, though I was cloudy mentally and cumbersome physically—I kept thinking (to choose a grandiose example) of the nearly gaga Richard Wagner in Venice at the end of his life, writing the exquisite Parsifal's rose maiden orchestration though he was drooling on the page. Senile but gifted—we should all be so lucky.

Precision is easier to master than artful vagueness, especially now when, thanks to Google, novels are fact-heavy. We no longer refer to "flowers" but to particular varieties of roses. The whole valuable distinction between foreground (precise) and background (blurred) has been lost, and now everything is crowding toward the viewer, clamoring for attention.

Nevertheless, there is something to be said for precision (of description, dialogue, narration, metaphor, summary), since it is so lively and gripping. And there's a quasi-scientific pleasure in reading something that is both new and accurate; ah yes, that's how kids really do talk, pines really do look; a boy's ear really does resemble a dried apricot.

Chapter 2

When we're young and impressionable, we're led to embrace the books our first lovers love. In my case, I was still in college when I met Charles Burch on the Oak Street Beach in Chicago on Lake Michigan. It must have been the summer of 1961, because I was still a student and I graduated the following year. I was reading *Lolita*, and Charles was reading *Cain's Book*, a New York heroin novel by the Scot Alexander Trocchi. Both books are worth rereading today, though *Cain's Book* was definitely hipper. I soon found out Charles himself was shooting up, which scandalized and thrilled the petit bourgeois in me. I was twenty-one and he was thirty—an age difference that seems insignificant after one is fifty but which young people think is daring.

Charles was a lean, sexy ad man we'd say now was right out of the TV serial *Mad Men*. He even had his suits made by Meledandri, just like one of the characters. He lived in my mother's building on Chicago's Near North Side near the Water Tower, where I was spending the summer alone while she was in Munich on work.

He had everything to impress a twerp like me. He had American Indian blood and the Tecumseh nose and hairless body to prove it. He'd played the jazz trumpet and sired a son with a black jazz singer. He'd been hospitalized for schizophrenia at an expensive funny farm where he'd met and come out with a crazy concert pianist. He found everything about gay life appealing and sordid and outlawed; he resented efforts to normalize it. He wrote poetry. I remember one line about his pianist lover's embrace: "Darker and more glamorous than roses."

Charles worshiped Ezra Pound, and to this day (at age seventy-eight) I keep *Cathay* by my bedside and reread "The River Merchant's Wife," "Exile's Letter," and "The Border Guard." Although he was very masculine, he was also very expressive and would place his hand over his heart and almost swoon as he whispered Pound's beautiful lines, especially his repetitions like "drums and kettledrums" in "The Border Guard" or the strangely beautiful, far-fetched paradoxical simile in Canto IV:

> . . . The sunlight glitters, glitters a-top,
> Like a fish-scaled roof,
> Like the church roof in Poictiers
> If it were gold.

Charles would exclaim, "*If* it were gold—oh, Ed, is anything more beautiful!" He felt inferior because he hadn't gone to college (though he lied to his Chicago ad agency, Leo Burnett, that he had). He'd been committed instead of enrolled. The few times I knew something he didn't, he'd say, "Well, of course, you're a college graduate." I'd sputter and protest that college students were morons and he knew more than any PhD. (I was in love.)

The problem was that he could hold contradictory opinions depending on who pronounced them. Normally he was a good liberal and defended a woman's right to abortion. But one time we were in a bar watching TV and the pope came on arguing for the right to life—and Charles sprawled and draped his face on his arm, which was already stretched out on the bar, and crooned in his beautiful modulated tenor voice (which reminded me of Chet Baker singing), "Isn't that haunting and convincing? Of course, life is fuckin' sacred! Isn't he a beautiful old man defending life? A poor little baby's right to live?"

Charles wasn't really asking me for my opinion. I was bristling with liberal indignation that he should find that frightful old baggage in the Balenciaga gown "beautiful," but Charles spun like a weathervane depending on which wind blew hardest. He quoted a favorite Pound line: "They will come no more, / The old men with beautiful manners." He could intoxicate himself with his enthusiasms, and only now do

I wonder whom he loved, who imbued him with his taste for Pound. (And did he understand that Pound line?)

It was a respected but unusual taste in the 1950s. Pound was considered a traitor for his wartime broadcasts in Mussolini's Italy against American economic policy. More crucially to us snobbish readers, at the time he was ranked below T. S. Eliot and Wallace Stevens, "difficult" poets to be sure but not as unapproachable as Pound with his Chinese characters, phrases in Italian from Dante, and quotations from the Greeks in Greek. I started on the Eliot habit early; my stepmother gave me the *Collected Poems* inscribed "To Eddie—who is thirteen!"

Besotted as I was, I still had my own standards. When Charles enthused about Lawrence Durrell's *The Alexandria Quartet*, I dutifully read all four volumes and then dismissed it as "gaudy twaddle." No doubt Charles felt justified in his endorsement, since the whole culture back then was raving about its lush Orientalist evocations and its complex multiple perspectives, its "Cubism." Now I doubt anyone but a specialist can rhapsodize about prose so purple it's indigo.

Of course there are other writers once celebrated but now looked at askance. When I was young, James Gould Cozzens was rated as highly as Saul Bellow or John Updike, reputedly because there were two New York newspaper critics who loved him; after their retirement, he was forgotten. Sir Walter Scott—in no way a forgotten writer—was once considered the leading European novelist, even in the antebellum South, where a million copies of his books were sold (the same ideas of heroism and loyalty to the clan?). Today does anyone read any of his novels other than *Ivanhoe*?

Ten years later in New York I met Richard Howard, poet, essayist, and translator, and had a big friendship and a little affair with him. One day I went out to Princeton with Richard to attend his class. He always spoke with authority, and now he told his students, "The two poets with the best ear in English are George Herbert and Ezra Pound." I was gratified that my love for Pound was confirmed. And I started reading Herbert, refusing to be put off by his Christian piety. Recently, when I interrogated Richard, he confirmed his taste for Herbert but not for Pound.

If Charles in my late teens and early twenties shaped my taste for Pound's muted lyricism and cultural bulimia (despite his crackpot economic theories and his "suburban" anti-Semitism), another person, one I met when I was in my teens and fell in love with, Marilyn Schaefer, was an Apollo to his Dionysius. She too was seven or eight years older than me, and she too held strong opinions, but less aesthetic and more moral and rational. I first met Marilyn when she was a painting student at the Cranbrook Art Academy, a sort of college right across the street from my Michigan prep school, the whole complex an architectural gem built in various styles (modernist, Gothic, Japanese) by the Finnish architect Eero Saarinen. Now, sixty years later, I'm in mourning for her. As an adolescent, I wanted to marry her: before dying, she said we had the perfect marriage because we didn't tie the knot.

Marilyn was a slender, pretty Iowa girl who seemed unlike anyone I'd ever met—as original in her diametrically opposed way as Charles, as cool and logical as he was unpersuadable by anything other than glamour and lyricism. She was a product of the University of Chicago of Robert Maynard Hutchins's time, with its Great Books, its Aristotelianism, its Socratic teaching methods, its skepticism. She was always skeptical about the so-called free enterprise system, about Christianity, and about Freudianism. In fact she was the one in the 1970s, after I'd lain on the couch for two decades, who said over dinner, "I don't think I can continue seeing you if you keep mouthing that Freudian rubbish. It's as dogmatic as Catholicism, and it's destroyed your mind." As you can imagine, that made a powerful impression on me. Charles, of course, was deep into group therapy conducted by a celebrated and expensive shrink; Renata Adler, the author of *Speedboat*, wrote up the same group in the *New Yorker* and left all the members feeling famous and betrayed. Charles was in therapy because he wanted to go straight; he thought correctly that he'd earn more money in the ad business if he were perceived as heterosexual. With his dramatic naïveté, he asked me (of all people), "How do you go straight?" I said, "By marrying a straight woman." "Do you know any?" he asked. Yes, I did and introduced him to the talented, attractive Thayer, whom I'd known since adolescence. He married her, though his continued addiction to drink and drugs led them to divorce. Then he asked me to introduce him to another woman; this time I chose a straight girl, Pat, who liked only gay men. They married, and eventually Charles became sober through AA, which he embraced with his customary fanaticism. After many years and a move to Vermont, Pat fell in love with the (heterosexual) warden of a local prison—and married him! For his third wife Charles answered a personal ad in a community paper that read "Sadist seeks slave"—and the sadist turned out to be a female hardhat who worked in construction. Charles joined the Vermont chapter of TAIL (Total Anal Involvement League), and he and his new wife would hook up with other members. When that marriage failed, he married a psychiatric nurse with a shaved head—and that marriage was completely successful up until his death in a bike accident. The nurse had the unfortunate habit of nibbling garlic all day long.

Marilyn's ways and views were much less violent, but she was equally eccentric in her quiet fashion. She was a bisexual who once said she was more attracted to men physically but women emotionally; she could only fall in love with a woman. She once made a list of all the men and all the women she had gone to bed with. There were fourteen names on each side. Conveniently she went to an all-girls' junior college, Monticello, where a charismatic woman teacher conducted a great books course, which awakened Marilyn's desire to go to the University of Chicago. Marilyn wrote the obligatory essay on T. S. Eliot, a paper she herself considered quite "brilliant."

The University of Chicago was thrilling (despite the fact that all Marilyn's teachers were male). She learned to question every received idea—something reinforced years later when she attended summer sessions at St. John's in Santa Fe or a special summer program for University of Chicago graduates at Oxford. She acquired a lifelong allegiance to Aristotle; I can remember how flattered I was one long, hot, dull summer in 1958 with my father in Cincinnati to receive a letter from her, in which she wrote, "To use Aristotle's categories, what are you doing, thinking and making?" What she was doing was working for a socialist newspaper in Iowa doomed to a tiny circulation but determined to make an impact. What I was doing was dull rote office work for my father.

In the 1950s the three most heinous things in America were heroin use, communism, and homosexuality; through Charles and Marilyn I was already on familiar terms with all three. (Now the only unforgivable crimes in America are pedophilia, anti-Semitism, and "insensitivity" to "trigger warnings.") If I had Freudianism as a dogmatism, Marilyn's was the Soviet Union. She chalked up all the accounts of the gulag and the show trials and the mass extermination of kulaks and Jews to American propaganda and disgruntled dissidents. In the 1950s there were still few exposés written by insiders—just Victor Serge's *Memoirs of a Revolutionary* and *The God That Failed*, an anthology of André Gide, Arthur Koestler, Ignazio Silone, Stephen Spender, and Richard Wright.

Marilyn admired how women were trained as doctors in the Soviet Union and how examinations funneled the brightest students into higher education. The early Soviet hostility toward marriage also appealed to her. When I pointed out to her how homosexuality was branded by the Russians as a form of capitalist decadence, she murmured, "Maybe it is." She read Lenin and Trotsky and always refused to read Nadezhda Mandelstam's *Hope Against Hope* and Aleksandr Solzhenitsyn. She didn't want her illusions shattered.

In "progressive" circles in the 1960s we were accustomed to taking positions exactly contrary to our own interests. We thought all privileged kids should be sacrificed to the Revolution. We weren't averse to seeing the death by firing squad of our own parents and their "capitalist" friends. Our poor parents, who lived from paycheck to paycheck and never accumulated any capital, what with our steep tuitions and psychiatric bills . . . Although we loved avant-garde art, we knew that the "workers" detested it and preferred social realism (on Marilyn's socialist newspaper in Iowa they'd tried out some arty sketches, but the union members said they liked photographs more). The people had decided.

Marilyn, who certainly wasn't wild-eyed, declared that as far as she was concerned the Louvre could be burned down if it could save one child from hunger. Fortunately we weren't called on to make such choices.

Because of her militant atheism, Marilyn was hostile to the 1960s craze for Buddhism in general and Zen in *Zen and the Art of Motorcycle Maintenance*. As a rationalist who believed in method and abhorred Zen's sneaky tricks on the conscious mind, Marilyn was suspicious of all these trendy koans. In general she preferred American authors to all the foreigners the other art students were reading (the existentialists, and surrealist works such as André Breton's *Nadja*, one of the first novels to integrate photos, and the Comte de Lautréamont's *Songs of Maldoror*, the first really vile book I ever read). Marilyn preferred Walt Whitman (a poet worshiped now but who seemed to me barbaric then), whom she wrote her master's thesis about, or the rather dowdy but powerful *Sister Carrie*, the transcendentalists, or Sherwood Anderson. I was slow to follow her path. My mother, for pete's sake, warbled on about Ralph Waldo Emerson and his "wisdom." A follower of Mary Baker Eddy and Christian Science, Mother was no intellectual giant. As children my sister and I had attended the Church of Christ, Scientist and listened to the two "readers" dip into Miss Eddy's thoughts. My mother read daily from *Science and Health with Key to the Scriptures*, which she found as soothing as a highball after a hard day's work. Ideas were not to be scrutinized and debated but relaxed into like a hot bath. When I asked her if she believed in free will or determinism, she replied, "A little bit of both, dear," which doesn't seem so inane to me now.

What she took away from Christian Science was, fortunately for us, not its distrust of modern medicine but its conviction that evil is only a form of ignorance and that as individuals we are just waves swelling out of the ocean of humanity and collapsing back into it. Ideas weren't a challenge to credulity, as they were for Marilyn, but an invitation to exaltation. We lived in Evanston, Illinois, not far from the Bahá'í Temple in Winnetka, which was meant to be a synthesis of the world's major religions. The temple, white as bone, had nine incurving arches that met at the summit. We called it "God's lemon squeezer," symbolizing how all the world's religions were really one, an idea that I found repulsive. Buddhism and Islam the same?

I wanted to divide the world into distinctions; my mother wanted to globalize them (one of her favorite words was *gestalt*). Today it would probably be "the big picture." If she had a unifying, stereoscopic vision, I had an insect's mosaic eyes. I loved distinctions and felt that only in difference lay the truth.

As a Texas-raised Baptist my mother had a profound respect for religion but preferred Mary Baker Eddy's spooky vibraphone to Baptism's wheezing organ in "The Little Brown Church in the Vale," a hymn my maternal grandmother played on the organ. She was enlightened enough to think that after I grew away from Christian Science, I should choose my own religion, just so long as I had one. I went to Northwestern's library and dipped into Max Müller's *Sacred Books of the East* in fifty volumes. Zoroastrianism? I liked the war between good and evil, but I wasn't quite sure about leaving corpses out on a ziggurat to be picked clean by vultures. Taoism? Sounded good with the pronouncements of the Tao Te Ching ("Rule a country as you would cook a small fish"). I was only ten and was puzzled by the injunction to conserve your semen so that it would fertilize your brain. What did that even mean? Confucianism was plain dull.

My chosen religion was Buddhism, but the early austere kind, Hinayana, in which the lonely monk pursued extinction, an escape from the Wheel of Rebirth in a universe without a God or interceding saints. My mother drove me all the way to the South Side and the Chicago Buddhist Church. I seemed to be the only Westerner, and I was put off by its gaudy, cheerful polytheism, with its swarm of kindly Mahayana bodhisattvas who might lift us to a Western Paradise where we could achieve nirvana in comfort. Mother and I had lunch at the Wisteria Tea Room (my first sukiyaki!) and never went back to the Buddhist church. The elderly Japanese proprietors of the restaurant had only recently emerged from the American prison camps of World War II, and the place looked shabby and nearly deserted, despite a few deft placements of painted herons.

Buddhism was something I'd pursue through my boarding school on my own, which suited me fine. I was so tormented about being gay, and thus inferior, that I longed for the extinction of all longings. Typically, my worst fear about homosexuality was not that it would stigmatize me as a person but that it would limit me as a novelist. In those days I couldn't name a single great gay writer (that information was suppressed, and the panoply of biographies made possible by gay studies lay twenty years in the future). How would I be able to write about all the key Tolstoyan literary occasions such as marriage and childbirth, stunted as I was by homosexuality, which according to the Freudian theory of the day was a halfway oral house on the road to full genital maturity? In the same way, the male painting students I was meeting couldn't name a single modern gay artist, certainly none of the giants you were likely to meet (and brawl with) at the Cedar Tavern. You had to be heterosexual (and heavy-drinking) to wield a brush in those heroic abstract expressionist days. That Michelangelo and Caravaggio were queer was irrelevant. The Renaissance wasn't now, and back then men could be real men, apparently, even if they fancied a boy. (Charles used to say, "If God had meant boys to be fucked, he would have put a hole in their ass.")

Charles insisted on the glamour of gays as a race of cursed men and disliked the efforts of emerging homophile organizations such as the Mattachine Society to normalize their vice and start magazines like *One*. "Imagine," he would say, "a bunch of safecrackers launching a magazine called Rob." Then he would laugh in an exaggerated, unconvincing way, a sort of neighing produced by someone without a sense of humor. Nor did Marilyn ever take homosexuality seriously as a cause. For her it was just a bit of "sophistication" that swirled like gauze around names such as Marlene and Garbo; certainly it shouldn't be allowed to compete with feminism, which was fighting for equal pay for equal work and legal parity—a political fight designed to protect women in poverty, a fight long since won in the paradise of the Soviet Union.

Marilyn and I would argue for hours, which gave us headaches but hid from our own eyes how powerless and insignificant we were. What did it matter the direction we wanted the Revolution to move in (usually Jacobean)? Maybe people were less depressed in the 1960s than now because they imagined that what they thought counted. But there was little or no coherence between our true interests and the positions we took. We should have been for an aesthetic elite of homosexuals, but in fact we were as puritanical and utilitarian as the Soviets. We were on the side of workers (none of whom we knew personally), and we embraced social realism in principle if not in fact. Later I would know some real workers—heavily tattooed, hair worn in ponytails, motorcycle-riding, manga-reading, and pill-popping—and I realized they were as batty as we were, far from the standardized robots of our fantasies. Americans, rich or poor, were a nation of weirdos.

Ideas interested Marilyn more than me, though I thought I had a peculiar gift for grasping and synthesizing them, a turn for abstraction that I didn't take seriously since it came so easily to me. Perhaps this skill had been honed in school or in debating club (I disliked debating either for or against a position; that seemed jesuitical to me, and it violated Plato's rules for rhetoric, which demanded that an orator embrace the truth, which to be sure he could later elaborate through the arts of persuasion).

My first job at age twenty-two was as a writer for Time-Life Books, and I worked on a host of subjects, everything from the giant molecule to Japanese gardens. I wrote the introductions (signed "The Editors of Time") to many books, including *The Leopard* and Laurie Lee's *Cider with Rosie*. Everything we wrote was submitted to the editors above us, grizzled Korean War pilots with buzz cuts and an encyclopedic knowledge, who would routinely bounce our copy back and demand "fixes" ("More color," "Doesn't track," or simply "Huh?" written in the margin). We had vast acres of time in which to write and rewrite, which allowed us to become mini-experts in hundreds of subjects. While working on the American History series, I was endlessly perusing the multivolume *Dictionary of American Biography* (DOB), where I first read a short life of Frances Wright, the Scottish utopian visionary of the 1820s who much later inspired my novel *Fanny*. Wright was opposed to religion and marriage (just like Marilyn!) and thought children should be raised by the state. She started a "failed" experimental colony in Memphis where slaves could earn money and buy their own freedom. She was the young mistress of the old General Lafayette and asked him to either marry her or adopt her. When he refused both options, she dropped him.

In the 1960s, women at Time-Life were the researchers and men were the writers—a division that seemed as god-given to us as the division of black slaves and white masters to the Confederates. A researcher (often a classy Ivy-educated heiress named Auchincloss with a limo waiting for her after work) would use her Vassar-honed skills to assemble a pile of Xerox documents that the poorer, state-schooled male writers (often sort of schlubby midwesterners like me) would ingest, and then extrude the yard of research into an inch of stylized prose.

On the twenty-sixth floor of the Time-Life building there was something called the Morgue, where dozens of women clipped articles from newspapers and magazines from all over the country and filed them in labeled folders. When I was writing my mammoth biography of Jean Genet, I was no longer working for Time-Life Books, but I convinced a friend of mine to steal the folders on Genet. The hundreds of snippets about Genet's travels through America in the early 1970s would have never made it to Google. This was an invaluable source that my friend immediately restored to its usual place. For the first time I could trace Genet's many appearances day by day on behalf of the Black Panthers.

I once joined Marilyn in Santa Fe at St. John's College, where she and other students in a seminar discussed Plato's *Republic*, pro and con. I had such a historical bias that I was grumpy about all these kids debating these propositions as if they'd just been coined by a contemporary, also from Idaho. It wasn't elitism that prompted my objections but rather a sense that each of Plato's words was loaded and meant something different to him than to us. Years later my reading of (and friendship with) Michel Foucault and my reading of Paul Veyne confirmed me in my historical caution in reading ancient texts.

One of Marilyn's strategies for dealing with my characterizations of her (I wrote about her in my first published story, "Goldfish and Olives" in *New Campus Writing*, in my novel *The Beautiful Room Is Empty*, and in several other books, usually under the name of Maria, which she chose) was to say I was given to terrible exaggeration, to tall tales, to imaginative overdrive. It was the sort of perennial joshing dismissal typical of siblings ("Oh, you know George, always putting icing on the cake"). I resented it since I considered myself a scrupulous realist, a chronicler unusual in that I did not correct past memories so they would dovetail with more recent opinions. I claimed that I didn't update or whitewash my recollections but that they remained airtight in the various archaeological strata of my memory. Almost everyone adjusts the past so that it will cohere with the present and forgets embarrassing or painful past realities, but a novelist has a stake in remaining faithful to the undoctored script. So when I say I like vagueness, I certainly don't mean *factual* fuzziness. I want things—especially historical facts, dialogue, settings—to be as accurate as possible.

Now that Marilyn is dead, I sound guilty of score settling. But I want to emphasize she was the most exciting intellectual companion of my life and I loved her.

Marilyn liked fiction, especially of the nineteenth century, and she even took a course at Oxford in Anthony Trollope. When I first met her, she was reading Franz Kafka and Rainer Maria Rilke, two stars in the 1950s firmament. Her real meat, however, was books about politics, economics, history, and philosophy. After she died, she left me her journals, which were disappointingly absent of comments about me but contained discussions of her reading. She had a brisk, refreshing way of asking of a new book, "What's the gist?" or "What's the main idea?" thereby cutting through the sort of long-winded obfuscation endemic to American campuses, the kind that has won Judith Butler booby prizes for her strange prose. Marilyn would subject every theory to the acid test of her trained skepticism, her desire to clarify. I can remember when a fashionable anthropologist of the 1960s (Desmond Morris) claimed that the function of breasts was to transfer to the front of the body all the allure of the buttocks. Marilyn did no more than raise an eyebrow.

I could find her skepticism irritating and frustrating, especially when I was in full flight toward the latest crackpot theory; we had so many in those days proposed about sex, gender, intelligence, race. When it was still okay to discuss homosexuality as an aberration, there was a new idea every year about it: due to a birth defect, gamma rays, the consumption of hormone-laden milk, or nature's way of controlling overpopulation. I even remember the "gay uncle" theory that held there was an evolutionary advantage to having a doting but childless older relative who would selflessly help his nieces and nephews along in life, just as people now argue that the function of grandparents is to serve as babysitters. No matter how stridently these notions were argued, they were forgotten a year later. Marilyn was very good at poking holes in their logic or cooking up counterexamples; she was credulous only when it came to the Soviet Union.

Marilyn had grown up in Iowa among the descendants of a German-speaking religious sect, Amana—not unlike the Mennonites. Her oldest brother Dick always had his nose buried in a book or in the *Encyclopedia Americana* or in an anthology of poems of the American people. The three older siblings memorized poems (which Marilyn could still recite seventy years later) and devoured any book that wasn't religious or in German (Booth Tarkington, Charles Darwin). "Dick's the one who introduced me to *Catcher in the Rye*, which we fiercely identified with—curious since Holden's life was so unlike ours." Dick later became a Communist who studied philosophy in Vienna and afterward became a worker, a longshoreman in California. Late in life he converted to Catholicism and Republicanism. When he and Marilyn argued over the phone, she finally said, "I don't want to fight over religion or politics with my big brother, from whom I learned all my views"— and they agreed to disagree.

I suppose few people in my life have been as hypnotizing as Marilyn and Charles—and in each case my love for them made me want to espouse their tastes. Marilyn was cozy; one of her favorite adjectives was *gemütlich*. She liked the lace curtains in the windows of French concierges and bought herself some. She preferred homey restaurants to grand ones. She pretended she was a beginning cook, but she turned out some extraordinary meals, especially if they involved ham from Amana. She served her guests Manhattans and cigarettes because both had become forbidden pleasures. She had a beautiful kneehole side table that her father, trained as a carpenter, had made. Although her family had been rich at one moment, she never distanced herself from the working class and wondered why our snooty but impoverished friends wouldn't become part-time waiters or salesclerks. Several of her aunts had been waitresses. Amana was her baseline, and since Amana was socialistic or at least communitarian (where everyone earned the same), she looked at the whole world of capitalism and its codes with the blinking innocence of a newborn. She liked calm, unpretentious gatherings at her place, which she called "dumpling evenings." If she'd recognized your voice on the telephone, she'd say, "Hello, dumpling," in a slightly dismissive voice, or as if your dialogue was habitual, disappointing, and all too familiar.

Charles was so wired that I doubt if he ever registered Marilyn; she acknowledged him politely, coolly, the one or two times they met—cool, perhaps, because she was puzzled how someone so different from us could appeal to me.

I remember in college sitting in a coffee shop with a classmate. I told her, as ambitious kids will, "If I ever become famous, I'll have to attribute my artistic education to Charles." And to Marilyn, I might have added. Her influence was subtler but more enduring and pervasive. If I can write a reasoned essay, I owe it to her, whereas my romantic vision of gay life I owe to Charles. For my rambling style, I take full responsibility.

Chapter 3

I always wondered if my mother was sending me some sort of message when she gave me Romola Nijinsky's biography of her husband, the Russian dancer who had sex with men and went mad. I was twelve. Was it just that he was an iconic artist (ballet dancer, choreographer) and she wanted to stoke my artistic fires? Or was it innocent compliance with a sissy streak I'd already manifested? Or was it something more sinister— gay men never leave their mothers, and I'd become the man in her life ever since my parents' divorce when I was seven?

Although my mother worked as a psychologist, she was quite naive about what we called "depth psychology." Her specialty was brain damage and mental retardation, and she would have thought a homosexual male was a "glandular case" and a lesbian unimaginable. She certainly didn't subscribe to the then-fashionable "suffocating mother/ absent father" etiology.

She was interested in the charlatan Bruno Bettelheim, whose work was later discredited. She entreated me to read out loud to her from Bettelheim in the car on long trips to Texas, and every few pages she'd shake her head and say, misty-eyed, "Isn't that deep, isn't that uplifting?" If she felt truly excited, she'd drum the steering wheel with her hands and, a true Texas gal, croon, "Oo—ee!" A cattle call possibly.

I may sound disabused now, but at the time I was wrapped up in her myth of "great men" and what they could "teach us." Later, when I was writing gay novels, she thought of me as a "leader" and "spokesman" for "my people." I was thrilled to be able to provoke such ecstasy in her just by reading to her, as if mere recitation were collaboration. She would often say, with a vague hand gesture as if she were seizing a cloud, that she and I were uncannily close on a spiritual level. Everything she said about the spirit was a clear echo of Mary Baker Eddy. I can remember as a child going to the Church of Christ, Scientist and listening to the two readers (usually a man and a woman) standing behind lecterns and reading Eddy's *Science and Health with Key to the Scriptures*. They seemed vague to me in the squishy, repellent way I associated with "wisdom" double-talk, not the poetic, generalized, distancing vagueness I admired in some fiction but rather the spineless, unrigorous hogwash perpetrated by suburban preachers.

As an excellent student (if not exactly a prodigy) I sometimes felt superior to my mother. Then, one day, I picked up her master's thesis on children and religion, written under the auspices of a Dr. Arlett. I was shocked by how big and polished my mother's vocabulary was (she never used those words in conversation), how fluid and convincing was her presentation. Suddenly I suspected erudite depths in this seemingly mediocre woman.

For me, as for many kids, words had a magical (and sometimes sexual) aura, and I would look up in my mother's medical dictionary words such as *penis*, *intercourse*, or *homosexuality*, exciting words no matter how dispiriting the definition, exciting just because they appeared in print.

In those days there were few mentions of homosexuality in books, at least to my knowledge, marooned as I was in a Michigan boarding school in that pre-Amazon age. I would do all my homework in the afternoon while the other boys were playing sports so that the two-hour obligatory evening study period, when we were each confined to our room seated at a desk, I could devote to writing fiction.

I was very troubled about being a homosexual, and my first novel, written when I was fifteen, was a coming-out story, although I'd never read one. It was called, alternately, *Dark Currents* or *The Tower Window*. I wrote it out longhand (as I still do), and my mother's secretary typed it up. It came to over a hundred pages. When I first started writing it, I included the boy's thoughts (he was, significantly, called Peter Cross).

Almost immediately the fragile craft of my narrative started taking on water from so much introspection, and in my first act of manipulating point of view, I decided to exclude rigorously everything he was thinking. The reader had to intuit, rather clumsily, his hopes and fears from his facial expressions, a method that relied virtually on a system of interpretation as cumbersome as phrenology. Nevertheless that provided me with the necessary economy and speed to move forward my story of a teenager torn between a lovely girl his age and a sexy Mexican male college student. The girl rejects him, and Peter is forced to find solace in Pedro, a scene accompanied by pelting rain and gale-force winds (I hadn't learned yet about the pathetic fallacy, as when it rains because we're sad). Peter's "choice" of homosexuality wasn't an independent act but due to a paucity of external options, neither nature nor nurture but the short end of the stick.

As a Buddhist I was determined to root out all desires, including especially my "sick" desire for other boys and men. Only through ridding myself of all "hankerings" could I achieve nirvana and escape the endless cycle of rebirth. The odd thing is that the transmigration of the soul from one body (old and ailing) into another (a happy baby's) didn't sound so bad—in fact, it was what most Americans longed for. The idea that existence was invariably tragic didn't quite jibe with midwestern optimism, but I accepted it on faith. I could certainly subscribe to the notion that life ends in old age, sickness, and death—but later, later.

I liked Theravada, or Hinayana, Buddhism because it dispensed with God. You could be an atheist and a Buddhist, at least in the primitive sort of Buddhism that I embraced. I located this austere branch in Southeast Asia and was sadly disappointed when at my prep school we admitted a Thai kid who'd just spent, as all Thai boys did, his thirteenth year as a monk. His hair was just growing in. He had a long, elaborate Hindu name that he, as a Chinese speaker of monosyllables, could scarcely pronounce. "Samsaki" became "Sam," which also suited his American classmates.

I asked him what it was like to live in a monastery and meditate for a year. He said it was a waste of time, that he never meditated, and that the older monks were interested only in feeling up boys, playing cards, and telling fortunes, that they were a dirty, lazy, superstitious lot. They filled up their begging bowls at the school cafeteria. Later I would know pale, big-boned, tonsured white guys who would sit in the lotus position at a Zen "peace center" and then begin to list to one side from lumbar agonies and their "master" would thwack them back into the upright posture— but that was more Oregon than Thailand, which was obviously a more laissez-aller place.

I would meditate in my dorm room after lights out—and once I even levitated in the air! Though I concentrated on my breathing and tried to empty my mind, my thoughts continued to sizzle like contemporary jazz around sex and resentments and my schedule. Each boarder had his own room, a plan designed to cut down on buggery, so I would meditate in privacy.

But I was miserable. There was no one I knew who condoned homo-sexuality, much less accepted it, except one very hairy man I tricked with one night in Chicago. I was eighteen, he forty. He seemed so kind and self-accepting that I went back uninvited to have breakfast with him. He said he knew I would come back. I don't remember what he said exactly, but he had told me in bed I was all right and that what we were doing was a pleasure, not a sickness. He was a businessman from San Francisco, and I imagined his city was more progressive than mine.

And yet I suffered, and even contemplated suicide. I broke a bit of stained glass I owned and cherished (Jim Valentine, an art student, had given it to me) and held the cobalt-blue shard to my wrist, but lacked the courage to go on. I wept and moaned and resolved to meditate more. At age sixteen I began to see a colorful but cracked shrink who assured me that my homosexuality was just a symptom of a deeper disorder and fixed me up with a girl patient, an anorexic wannabe model who would peri-odically be hospitalized and force-fed, though she would tear the feeding tubes out of her arm and run up and down seven flights of hospital stairs to lose the gram she might have gained. That wasn't exactly the cure I needed, since she was also bulimic and her breath usually smelled of vomit.

In *The European Witch Craze of the Sixteenth and Seventeenth Century*, published in 1967, the English historian Hugh Trevor-Roper argued that it was precisely educated and intellectual men who believed in witchcraft and tortured condemned eccentric women as witches. The ecclesiastical authorities hoped thereby to save the witches' immortal souls from damnation, and several witches were grateful to them. This speculation explained to me why I, as a would-be "intellectual," believed so fanatically that homosexuality should be uprooted completely, whereas a more ordinary kid might have accepted it as a fun way of getting off or something. In my twenties I was impressed by Karl Popper's *The Open Society and its Enemies*, which argued that the intellectual's urge toward unifying, simplifying big theories was the origin of fascism and that regular-guy democracy relied on messy, incoherent explanations. Precisely to the degree that I was smart, I was able to torment myself for being gay—a notion that was at once flattering to my vanity and critical of my conduct. Like a Puritan divine sniffing out the faintest whiff of sulfurous sin, I could see my own abnormality in every gesture, every intonation. I read Freud, especially *The Psychoanalysis of Everyday Life* and *Civilization and Its Discontents* as well as key essays such as "Mourning and Melancholia"; that they were so well argued and sonorously titled made them all the more seductive. Other people might have Marx or Darwin, I had Freud. Yes, the universe might have been unimaginably ancient and without any moral design or purpose, and human beings might be on earth for a nanosecond for no reason at all (teleology replaced by random variation and natural selection), but our holy trinity of Freud, Marx, and Darwin could lend a rigor and system to all these meaningless events.

Personally I never allowed a bleak metaphysical chill to creep up on me. I'd already been inoculated by Buddhism and saw everything as illusion. But the one thing that did seem an unacceptable problem was my homosexuality. I believed it marginalized me and cut me off from the great human occasions, a disaster for a writer. It skewed my values and kept me immature, with no chance of obtaining Freud's prized and coveted genital stage. Whereas Freud had postulated that altruism was a sublimated form of homosexuality, I couldn't even cultivate that virtue, since from age twelve on I had been "acting out" (i.e., getting laid).

That was the heyday of psychotherapy and self-help. Erich Fromm was immensely popular with his bestsellers *Escape from Freedom* and *The*

Art of Loving. I devoured them though they struck me as Freud lite. He had a historical and sociological dimension. In fact, he was a neo-Freudian along with Karen Horney and Harry Stack Sullivan, both household names in my house. I liked Fromm's uplifting humanistic ethical bromides, but they did seem a letdown after Freud's much more dour and inarguable concepts, just as Sergei Rachmaninoff, though lovely, was a step down from Robert Schumann, say, and Raoul Dufy a sweetened version of Henri Matisse. I loved Fromm and Rachmaninoff and Dufy, with his cheerful boat scenes smeared with ambient color, but I was already a snob and preferred what was depressing to what was reassuring. I'd learned that reassurance was tawdry. Beckett, with his grimness, his complete lack of hope, was irreproachable, rated by a New York newspaper survey of American writers in the 1960s as the world's most esteemed author.

When I was fourteen or fifteen, I spent the summer on Walloon Lake in Michigan. My father, who'd already been alerted by my mother that I was having "object choice" difficulties, though I'd pledged her to secrecy, thought he could cure me through yard work. Without knowing why, I was subjected for weeks on end to the "yard work cure," which in this case meant loading up a wheelbarrow with the luxuriant carpet of brown pine needles that covered the lakeside hill my father's house was built on. The work was as pointless as a gulag task—and in *Forgetting Elena* I assigned raking pine needles as a lonesome, senseless, inexplicable punishment to the prissy, pedantic narrator.

My only consolation was that somehow I got my hands on Thomas Mann's *Death in Venice*, which I'd read in my bedroom for hours at night, stared at accusingly by the knotty pine eyes on the planks lining the walls. Teenagers, flooded with destabilizing hormones and a longing for elsewhere, are particularly prone to the seductive power of dark narratives. I gloried in this tale of a German adult on the Lido in Venice falling in love with the beautiful Polish adolescent aristocrat. Years later I saw Luchino Visconti's film, which choked me up though I made the mistake of watching it with a bunch of rowdy, impious gay boys who found it a ludicrous piece of kitsch. Years after that I skimmed a book about Tadzio. Mann's real-life boy (ten at the time Mann saw him) had become a prosperous heterosexual Polish aristocrat who resented all the fuss.

Death in Venice made me hope that there might be others like me, somewhere out there, possibly in the ritzy nearby community of Charlevoix. He'd be older, rich, devoted to me and my magical youth. I wrote a sonnet to him. The final couplet was about the tide obliterating our footprints, "rings of melting sands." I'd bought a rhyming dictionary that also had a guide to various poetic forms. I tried the most difficult ones, including the sestina and the triolet. At my prep school in Latin class I was translating *The Aeneid* and Catullus into graceless English verse. I thought I was a genius, but I would have traded in all my exceptional talent to be normal, athletic, heterosexual, handsome, and popular. I had no desire to be eccentric. If I'd been an adolescent in the 1980s, for instance, I would have opted to be preppy, not Goth.

Although homosexuality wasn't often spoken of, it kept creeping into Broadway plays as a perennially "sophisticated" subject. I heard dim echoes of Lillian Hellman's *The Children's Hour*, in which two women teachers are unfairly accused of being lesbian and then, strangely enough, become lesbians. Or *Tea and Sympathy*, in which a teenager is suspected of being gay until a teacher's wife generously volunteers to sleep with him. Or a stage adaptation of André Gide's novel *The Immoralist*, in which a French tourist, honeymooning in Algeria and stymied in his lovemaking to his new wife, goes off with an Arab youth. His succumbing to the boy is just barely hinted at in a bit of wordless business at the final curtain.

Gide was the tutelary god of my adolescence, and I immersed myself in his work. He wasn't a very good role model, since he made it clear that he was a pedophile, not a homosexual, and genuinely immoral. When an old friend, a Protestant minister, entrusted him during the war with the care and protection of his family, Gide abandoned his own wife and ran off to London with the minister's fifteen-year-old son, Marc Allégret. Gide's spurned wife was so angry that she burned all of his letters to her, which he considered his best writing. She thought burning the letters was the only way to even the score and to continue living with him. Years later, imitating her, I stopped sleeping with my French lover; it was the only way I could see to punish him for his childish cruelty to my previous boyfriend, dying of AIDS—the only way I could go on living with him. I doubt if he caught the allusion.

Gide's journals were a revelation, as was *If It Die*, his memoir. In it he encounters Oscar Wilde in North Africa, who credits himself with first urging Gide to live out his same-sex yearnings with a twelve-year-old Arab musician, though in fact Gide had acted out much earlier in Algeria. Perhaps I was most envious of Gide's wealth, which enabled him to practice the piano for hours and to travel somewhere almost every week. He was paralyzed when he sat down like a grown-up at a desk in his study; he was free to scribble only in a train or in a hotel room. How he would have loathed Michel de Montaigne's manner of writing, dressed in his best clothes, a footman holding a candelabra on either side, the great man approaching the page as the highest representative of his period. F. Scott Fitzgerald also liked to dress up for the page.

I was enlightened by Gide's way of mentioning his sexuality in passing while he recorded directly his conversations with his wife and his correspondence with novelist (and Nobel Prize winner) Roger Martin du Gard. His example of being open about his "perversion" left an impression on me, much greater than did *Corydon*, his defense of homosexuality, which argued that sex among boys (and with their adult lovers) was the best way to preserve the virginity of our young ladies—and besides, other primates do it and so did the ancient Greeks.

I admired Gide for defending homosexuality, no matter how foolishly, just as later I admired him for being one of the first progressive intellectuals in the West to denounce the Soviet Union and Stalin's crimes. Gide was fortunate that in Russia his guide and translator was an ex-Communist French friend who'd defected years before to Russia and by now was thoroughly disillusioned with Stalin. Whereas other foreign visitors were treated to mind-numbing factory tours (they'd never visited a factory in their own country) and met only party hacks presented as "distinguished writers," Gide had a thorough look at the barren, bloody landscape behind the pretty Potemkin village.

It was so strange (though it didn't feel odd) to be a midwesterner sitting in a Detroit boarding school reading André Gide, who'd only recently died. I loved everything French: I drank espresso on a forbidden hot plate in my room and listened to Juliette Gréco on my turntable during the half hour after study hall and before lights out, the only time slot when we were allowed to make noise.

I learned from Gide's journals that he'd rejected Proust's *Swann's Way* without reading it, on the basis that someone who'd written society items for a conservative newspaper couldn't possibly be a novelist of interest. He'd rejected it on behalf of the *Nouvelle Revue française*, which grew into Gallimard, France's premier publishing house. A few years later Gallimard had to eat crow in order to lure Proust back. I was thrilled when years later Gallimard published my biography of Genet.

I wrote a senior paper in high school on the Madame de Sévigné theme in Proust. I read Proust entirely in C. K. Scott Moncrieff's faulty but brilliantly fluent translation (an English classic). Of course I recognized that the most vivid character, Charlus, was a homosexual in love with the younger violinist Morel, and that many of the characters turned out to be lesbian or gay—though the narrator himself remained a mama's boy, neurasthenic but resolutely heterosexual. In Proust's pages I learned that through the secret world of homosexuality (what would later be called the "homintern"), one could rise socially, sleep with one's elders and betters, get beaten by male prostitutes in a brothel—and become sexually aroused by profaning and spitting on photos of revered friends and parents. Proust must have been one of the first writers to describe cruising and intergenerational sex, using elaborate but botanical and entomological comparisons as Charlus responds to the advances of Jupien, a servant. Nor did Proust have any clear idea of what caused homosexuality, except that he assured his readers it was accursed (much like being a Jew, which in real life he was, through his mother, though he seldom acknowledged it publicly).

One could easily (and too hastily) dismiss Gide's relentless pedophiles and Proust's sadists or gerontophiles or cash-masters as unhealthy role models for a teen in Michigan, but youngsters can plunder a text and find what they want in the margins. I found Gide's willingness to treat such a

39

forbidden topic at all courageous, just as Proust's way of revealing the hidden empire of homosexuals was an empowering show of force. In those days everyday American homosexual males were dismissed as skinny sissies; a real man could safely kick sand in his face or rob him. I myself had been robbed several times, powerless to call the cops since homosexuality itself was a worse crime than theft. So to read about the ways in which attractive men schemed their way to the top by manipulating older, wealthy "patrons" was enviable somehow. These guys weren't effeminate caricatures willing to be pushed around! And they were thoroughly (if not openly) integrated into society, not living somewhere at an isolated (if ultimately tragic) distance from the normal world. It was thrilling to read about a frightening, tyrannical gay social arbiter such as Charlus or a scheming, treacherous one like Morel—or magnetic, deceiving cruel lesbians such as Albertine, or dashing, aristocratic (and secretly gay) soldiers such as Saint-Loup. At least they weren't pansies or victims!

So much of the gay fiction of the 1970s that was considered politically correct (though we didn't yet use that term) took the gay couple out of the world, certainly out of the ghetto, which was stigmatized as poisonous. Even though progressive gays complained of John Rechy's bestselling *City of Night* because it reinforced the stereotypes of the hysterical drag queen and the macho hustler, nevertheless it showed gays living among other gays—an anthill rather than a solitary ant or ant couple. Even Larry Kramer's tedious, sex-negative, and much reviled *Faggots*, which was written to show how gay men were leading reckless and unfulfilling lives by hooking up so often (and this years before the advent of AIDS), at least had the unintended advantage of showing gays living together.

Other early gay books I read were what the French called "rosewater" romances, such as *Quatrefoil* and *Finistère*, and serious fiction such as James Baldwin's *Giovanni's Room* (in which, curiously, there are no black characters and in which we're led to believe a man is desirable only until he succumbs to a same-sex attraction).

The best of these books was Christopher Isherwood's *A Single Man*—precise, selectively detailed, compressed. The hero wasn't the usual stud or sad sack or sensitive youth; nor was the background a ruined castle along the French coast. In the vague-precise continuum that haunted me, it was very much toward the precise end of the spectrum. The hero was a middle-aged Englishman teaching in Los Angeles, grieving for his deceased lover. Although the prose is very lean, there's room for little meditations: on how we perform most of our daily tasks (driving, small talk, even teaching) on automatic; on how Americans are the least materialistic and most spiritual people on earth, living entirely on a symbolic level—in symbolic houses decorated with symbolic furniture; and on how the self assembles itself upon waking and breaks down in sleep or death. Although there's no explicit reference to Hinduism, Isherwood was an adept and even spent time in an Indian ashram—and the awakening and dispersal of George's identity is a secular parallel to the Hindu (or Buddhist) notion that the self is an illusion compounded out of various illusory elements (the five *skandha*s). Whereas most gay novels of the times provided an etiology and apology for the regrettable aberration, Isherwood avoided such explanations and plunged the reader directly into George's experience; whereas most of the novels of the period touching on gay themes (Gore Vidal's *The City and the Pillar*, Hugh Selby's *Last Exit to Brooklyn*, or Jean Genet's *Our Lady of the Flowers*) portrayed freaks, transvestites, criminals, or other marginal characters, George is solidly middle-class and respectable in deed if not in thoughts. Years later I met Isherwood and Don Bachardy, first in New York and later in Los Angeles, and ever since I've been a minor cog in the Isherwood industry (writing reviews or prefaces to his posthumous publications). He was lively company, charming, witty, and he and Don seemed to have a perfect mutual understanding, though the journals about the 1960s showed it had been a rocky relationship initially.

Over the years I enjoyed reading the first European gay novels I could find—Mikhail Kuzmin's 1905 *Wings*, Georges Eekhoud's 1899 *Escal-Vigor*, Umberto Saba's *Ernesto*, written in the 1950s; going way back, I relished Moses Hadas's translation of *Three Greek Romances*, in which one of the tales ends with a double wedding—two men and a man and a woman.

Why did books play such an important part in the formation of my sexual identity? At that time there were no "out" actors or politicians, and as a teenager I found it hard to meet older men who shared my erotic and intellectual interest. I was "jailbait." Or they had migrated to New York, Los Angeles, or Europe. When a daring young professor brought me as a nineteen-year-old to a gay faculty party (all Mabel Mercer and martinis), his colleagues at the University of Michigan were furious at him for this breach in secrecy. I was delighted by the witticisms that were bandied about, by the look of all these adult men in Brooks Brothers suits, the haze of alcoholic sweat bathing their faces. They were heavy-drinking and smoking, all slender and campy, for once not afraid of laughing too loud, lisping, or making exuberant gestures. In those days, as I was discovering, gays discussed authors on familiar terms—and as if all of them were gay or female. "Oh, Norma Mailer, she's too much in *Advertisements for Myself*, going on about anal sex. How come she knows so much about it?" The remarks were mostly idiotic, but it was so exhilarating to see the whole world of the arts as gay. We all laughed in complicity. "Miss Hemingway with her butch lesbian act shooting tigers, she's fooling no one. She's just a big bull dagger, nothing more." I got the inside scoop on "Miss Baldwin" from someone who claimed to have "browned her" in Istanbul. The insinuation that someone had once been sexually available served to excite us and denigrate him: "Leonora Bernstein? She's nothing. I've had her." There was something mildly creative, I suppose, about all these gender reversals (one young assistant professor was working on "William Cather" and discussed that frightful old butch, "Bertrude Stein"). In my short biography of Proust I once argued that the shift from male friends to female characters in *Remembrance of Things Past* was an act of imagination, a constant exercise of Proust's myth-making talents.

In my own writing I didn't feel the need to disguise men as women, though *Forgetting Elena* has a weirdly lunar straight-sex scene (the narrator, an amnesiac, doesn't even know what sex is and wonders if it's some sort of ceremony). Elena herself was based on Marilyn.

I wasn't a compulsive reader, nor was I as widely read as many of my friends; I feel slightly presumptuous tackling the subject of this book when I look at the overflowing libraries of people I know and hear their conversations. My feeling of fraudulence has diminished somewhat now that I've outlived everyone; just by dint of reading (no matter how slowly and without discipline) for many decades, I give the illusion of being well read.

When I was reading what could be called how-to books about gay life, it was all mixed in with the camp chatter of a previous generation that has all but been expunged from the face of the earth. Only a few diminutive old men, perfectly turned out and with a twinkle in the eye, can still switch genders or say something devastating, almost as an aside and intended to be heard only by wicked old-timers (certainly not by the blue-lipped puritanical young with their political correctness). "Where did that young man go? Off in a huff—hired no doubt." Young people dislike and even fail to understand our slang; my gay students ask me what "tricking" means. It's all old whore's slang, of course. A whore "turns a trick" (sleeps with a customer), and for gays a "trick" was a quickie, a one-time partner. "Gay" itself seems to be whore's slang for "loose morals," as in, "She's definitely available. She's gay, she's in the life." A whore's customer is a "john." If an older partner was "generous," in today's gay slang, we used to call him a john.

But gay slang was much more fanciful than that. We'd pretend to be Victory Girls during World War II with our hair in Victory Rolls and Lurex snoods, playing at being comfort women to our "boys in uniform." Once when I asked the painter John Button if he knew the poet John Ashbery, he said, "Know each other? We were crumb girls together at the Last Supper."

When I was still a boy, my father took me to New York for the first time. We ate at Asti's, where we befriended an English soldier at the next table. I was so excited to be with my first Englishman, who I assumed must be catty and wicked. Stoked on Oscar Wilde, I blurted out a bit of his dialogue, which was relevant to nothing in the conversation. Exhilarated and blushing, I referred to a "widow we know" (entirely invented) "whose hair has turned quite gold with grief." The soldier actually sneered at this batty little fairy. My father was intensely embarrassed. And yet I was puzzled that this Englishman, with his exotic accent, didn't smile at this ancient, irrelevant camp witticism.

I came close to losing a college boyfriend when I started talking like a character in Evelyn Waugh whom I was reading at the time.

Even for my generation, camp was already passé. I remember how disappointed the great Russian scholar Simon Karlinsky, twenty years older than us—who'd fought long and hard for gay liberation and gay studies (he wrote *The Sexual Labyrinth of Nikolai Gogol*, an early gay revisionist biography)—was with me and my friends when we gender-switched and camped it up. He was just as exasperated with us for our "socialist rhetoric" (this was in 1970). Politically we dismissed him as a "White Russian," and socially we tried to convince him that our brand of camp was a late acquisition, ironic and second-degree, almost historical. We studied Susan Sontag's "Notes on 'Camp'" and read carefully Isherwood's paragraphs on it in his earlier novel, *The World in the Evening*.

For some reason (exhibitionism? overwhelming confusion?) I always wrote about homosexuality. When I started out in prep school, I had every intention of publishing my maiden effort, becoming rich and famous and leaving my parents in the dust, but somehow I couldn't get myself to send the manuscript, neatly typed, to—who? An agent? An editor?

All through my twenties I was writing unpublished gay novels—until I was thirty-three and sold my first crypto-gay book, *Forgetting Elena*. My very next novel, a bisexual book that took me five years to write, I couldn't get published, and it's still sitting in my drawer. Finally I became a "gay writer," a niche market that has carried me through more than twenty-five books over the years. The other day I saw my name (and Camus's) endorsing the writings of the French mystic-activist Simone Weil, who died after World War II; I must have endorsed that book decades ago, I thought, before my name became synonymous with "gay." They'd never cite me now on a book about something else. When the great Serbian writer Danilo Kiš died, I dictated an obituary for him for an English newspaper over the phone, but when I named his partner it came out "Dominic" instead of "Dominique," and someone reproached me for the confusion—"Especially given your reputation."

But it was thrilling to be a gay writer in the late 1970s, when we first broke out. We had this whole scarcely explored subject to explore; the first black writers must have felt the same exhilaration. Gay readers felt on intimate terms with gay writers, and since there were no out actors or politicians, we were minor celebrities and opinion-makers in our ghetto. I remember saying to someone at the time, "I may never be so well known as John Updike, but to my few readers I'm indispensable."

Chapter 4

I disliked my piano lessons, since I decided I'd never be a concert performer. I tried many instruments (harpsichord, harp, recorder) and arts (composing, painting, acting, and writing poetry and plays). I took voice lessons; I was the captain of the glee club. But the instant I understood I wasn't outstanding at something (already outstanding, at the beginning), I'd lose interest in it. I wrote a score for an opera—well, a few pages of it—and submitted it to the father of a school friend. The man was a professor of music at Northwestern, and he played through my primitive little score with lots of arpeggios, chords, trills, and octave doublings, which he threw in generously, but he seemed reserved in his praise. I would improvise on the piano until I got too old (ten) to be precocious, and my mother gave me a sickly smile of the you've-delighted-us-quite-enough variety. My abstract paintings were okay, but Marilyn suggested a form or color should dive behind another and then emerge on the other side of an intervening shape—that I weave it all together and not invent curious little asteroids and set them adrift in limitless space. That "weaving" became a principle of literary creation.

The least reservation or hesitation was enough to discourage me definitively. My mother suspected I was a genius, and so did I, and a genius must never be seen struggling to master his craft. He starts out already accomplished. The curse of being great at something without working up to it was a malediction my mother placed on me. On the other hand, she had the same exalted but easily crushed esteem for me that she had for herself. I've had many reversals in my professional life, and *Harper's & Queen* magazine once called me "the most maligned man in

America"—a badge of honor, in my eyes. My mother always doubted me as much as she overpraised me.

I went to a Deweyite public grade school in Evanston outside Chicago, where no grades were handed out, only long written comments by teachers on how successfully a student was realizing his potential. That whole system of education was scrapped after the Russians launched *Sputnik 1* in 1957; Americans feared they were falling behind in the Cold War. But in that happy pre-Sputnik era of "progressive" education, we were contentedly smearing finger paint, singing a cappella two hours every week, helped along by our teacher's pitch pipe, and trying to identify Debussy's *Jeux* or Prokofiev's *Peter and the Wolf* in music appreciation class. Richard Howard, the poet, and Anne Hollander, the costume historian, had attended a similar public school in Cleveland. A poem of Howard's starts with the line "That year we were Vikings."

The high point for me every day was something called "creative dramatics." We'd read something about Joan of Arc, maybe even Shaw's *Saint Joan* or Jean Anouilh's *The Lark*, we'd assign roles (Anne Miner was Joan, I the weak-willed dauphin), and soon we'd be onstage, improvising our words and movements. About one-third of the stage was composed of yard-square wood blocks; when they were all assembled, they lay flat as an extension of the apron, but we could stack them and create battlements and chairs and trenches if we wanted.

It was exhilarating to wear costumes and makeup and entreat a maiden in shining armor to conduct me to Rheims that I might be anointed and crowned. We gave the play only once to cheering parents and jeering siblings. I was so myopic I couldn't see anyone in the audience. Theater enabled the fantasy of being the center of everyone's attention, of impersonating someone, not vague and shape-shifting like people around me or myself, but characters with clear-cut traits and a destiny: an adult of the past, someone in history.

Rulers were my favorite roles. Maybe as a scrawny gay boy, virtually friendless and powerless, I was drawn in my imagination to all-powerful tyrants. In third grade in Dallas, Texas, my mother and I went to a costume shop and rented a gold crown and a blue velvet doublet; I played the king in my own adaptation of Maurice Maeterlinck's *The Blue Bird*.

Except I didn't confess that I'd copied an already existing play; I pretended I'd thought it all up, maybe as an additional form of falsehood. A fake heterosexual and a fake writer . . .

Plagiarism, Simon Leys writes in an essay, is the first step toward literary creation; later it might be subsumed into the more respectable pursuit of translation. I've always been astonished how many famous writers have been guilty of plagiarism: Susan Sontag in a novel; D. M. Thomas in *The White Hotel* and also his translation of Pushkin (he just wrote out the standard prose translation in lines of verse); two books by Doris Kearns Goodwin; Jacob Epstein (who lifted whole pages from Martin Amis's *The Rachel Papers*). And then the pure inventions passed off as prosaic fact—notoriously James Frey in *A Million Little Pieces* and Edmund Morris's *Dutch*, a biography of Reagan "with fictional elements." And then those nonfiction books that have openly avowed fictional additions: in both Martin Duberman's *Black Mountain* and Peter Ackroyd's biography of Charles Dickens, the biographers appear in scenes that never took place in real life. Fair enough, since they admit that that's what they're up to.

But why do so many famous and otherwise respected writers place themselves in such obvious and inevitable danger? Now, especially, when Google can identify any recent quotation? Do they want to tempt fate and become pariahs? Are the writers like ballet dancers (or respiratory therapists) who smoke? Do they hope their magical status will protect them from all harm? Have they run out of inspiration or time? Or do they like living dangerously? Barebacking and then rushing to be tested? Is it a kind of Russian roulette?

My next plagiarism was *The Death of Hector*, drawn directly from *The Iliad*. I was in fourth grade in Rockford, Illinois (where Homer was unknown), and I, of course, played the slain Trojan prince and cast the best-looking boy in my class as Achilles, who stabbed me. That way I got to be royal and a victim, done in by a handsome straight boy. That summer I was in Camp Towering Pines, outside Racine, Wisconsin, and I played Boris Godunov; again I was the tsar and mad and dying with the Kremlin bells tolling in an Alexander Kipnis recording, as I wore a

Hudson Bay red wool blanket as my royal robe. I gesticulated effectively as I beheld the ghost of a prince I'd slain, and fell to my knees.

With my Texas cousins Sue and Jean, I was always playing king and slave. It didn't matter which role I played, as long as everything was done properly. In fact I often preferred to be the slave, since I could do it better than the girls could, and I didn't giggle. That was the same year I would ride around on my bike in Preston Hollow outside Dallas and make it thunder by shaking my hand in three series of three gestures. I was Jupiter. I mean, I seriously believed I was Jupiter. My favorite fantasy was about my resurrection from the grave on the back of an eagle. I'd be in all my immense glory, and my mother and sister and my cousins would all fall back in terror and awe and regret that they hadn't worshiped me enough when I was alive.

Later I had the dream of conquering the world. I started to write the biography of Frederick the Great. I was ten and read two other biographies. I quickly became bored. Three years later, in my Buddhist years, I tried to write the life of Prince Shakyamuni before he became the Buddha. It was in blank verse, with copious illustrations I drew myself. As a sophomore at Evanston High, I let it be known I was dying of leukemia. I received lots of sympathy from a few girls. In fact I had mononucleosis, and I stayed home from school ailing for weeks; I would lie on my mother's bed while she was at work. The bed was situated in a bay window lined with stained glass. I loved the way the sun shot bars of light over the page as I read Alexander Pope's *The Rape of the Lock*. I saw right away that it was supposed to be mockery. Children are good at mocking each other but seldom have a real sense of humor; they laugh hollowly only at silly or cruel things. Perhaps that was the first moment I saw the point of genuine humor. The verse was so delicate and formal and surprising and stinging: razor-sharp, cut-metal filigree. I was so happy lying in bed reading Pope and chuckling while everyone at school felt sorry for me. I guess I was a strange adolescent.

I loved to read plays about dying monarchs. When I was in seventh grade, I read Henrik Ibsen's *Emperor and Galilean*, about Julian the Apostate in two parts of five acts each. And I liked his *The Master Builder*, in which the architect falls to his death from one of his overly ambitious buildings. *Ghosts* suited me fine, since the young hero goes mad at the end due to the syphilis he's inherited from his father.

Once in my thirties I confessed to my group therapy that I'd always had these fantasies of being a king, preferably a dying one. My therapist asked me to stage a scene, with the other patients acting as courtiers. But I couldn't get beyond the grand entry and the crowd bowing before me. How pathetic! I hadn't elaborated the fantasy any further. Perhaps I was afraid to admit I wanted to die and be mourned. For about ten years, between thirty-five and forty-five, I was a sexual masochist and occasional sadist. I never liked the ouch! part; verbal submission was my forte.

Opera was the perfect medium for me—as much for its plots as its heart-stopping music. I checked out of the Evanston Public Library heavy albums of eight or ten 78s—and the scores! I wasn't very good at reading music, but I loved the old art nouveau illustrations on the covers of the scores to *Tosca* and *Madama Butterfly*. They gave me a vivid sense of how recent this music was, published only fifty years earlier. Why, *La fanciulla del West* had been written for our very own Metropolitan Opera in 1905 or something, and Giacomo Puccini had attended the premiere! I loved his cowboys demanding "ancora di whisky!" Kids are attracted to melodrama for its emotional highs, its passionate love scenes and violent declarations of vengeance, its touching deaths and its picturesque poverty. With my tracking index finger I'd follow the rising and falling notes, the rapidly turning pages of full orchestration played presto, and the slowly turning score of the languid flute solo. My main interest, of course, was the words in Italian (or French or German). Sometimes the heavy 78s were scratched from frequent listening (the "Habanera" in *Carmen* was pretty well mutilated), but most of the records were pristine; an entry in purple ink on the card in the front pocket revealed that the *Fanciulla* had last been checked out in 1944.

I suppose it comes down to role-playing in a heightened, Technicolor world. When I write entirely invented (as opposed to autobiographical) fiction, I daydream my way through the various roles and for days keep up a subvocal intoning of everyone's dialogue. I'd argue that for many writers, dramatic scenes are the rudimentary building blocks of their novels—certainly for Fyodor Dostoevsky, with his prostitutes defiantly throwing rubles into the fireplace. In my creative writing classes I point out to students that there's no need to compress all the action into one big toe-to-toe confrontation; they can spread the action out over many discrete scenelets and mix the melodrama with meditation and description—a far more lifelike method.

Chapter 5

When I was first a Buddhist, I took an interest in everything Chinese and Japanese. I remember when I discovered Japanese prints in a big art book I checked out of the library—*The Floating World* (1954) by James Michener—and books on the kabuki by Faubion Bowers, who was General MacArthur's translator and served as the interpreter at his initial meeting with Emperor Hirohito. Bowers has been called the man who saved the kabuki, which was slated to be closed by the American military occupation (and was in fact briefly shut down) because, it was claimed, it promoted feudal values. Bowers, a cultured American from Oklahoma (who years later manned a gay suicide hotline with a friend of mine), argued that the kabuki must be preserved as a sacred Japanese institution. He lived in the American embassy with the MacArthurs and promoted Japanese culture persuasively, along with Michener and the theater director Joshua Logan, who in 1952 co-wrote with Michener and directed the musical *South Pacific*.

In 1954, when I was fourteen, I saw a dance group called Azuma Kabuki, an effort to promote Japanese-American unity in the postwar period that (atypically) was made up of mostly female performers and (atypically) omitted the spoken drama and included only the dances. It was a memorable evening for me, since I sat next to my mother's fiancé's twenty-two-year-old son, a hottie doing construction work for the summer, and pressed his leg so insistently that during intermission, while our parents were at the bar, we decided to meet and spend the night together. "What shall we do?" Bob asked, red as a radish. And, cool as a cucumber, I said, "You like Perry Como, and we have a TV and you don't. Come over next Friday to watch the Perry Como show and drink so many beers you can't drive home. Ask my mother if you can sleep on one of the twin beds in my room." He was astonished by my sangfroid at age fourteen— something I no doubt picked up from the novels my stepmother read, books like *Forever Amber*. I wrote about Bob, my night of passion, and a rematch in Paris fifty years later in a story called "Reprise."

As a teen I'd look for hours at Japanese prints—Torii Kiyonaga's tall, stately ladies standing in a boat under a bridge and holding long-stemmed pipes, Kitagawa Utamaro's courtesans looking into a mirror to blacken their teeth or to play with a cat, Tōshūsai Sharaku's bold actors, their grimaces outlined in heavy makeup. I daydreamed over lovers under paper umbrellas running through the rain on clogs; I was especially struck by their mismatched fabrics (a Scottish plaid next to white paulownia blossoms on black silk). Later, when I had some money, I bought a print of a bare-chested, long-haired fisherman sitting cross-legged on the beach and shucking oysters for an effeminate, overdressed, carefully coiffed city slicker.

As a teen I had seven small bronze reproductions of T'ang-dynasty horses in various poses (galloping, grazing), which I would play with for hours along with the square metal boxes of tea I collected and a green jar of candied ginger with a round cork lid, empty now of its gooey contents but still redolent of them. I'd never had toys as a child, so now, at fourteen or fifteen, in the strictest secrecy, I staged triumphal marches for an emperor with my Asian gewgaws, though I locked my door, afraid of being discovered at this embarrassingly childish play.

I even tried to listen to some Peking opera, though I was defeated by so much squealing and twanging. The fault was all mine, I thought; I hadn't been sufficiently initiated into this superior art form. Like most educated Americans of the period, I had an almost holy respect for other cultures. That was the main difference between the solemn, diffident Americans and the mocking, ethnocentric English—our cultural relativism is deeply rooted.

Maybe I was motivated by my distaste for our own boring, middlebrow, overly obvious world. I was attracted to the exotic, to which I ascribed refinement, tolerance, a mystic universalism. I was drawn to the utterly foreign. I was convinced all these unfamiliar symbols and signs disguised a greater wisdom. What we would have called back then "primitive" cultures interested me not at all; to catch my attention a culture had to be old, sophisticated, and nearly incomprehensible.

In boarding school I was drawn to an English dorm master who'd studied Chinese. When I told him I wanted to be a novelist, he said that few writers could earn a living, and I should study something I could teach: classical Chinese, for instance. As a Buddhist I already felt half Asian. I liked the idea of classical, as opposed to modern, Chinese, since I thought with classical I'd have a safe sinecure, spared demanding students and free to write.

As an undergraduate I studied Chinese every semester but never made much headway in the spoken language. The only classmate who did was an extroverted weirdo who didn't mind making all those funny sounds. I did slightly better in the written language and made hundreds of flash cards with the Chinese character on one side and the English meaning and pronunciation on the other. I learned how to use the Wade-Giles Chinese-English dictionary, no mean accomplishment since looking up a character meant recognizing the radical (the root signifier) from among 214 possible radicals and then counting the remaining strokes. Aside from my nearly pointless language classes, I studied Buddhist art with the great German scholar Max Loehr, who traced the image of the Buddha from Gandhara (now part of modern Pakistan) where Greek sculptors in Alexander the Great's retinue fashioned the first ever busts of the Buddha in the likeness of Apollo, complete with snail-shell curls and dagger-straight noses. From there we followed the Buddha image through Southeast Asia and on to the Gupta dynasty in India, and then to China, where the literal-minded Chinese took one look at Avalokiteśvara, a bodhisattva so spiritual he didn't have a penis, and assumed he must be their female goddess Kuan-yin. On to Tibet, where females sat on male organs as a metaphor for the mind penetrated by the body or something. In China we lingered over Sui-dynasty buddhas, with their intricate folds sheathing their slender bodies in contrapposto, and the paintings of the

Ch'an buddhas (predecessors of Zen in Japan) in which a crazed monk with a tangled beard would be shown ripping up the holy scriptures, the sutras, as an act in favor of the anarchic and irrational against the conventional. We learned what a centuries-long ordeal it had been to translate Buddhist texts from Pali to Chinese—two languages no more related than English and Chinese. We read a T'ang-dynasty Confucian protest by a courtier, Han Yu, written in 819 A.D., against Buddhist superstition (the worship of the Buddha's finger bone, "his ill-omened and filthy remains"). We studied the hundreds of small buddhas installed in the caves of Tun-huang as well as some of the world's first examples of printing: woodcut prayers, printed as multiples to increase their efficacy as petitions to the Buddha. I remember translating a few paragraphs of a modern Chinese text on the Buddha written in the gnomic ancient style. Three characters, "sun," "west," and "die," had to be translated "Just as the sun sets in the West, so the Buddha died."

What makes Chinese difficult is that there is no tense to the verbs, the nouns are both singular and plural, and meaning (as in English but not Latin, say) is determined by word order. In the classics there are no commas or periods, so punctuating them was a scholarly test—and also an interpretation of the text. Since Chinese is the world's oldest continuously spoken language, a single character can mean many different things, depending on which century it was written in: meanings evolved. The character that meant "throne" in one century could now mean "mister." Of course the most demanding aspect of written Chinese is that it doesn't use a limited alphabet but an almost limitless number of unrelated characters. Over the centuries there were naturally efforts to simplify or alphabetize the written language (the Communists did succeed in limiting the number of strokes used in certain words, so that the character for "nation" lost five or six strokes, as I recall). In traditional China, however, the mandarinate had a stake in keeping the language fiendishly difficult. Since there was no hereditary nobility but only scholar-officials selected through the world's first civil service examinations, the only way mandarins could pass on their high positions to their children was by providing them with the twenty or so years of tutoring necessary for passing those tests (usually based on the Confucian classics). Sometimes, exceptionally, a whole village would band together to finance the education of its brightest son—a strategy that occasionally worked. Once a peasant became the governor of a province, say, he could use his immense power to favor the people of his village. The government tried to cut down on nepotism, however, by forbidding officials to serve in their native districts. Hence all the sad poems of separation and farewell—the Chinese poems, for instance, that became the texts of Gustav Mahler's haunting "Abschied" ("Farewell") in his *Song of the Earth*, or Pound's "Exile's Letter" in *Cathay*.

I read lots of T'ang- and Sung-dynasty poetry, mainly in English translation. The feeling for the hermit, for the beauty of the landscape, the melancholy of lost friends, the thrill of getting drunk in the spring—these were all subjects of such poets as Li Po, Tu Fu, and Wang Wei and poetic topics I could embrace, things I wrote about in my own feeble poetry. I was pleased in an infantile way that the "Po" in Li Po's name was pronounced "Bai"—the word for "white," my name. My favorite translator into English, after Pound, was Kenneth Rexroth.

Simplicity, formalism, ritual, and a muted eroticism were the elements I admired in Chinese poetry. I found those same elements, more expansively developed, in Japanese fiction.

My real romance with Asia began in my late twenties and early thirties, with the reading of Japanese fiction of the Heian dynasty. I loved *The Tale of Genji* and *The Pillow Book of Sei Shonagon*. I read the eleventh-century *Genji*, sometimes called the world's first novel, in the Arthur Waley translation and later in the more scholarly Edward Seidensticker version. I've never read the third translation by Royall Tyler.

Waley did for Lady Murasaki, the author of the *Genji*, what Scott Moncrieff did for Proust. These Englishmen may have made mistakes, but they naturalized each book and turned it into an English classic.

Genji (six volumes in the Waley translation) tells the story of an eleventh-century prince and his gallantries. Although he does not stand in the imperial line of succession, Genji has all the power and privilege of a prince royal and none of the responsibilities. He is especially powerful after his illegitimate son becomes the emperor. Affectionate, psychologically complex, and subtle, Genji devotes his time to devising living quarters for his various mistresses, to whom he remains loyal despite the vagaries of romantic desire. Like the other courtiers, he sends friends and officials short poems on almost every occasion (an outing, for instance, to view the cherry blossoms). These poems, especially if they are composed by a superior, must be answered almost immediately by the recipient's poem, which ideally should echo words and images in the original. The elegance and appropriateness of the impromptu poem is judged on the beauty of the calligraphy, the cleverness of its allusions, and the originality of the attached object—a cherry blossom branch, say, or a bit of moss from a sacred Shinto shrine.

The plot deals mainly (at least in the first two-thirds of the book) with Genji's exhausting and often secret romantic life. Handsome and respectful enough to satisfy most feminist readers, Genji is always finding himself in remote and picturesque places, courting a beauty who's renounced the world (as a nun or a widow, say). He falls for a prepubic girl—possibly the author, Lady Murasaki. He brings her to his palace and raises her until she's the right age for sex (fourteen).

Of course he never actually sees any woman. Maybe he'll glimpse the tastefulness of the various layers of her gowns as she trails a sleeve from the shuttered window of her passing litter. Or he might judge her character from a sample of her calligraphy. Or he might hear her breathing, singsong voice as she sits behind her impenetrable curtain of state. If he's invited into her bed, it will be in darkest night. As soon as he returns home before dawn, he must dash off a morning-after poem, of course.

If sometimes these nocturnal encounters seem frequent and random and even violent, they were as inconsequential and as natural as a gay man's tricks in the 1970s. Perhaps this heterosexual promiscuity was what appealed to me originally. And not always heterosexual. Genji, the inveterate womanizer, courts a young boy at one point because the boy resembles his unattainable older sister, an episode introduced without any special fuss.

The *Genji* was written by a female courtier for the reading pleasure of other women. The author, because she was a mere woman, wrote in the spoken language using the Japanese alphabet and avoided the stilted

Chinese words that a male author would have used, much as a Renaissance woman might have written in French or Italian, whereas a typical man (Erasmus, for instance) would have written in Latin. Of course Lady Murasaki greatly benefited from writing in a language she and her readers spoke every day, just as did Marguerite de Navarre and Dante and Geoffrey Chaucer, say.

With all its charm and delicacy and its gripping episodes of amorous adventure, the *Genji* remains a world classic, prized for its delicate sensuality. Murasaki's Japanese (like Chaucer's English) was unintelligible just a hundred years later, and over the next thousand years the ancient masterpiece was translated several times into a more modern Japanese; I've heard that some Japanese students find the English translations easier to understand than the classical Japanese.

There were two other books I read at the same time. Sei Shonagon's *Pillow Book* was one, a diary written roughly at the same time by another court lady (women slept on high, round wooden pillows in order to leave undisturbed their elaborate coiffures; a diary, it seems, could be secreted in the hollow center of the pillow). Snobbish, conformist, observant, Sei Shonagon gives a franker, less tinted picture of court life. She makes lists of "unsuitable things," such as "snow on the house of common people" or "eating strawberries in the dark." She lists rare things, such as two lovers (or friends) who stay constant over the years.

One of the dramatic moments occurs when a crazy woman runs around the courtyard naked; we realize that Sei Shonagon has never seen a nude body before, not even her own. She thinks it looks like a white worm. We're told that a cat should be completely black except for its belly and bib, which should be white—a "tuxedo cat," as we'd say.

She recounts a day when the dowager empress and all her ladies have gone on a nature outing; the emperor has sent a friendly poem, and no one can think how to respond. So much time has already gone by that the situation has become intensely embarrassing. No one can think what to write.

An irritating thing, I recall, is when a man one loves gets drunk and falls asleep. The male courtiers are polite and deferential, but occasionally ruffian soldiers invade the palace and rape the women. She doesn't like it, but Sei Shonagon accepts it as a fact of life.

The other book I read at that time was Ivan Morris's *The World of the Shining Prince*, which condensed and ordered all the information about Genji and his court. Morris's book was to the *Genji* as W. H. Lewis's *The Splendid Century* was to the many volumes of Henri de Saint-Simon's journals. I can't remember reading these books systematically. I just remember swallowing them whole.

All three books—*The Tale of Genji*, *The Pillow Book*, and *The World of the Shining Prince*—inspired me when I was writing my first published novel, *Forgetting Elena*. It, too, conjured up an island kingdom that was ruled by a prince; it, too, had replaced ethics with aesthetics; it, too, demanded of its citizens constant occasional poetry; it, too, fed on harsh but utterly capricious judgments and on codes that were never broken; it, too, had replaced titles (and even proper names) with evasive honorifics. The landscape had invaded the village; everyone was dressed simply and the same—but just under the surface, in both the world of my novel and in the *Genji*, the huge, crushing machinery of the state was ticking into inexorable, sickening motion.

If I combined the Heian court with the gay resort Fire Island Pines, I did so because they were both governed by nearly indiscernible rituals, because under the apparent egalitarianism lay vast differences of rank and power and because in both instances good taste had replaced the good. In Louis XIV's court, titles had been replaced by the innocuous-sounding Monsieur (the king's brother) and La Grande Mademoiselle (the king's cousin). At Versailles endless squabbling determined who had the right to sit in a chair or on a stool, who could enter a door first—all the hotly contested minutiae of precedence, disguised by an unfailing politeness. All of this fed into my novel, which John Ashbery called "terminally sophisticated." I was also influenced by the then popular notion that society can best be understood as something performed in reciprocal theatrical roles. Erving Goffman introduced this concept in his 1959 book *The Presentation of Self in Everyday Life*.

Soon I began to read twentieth-century Japanese fiction. My favorite writers were Jun'ichirō Tanizaki and Yasunari Kawabata; I disliked Yukio Mishima, whom everyone praised. Tanizaki must be one of the handful of great writers of the last century, especially for *The Makioka*

Sisters. Richard Howard first gave it to me, saying it was the Japanese *Buddenbrooks*. I dared not tell him I had never read the German classic (and still haven't) and that I found Thomas Mann rough sledding (I was upset years later when an angry German teen reader at a bookstore in Munich hissed at me that I was no better than Thomas Mann with my *Bildungsbürgertum*, a German word referring to the educated elite, given to people guilty of intellectual preening and "cultural" snobbism).

The Makioka Sisters was written by Tanizaki during World War II as an idealized memory of the happier years before the war—and perhaps as a reminder that Japanese traditions were not just military. The wartime government censored it on the grounds that it treated of the soft and "grossly individualistic lives of women." Indeed, the principal characters are Yukiko and her younger sister Taeko. Whereas Taeko is wayward, wants to open a dress shop, sleeps around, and has a miscarriage, Yukiko is maddeningly shy and traditional. As in a Jane Austen novel, the plot is mainly concerned with marrying off the girls. Taeko can't marry until her older sister is paired off; Yukiko is stubborn and haughty. When a Westernized, golf-playing suitor calls her to ask her out for a stroll, she refuses for ten minutes to take the phone, and when she finally hears his invitation she makes a sound that could mean either yes or no (corresponding to the ambiguous but oddly emphatic British *Hmnn* . . .).

The girls are endlessly being shuttled off to the senior branch of the family in Tokyo, a city they despise. Less and less frequently (Yukiko is approaching thirty and has a mark on her forehead during her period, and the merchant family's fortunes are wavering), a matchmaker arranges a ghastly formal meet-and-greet dinner (called a *miai*) in which the man's family and the woman's all attend, often in a Chinese restaurant—and conversation is predictably glacial. Each family hires a private detective to sniff out any signs of congenital disease or madness or scandal in the potential mate's lineage.

Although these rituals are stiff and grotesque, the Makioka family in its intimacy is extremely endearing. The little daughter of the house astutely guesses why her aunt is jaundiced; it must be the steak she ate yesterday. The whole family seems addicted to shots of vitamin B;

the various members are always complaining they're "low on B." The discreet, aestheticized, and unaggressive brother-in-law, who passes the sauna where the sisters are cutting one another's toenails, is delighted when he sees these clipped crescents of nail shining like moons on the floor.

A typhoon, serious operations, and always those agonizing *miai*s. The reader is immersed in traditional Japan, the war is on the horizon. By the end of this very long book, Yukiko has landed a husband she doesn't much like and is traveling in a train to meet him when she suffers an attack of diarrhea. Tanizaki has a Tolstoyan love of disease and death, as Richard Howard laughingly pointed out to me years ago.

Some novelists dote on the grotesque and are so horrid they're funny. In Jean Rhys's masterpiece *After Leaving Mr. Mackenzie*, there are some hilariously awful descriptions of bed-sit wallpaper, though the most amusing grotesque moment occurs when the middle-aged heroine, who's alcoholic, menopausal, and fat and has been put out to pasture by the man who has been keeping her for years, seems to have found a well-heeled admirer in a pub, one she badly needs, since she is penniless. She's bringing him home and precedes him up the stairs. When she's on the dark landing, he reaches up from the stair below to pat her hand affectionately. She screams, so drunk she can't remember who he is, alarmed. All the boarders and the landlady open their doors and turn on their lights, and the admirer dashes off, never to be seen again.

In the late Tanizaki novel *The Key*, a fifty-five-year-old man, frustrated by his forty-year-old wife's modesty, gets her drunk. When she has passed out, he strips her nude, arranges her limbs, and takes pictures of her on his new Polaroid. His son-in-law is strangely cooperative. In *Diary of a Mad Old Man*, the seventy-seven-year-old hero has suffered from a stroke but is still extremely horny. His beautiful daughter-in-law, a yen-digger and former showgirl, plays along with the old man's obsessions. In return for the gift of a diamond, she lets him take a cast of her feet, which will be placed on his Buddhist tomb. For a prudish American these novels (and in both books the family's easy complicity) were shocking. I also read *Some Prefer Nettles*, a novel that explores the difference between East and West—and systematically blurs the distinction.

Again it's a family novel, turning around a patriarch who makes his young mistress wear a kimono and wait on him like a subservient geisha.

In his two best stories, Tanizaki created a closed, suffocating world. In "The Bridge of Dreams" (the title is lifted from a late chapter of the *Genji*), a boy loses his mother when he is still a little child. His father takes up with a divorced ex-geisha who lives with the boy (now an adult) and nurses him from her breast. The son, encouraged by the father, lives with his stepmother in a half-erotic, half-familial way, even after the father dies. The son and the woman seldom leave their beautiful Kyoto mansion and its big garden. While I worked at my first job for Time-Life Books I wrote an essay on the Japanese garden—how water falling through a bamboo tube must be melodious, even if the tube must be cut and recut to attain the perfect sound; how the stepping stones must be placed awkwardly so that the visitor has to pause repeatedly to enjoy the view; how the miniature plantings and artificial terrain must be staged so as to give the illusion of spacious mountains and rivers. In the garden is the cottage for the tea ceremony, which should look casual and rustic (we learned about *wabi-sabi*, key aesthetic terms that sounded like the names of twin miniature poodles but meant "rustic simplicity," "imperfect," "flawed beauty"). The building should be radically simple, purpose-built, as natural seeming as a tree trunk.

The other great story, "A Portrait of Shunkin," is the hagiography of a Meiji-era blind samisen player and her faithful servant, who becomes her pupil. When the woman is mysteriously scalded with boiling water, the servant blinds himself so that he will always remember his mistress as beautiful. One scholar has suggested that it is the servant who has disfigured his mistress so they can live in seclusion far from the world. In any event it is a sadomasochistic love (definitely physical, since the couple have a child). Marilyn, usually so cool and skeptical, respected the unbridled passion that makes Don José kill Carmen, that makes Des Grieux join Manon in death in "the desert of Louisiana," and that causes Shunkin's servant to blind himself. The most beautiful image in the story is of the old blind couple tilting their heads upward to follow the song of a rising lark.

Finally, I looked at Tanizaki's essay "In Praise of Shadows," in which he extols Japanese bathrooms with their dim light and pine boughs and soft, faded wood fixtures, in contrast to the painfully bright, surgically clean contours of a Western bathroom. By the same reasoning, he praises patinaed bronzes as opposed to polished ones, muddy Japanese complexions over scrubbed white faces, and so on.

The other great modern Japanese writer is Kawabata, who won the Nobel Prize and later committed suicide. My favorite novel by him is *The Sound of the Mountain*, which I've taught several times in courses designed to show there's more to contemporary literature than American coffee-cup realism.

People assume that we read to see our reflection, but this reader, at least, prizes difference, strangeness. Just as I wanted to explore unfamiliar religions and languages, I wanted to discover strange codes of behavior. For instance, in *The Sound of the Mountain*, an old couple are delighted when they read in the paper a "romantic" account of the double suicide of young lovers. Suicide, instead of being interpreted as an extreme aberration or a sign of despair, is understood as a passionate declaration that life can never get better than this. Yukio Mishima, Kawabata's disciple, defended hara-kiri as a noble act, a way of "winning."

The Sound of the Mountain is a book about old age and its forgetfulness and remorse, but even so my young students always liked it best of the many books we read together. Even in translation, it is written in the simplest, most limpid prose. Though the book is about regret and decline, nevertheless it is animated with memorable nature descriptions. At the beginning of the book the old man (he's sixty-two), Shinko, is trying to remember if he must buy dinner for two people or three. On his walk home he passes some sunflowers. They remind him of crowned heads, and he returns to this indelible image several times. Themes get repeated frequently, which reminded me of Japanese linked verse, or *renga*, in which words (in this case themes) repeat in a regular pattern. In his introduction to Kawabata's *Snow Country*, the translator mentioned haiku as an influence, and certainly the compression and suggestiveness as well as the constant allusions to nature and to fleeting existence—these elements are all present in Kawabata's prose, but in large swaths of *The Sound of the Mountain* (its rumbling sound is the noise of approaching death) we find that thoughts and images are repeating in some sort of fixed pattern.

A delicate sensuality that can be traced back to *Genji* colors every page. For instance, Shinko is falling for his beautiful daughter-in-law (that again!). When she gets a nosebleed, he makes her lean her head back over a sink. After the bleeding stops, and she leaves the room to lie down, Shinko avidly laps up the blood-tinted water remaining in the sink.

Japanese fiction, with its stillness, its perverse eroticism, its affectionate observation of daily habits, its acceptance of death, had a big effect on my writing and an even bigger one on my sensibility. My friends and I read many of these books at the same time, and we would pretend we were exchanging poems or arranging the layers of our sleeves or submitting to a matchmaking *miai*. Marilyn and my first lover, Stan, and I—all three of us—loved to live in this simple but formal world. Simple because there was no Versailles-style grandeur, but formal because everyone was watching everyone for felicitous or mistaken deportment. Not that we were critical of one another; at worst we were amused by each other's gaffes (Marilyn, to be precise, tolerated what she considered my novelistic exaggerations). Simple and formal: my formula for a dinner party. I liked to set a beautiful table and prepare many dishes but let everyone wear jeans and drink too much and interrupt each other. I even wrote the menu in grease pencil on a small porcelain tablet and distributed silver knife rests to each guest—we were a long way from Illinois! The complicated food and the table suggested the evening was a special occasion, but the rowdy manners meant that we could say anything we pleased. The hors d'œuvres, the seating, the quality of the wines, the sequence of courses showed that I took my guests seriously, that I esteemed them, but the talk, I hoped, was anything but stiff. In an indirect way this mixture of formality and frivolity owed something, we thought, to the *Genji*.

Just as Proust provided us with a whole range of characters (Charlus, Norpois, Madame Verdurin) to recognize in the people we were meeting, Japanese fiction, from the *Genji* to Tanizaki, also gave us types to meet and especially rituals to observe and an aesthetic twist to lend to even the most banal moments of our daily lives. Whether preparing tea, spacing our steps, arranging flowers, perfuming the room, or lighting it, we suddenly saw every moment as an expressive choice.

I was grateful to Kenneth Rexroth, a sort of godfather to the Beats in San Francisco, for his translations of Chinese poetry, so slim but heavy with the significance of transience. One of the basic Buddhist "noble truths" is the recognition that everything is transient, an insight that became codified in the Chinese and Japanese aesthetic.

Here is Rexroth's translation of the great Chinese poet Tu Fu's "Full Moon":

Isolate and full, the moon
Floats over the house by the river.
Into the night the cold water rushes away below the gate.
The bright gold spilled on the river is never still.
The brilliance of my quilt is greater than precious silk.
The circle without blemish!
The empty mountains without sound.
The moon hangs in the vacant, wide constellations.
Pine cones drop in the old garden.
The senna trees bloom.
The same glory extends for ten thousand miles.

My love of Pound, acquired from Charles, has remained constant despite Pound's deplorable politics, especially when it linked up with my love of Asian poetry. When the *Paris Review* asked me to name and analyze my favorite poem, I chose Pound's "translation" of "Exile's Letter."

SO-KIN of Rakuho, ancient friend, I now remember
That you built me a special tavern,
By the south side of the bridge at Ten-Shin.
With yellow gold and white jewels
    we paid for the songs and laughter,
And we were drunk for month after month,

forgetting the kings and princes.
Intelligent men came drifting in, from the sea
    and from the west border,
And with them, and with you especially,
    there was nothing at cross-purpose;
And they made nothing of sea-crossing
    or of mountain-crossing,
If only they could be of that fellowship.
And we all spoke out our hearts and minds . . .
    and without regret.
And then I was sent off to South Wei,
    smothered in laurel groves,
And you to the north of Raku-hoku,
Till we had nothing but thoughts and memories between us.
And when separation had come to its worst
We met, and travelled together into Sen-Go
Through all the thirty-six folds of the turning and twisting waters;
Into a valley of a thousand bright flowers . . .
    that was the first valley,
And on into ten thousand valleys
    full of voices and pine-winds.
With silver harness and reins of gold,
    prostrating themselves on the ground,
Out came the East-of-Kan foreman and his company;
And there came also the "True-man" of Shi-yo to meet me,
Playing on a jewelled mouth-organ.
In the storied houses of San-Ko they gave us
    more Sennin music;
Many instruments, like the sound of young phœnix broods.
And the foreman of Kan-Chu, drunk,
Danced because his long sleeves
Wouldn't keep still, with that music playing.
And I, wrapped in brocade, went to sleep with my head on his lap,
And my spirit so high that it was all over the heavens.

And before the end of the day we were scattered like stars or rain.
I had to be off to So, far away over the waters,
You back to your river-bridge.
And your father, who was brave as a leopard,
Was governor in Hei Shu and put down the barbarian rabble.
And one May he had you send for me, despite the long distance;
And what with broken wheels and so on, I won't say it wasn't hard
　　going . . .
Over roads twisted like sheep's guts.
And I was still going, late in the year,
　　in the cutting wind from the north,
And thinking how little you cared for the cost . . .
　　and you caring enough to pay it.
Then what a reception!
Red jade cups, food well set, on a blue jewelled table;
And I was drunk, and had no thought of returning;
And you would walk out with me to the western corner of the castle,
To the dynastic temple, with the water about it clear as blue jade,
With boats floating, and the sound of mouth-organs and drums,
With ripples like dragon-scales going grass-green on the water,
Pleasure lasting, with courtesans going and coming without
　　hindrance,
With the willow-flakes falling like snow,
And the vermilioned girls getting drunk about sunset,
And the waters a hundred feet deep reflecting green eyebrows—
Eyebrows painted green are a fine sight in young moonlight,
Gracefully painted—and the girls singing back at each other,
Dancing in transparent brocade,
And the wind lifting the song, and interrupting it,
Tossing it up under the clouds.

　　And all this comes to an end,
And is not again to be met with.
I went up to the court for examination,

Tried Layu's luck, offered the Choyu song,
And got no promotion,
And went back to the East Mountains white-headed.

And once again we met, later, at the South Bridge head.
And then the crowd broke up—you went north to San palace.
And if you ask how I regret that parting?
It is like the flowers falling at spring's end,
     confused, whirled in a tangle.
What is the use of talking! And there is no end of talking—
There is no end of things in the heart.

I call in the boy,
Have him sit on his knees to write and seal this,
And I send it a thousand miles, thinking.

(Translated by Ezra Pound from the notes of the late Ernest
Fenollosa and the decipherings of the Professors Mori and Araga.)

Ezra Pound's beautiful "Chinese" poem, from his great early book
Cathay, is a compendium of all his many gifts. Somewhere he says that
the ideas in poetry should be simple, even banal, and universal and
human; he points out that the chorus in Greek tragedies always sticks
close to home truths of the sort "All men are born to die." "Exile's Letter"
has this universal simplicity ("There is no end of things in the heart") and
is about the sadness of parting from dear friends. As someone who was
himself often living far from writer-friends, Pound obviously knew all
about the exquisite melancholy of parting.

There is a historical dimension to this poem worth noting: the Chinese
had the world's first civil service and no hereditary nobility. All prominent scholar-bureaucrats could secure positions only by passing rigorous
Confucian examinations. Each advancement meant a new dislocation.
Since the empire was so large and transportation was so bad, friends and
lovers and family members were often separated for many decades. Such
separation is the subject of this poem. A modern counterpart would be

the American academic system, which often splits up couples and divides friends as scholars head to far-flung colleges in search of tenure-track positions—except that in traditional China, there was no rapid air travel or Skyping.

The pain of repeated parting and the precariousness of the scholar's life is played out here in a landscape of pellucid pools and beautiful pleasure pavilions filled with dancing girls and gifted musicians. We hear about the "blue jeweled table" and "water clear as blue jade" just as we hear about "vermilioned girls." Several times we're told that the participants in these transitory revels are drunk; in traditional China (as in contemporary Japan) drunkenness is seen as sympathetic, sociable, clear evidence of sincerity. "The Gentleman of the Five Willow Trees," a fifth-century Chinese text, celebrates a scholar who was always drunk when there was wine and who lived in poverty with no interest in advancement. Many of the heroes of Chinese literature were Taoist hermits who withdrew from the world and drank and wrote poetry. The most famous poet of all, Li Po, was said to have drowned while trying to embrace the moon's reflection when he was drunk. The traditional Chinese said that someone was a Confucian in office and a Taoist out of office; Taoism was certainly associated with eccentricity, drinking, writing poetry, while Confucianism was much more staid and official. This poem demonstrates the tension between the two religions and approaches to life.

The poem rehearses a favorite Poundian practice of repeating a word. Here we have "sea-crossing" and "mountain-crossing" and "cross-purposes" just as we have "valley" and "ten thousand valleys." Or typically we have "And thinking how little you cared for the cost . . . / and you caring enough to pay it." The "it" doubles for the word "cost."

Pound had a trot of the Chinese prepared for him by Ernest Fenollosa, who worked from a Japanese transliteration; that's why the names all sound Japanese rather than Chinese.

People say that Pound "invented" Chinese poetry for the West. Certainly for the English; the Germans, those great philologists, were a century in advance, and in France the study of "Oriental languages" and artworks has long been prized. There's a moment in Proust when a dying connoisseur pays his last visit to a museum to see a Vermeer exhibit (Proust himself did that); on my first trip to Paris in the mid-1960s I became deathly ill with hepatitis, but before I flew home I was determined to visit the Musée Guimet, one of the world's great Asian museums. Of course I knew the passage in Proust, and as I staggered up the countless stairs to the main collection, I fully identified with Charles Swann (though he was visiting the Vermeer exhibit in the Jeu de Paume). As a midwestern public library aesthete and would-be intellectual, I was determined to immerse myself in the Original.

Chapter 6

I've been asking writer friends what inspires them. Sheila Kohler, the prolific South African writer, responds, "There are books that have inspired me to write. It is something to do with the voice, I believe. Particularly when I was starting out, I would find myself parroting a voice that had entered my head: particularly a writer like Virginia Woolf—I find sentences still in the margins of, say, *Mrs. Dalloway*, or even Dickens, who propelled me to the page, giving me a springboard that launched me into the air so that my own sentences rang similarly (at least to my ears) though the story was my own. I'm still sometimes inspired in this way. Marguerite Duras was also a hypnotic voice, and her *Lover* helped me with the writing of *Cracks*. Even my first book, *The Perfect Place*. Also, Joyce Carol Oates—that rush of words. There are voices that seem to enter the unconscious almost directly. Now I'm actually embarked on a book based on a book, or rather a character in a book, and here I am inventing a voice for a character who doesn't have one in the book. When I wrote *Dreaming for Freud*, I was naturally using Freud's voice—in a way—such a direct one in his case histories, though half my book is written from Dora's point of view (there I used my own adolescent letters!)."

Books play an equally large role, though less directly, in the work of Maylis de Kerangal, the prize-winning French author of *The Heart*. She assembles a "collection" of maybe thirty books, not as references, not even as obvious influences, but ones that bear some family relationship to her subject. If she is writing about a teenage daredevil who dies in a car accident after an exhausting predawn bout of surfing, she might feel the need to consult a book about ancient Greek attitudes toward death.

Oddly enough, Andrew Sean Greer, the American novelist, also starts with a "family" of books that are related to a subject only in his mind.

In my own case I like to read great books not because I'm hoping to imitate them but because I want to remind myself how good you have to be to be any good at all. We won't be read in the light of other writers in our zip code or decade but as we compare to Proust, Joyce, and Nabokov. History has set the bar very high, and one must jump over it, not do the limbo under it.

Until I was about thirty I felt so close to a constant breakdown that I wrote to keep my head above water. My early, unpublished novels were virtually diaries, except I wrote about myself with frigid disdain in the third person as a lamentable character, not in the more natural self-justifying first person. No voluptuous smelling of one's own farts under the sheet for me—I despised myself more than anyone else could.

Yet I remember an exception: a novel called *The Amorous History of Our Youth* in which I glorify a young gay man who meets an Italian hustler—and falls in love, only to discover that Mario is his half brother. I entered it into the Hopwood Contest at the University of Michigan, and the woman novelist (anonymous) who judged the contest found my manuscript peculiarly distressing, even horrid. That was the era (1961) when gays were supposed to be sad, lonely, and certainly repentant. But everything in my book was impertinent and irritable. We didn't know yet how to be cool and assertive about our homosexuality. All I knew to be was to be lighthearted and baffling.

The title itself was an allusion to a seventeenth-century satire about court life by Madame de Sévigné's cousin, Roger de Bussy-Rabutin, for which the poor guy was exiled. Maybe also Mikhail Lermontov's *A Hero of Our Time*. I suppose I was pretending I was living in the aristocratic European past, which in my imagination was so much more insouciant and morally flexible, or at least indifferent. No one in 1961 knew how to plead for himself sexually as just another variant of normal human behavior. Freud himself, after all, saw homosexuals as regrettably arrested in the anal-aggressive stage or something, and in the

1950s one psychoanalyst recommended to my mother that I be institutionalized and the key thrown away—"unsalvageable," he said. I was just thirteen, and it's true I was unbearably cheeky.

Unlike Jean Genet, I didn't have the courage to be darkly evil or sinful, but I was, rather blindly, groping my way toward anarchy or rebellion—or as I would say, petulance. If all books are a blend of mimesis and longing, this book was heavy on the wish-fulfillment side of the equation. In real life it was based on an encounter I'd had at eighteen with a handsome gigolo, whom I met cruising in Chicago's Bug House Square on the Near North Side (across from the Newberry Library), the most celebrated free-speech center in America, home to soapbox orators (and later to cottaging homosexuals, and eventually, in 1970, host to Chicago's Gay Pride March). The gigolo must have been about my age, but beautiful, Italian, with curly black hair. I named him in my mind Mario. In my novel, the father whom Mario and my protagonist shared was a delightful bounder with children everywhere—rich, because my awkward, pale protagonist was rich and soon enough was supporting his brother-lover Mario. I think everything ended happily. In my case this turn of events is what George Meredith might have called "moral sculpture": You flatter someone (the reader in this case) for being more broad-minded than he actually is. "It's the finest of the Arts . . . adepts in it can cut their friends to any shape they like," Meredith wrote. The idea is that you can instill a virtue that may not exist by pretending it does and praising it ("You're the kindest, most generous man in the world," you say to a skinflint. "Everyone admires your generosity"). I was trying to train my reader (if there were to be one) to wink at all this perverse nonsense (straight and gay philandering). I considered such acceptance very "sophisticated." Years later, I found with my French boyfriend, Hubert, that what he meant by a "sophistiqué" was someone afflicted with silken double-talk—I guess he was returning to the root meaning of *sophistry* as a school of Greek philosophy. In any event, moral sculpture has always been one of my inspirations, the desire to show a world more accepting than ours, more loving, subtler, more alert.

Memorializing someone has also been one of my inspirations—capturing in words what made someone exciting, comforting or comfortable, knowledgeable, intimate. In *The Beautiful Room Is Empty* I portrayed (while they were still very much alive) Marilyn Schaefer (as Maria) and Charles Burch (as Lou), and in *The Farewell Symphony* I resurrected David Kalstone, a literary critic who was always warm, funny, interested in the new and the offbeat like a child attracted to a Christmas tree ornament that bubbles. He was also my best friend. He economized all year long on his professor's salary so that he could rent the top floor of the Palazzo Barbaro in Venice for the summer, where he lived a very glamorous life indeed. We were friends with Peggy Guggenheim and read to her in her private gondola from Henry James's *The Wings of the Dove*. David lived in an apartment where the kitchen had been John Singer Sargent's studio and the library had been Henry James's bedroom. In my Paris memoir I recalled my twenty-year friendship with Marie-Claude de Brunhoff. These were friends you'd talk to every day, who made you a front-row witness to their lives, who humanized you and immersed you in the trivial and the sublime, who invited you to visit every summer their castles in Spain (or, in Marie-Claude's case, her fisherman's cottage on the Île de Ré).

At my age (seventy-eight), I realize that everyone, or almost everyone except Hitler, will be forgotten from this period; if a writer can shore up an eroding coastline for a decade or two, that's the only "immortality" we'll ever know on this dying planet.

In writing *Hotel de Dream*, I began with an empty space in Stephen Crane's life. He had vast sympathies (his *Red Badge of Courage* is the best book about the Civil War, though he was born after the war ended). A friend of his wrote in his diary that he and Crane had encountered a young male prostitute and that Crane (who'd already written about a fallen woman in *Maggie: A Girl of the Streets*) resolved to write a portrait of the boy. The novel, which was to be called *Flowers of Macadam*, was never written. I decided to write it for him. Crane liked prostitutes and was even married to one, the madam of a Florida bordello called Hotel de Dreme (after the previous owner's last name). He was curious and open-hearted, as his journalism and short stories reveal, and he'd been raised the son of a preacher. As an adult he may have become a nonbeliever, but he remained "Christian" in his sensitivity to and love for other people.

Defending the higher morality of tolerance against the moralism of bigotry seemed to me a worthy literary project.

What could inspire readers? Taking infinite pains in the case of Proust or Flaubert or Knausgaard, a sign that one considers it worthwhile to give fictional lives (or one's own) the same finish a master craftsman, an André-Charles Boulle, might devote to a piece of marquetry. I suppose most readers are looking for admirable characters, people they would like in real life or whose faults they could identify with: redeemable faults. My friend Andrew Sean Greer says he prefers villains—Captain Ahab, Charlus, Humbert Humbert, Milton's Satan. They are certainly attractive—so energetic, heat-seeking missiles, monomaniacs. Someone once said Honoré de Balzac's only mistake was to lend his characters the driven purpose of his own genius (sublime mistake!). Whom do we admire in fiction? Atticus Finch, Greer claims, but *To Kill a Mockingbird* is for children.

In Stendhal's *The Charterhouse of Parma*, the duchess is emotional and impulsive but beautiful and loyal and loving. Her nephew Fabrizio is beautiful and impulsive, high-handed because high-born, not terribly bright, idealistic, courageous, courtly, consumed by romantic dreams. The duchess's lover, Count Mosca, is cunning, practical, regretful about turning fifty, besotted with the duchess—willing to do anything to prove his love for her, but with a keen sense of how to maneuver with the capricious despot, the prince of Parma. Are these characters admirable? While we're reading, we feel they are, but the next day we're not so sure that their arrogant aristocratic values are exactly ours. When Fabrizio kills an actor, we're led to think it's his right, that his life as a del Dongo is worth that of ten comedians. And yet . . .

It was the genius of Stendhal, who was constantly reading Renaissance tales of Italy, to instill his contemporary characters with the noble ideals or simply the arrogant behavior of the past, more suitable to the age of Orlando Furioso than of Balzac. Miguel de Cervantes had a similar strategy, but it was for comic effect—the discrepancy between banal reality and knightly fantasies. Stendhal melds the two periods seamlessly for heroic effect.

Are his characters sympathetic? Yes, for their ardor; for their *sdegno*, if that means disdain, or their *sprezzatura*, their "studied carelessness."

That is, if your idea of bliss is to wear rags and to be trampled by the fine horses of the passing royal carriage.

I think in fiction we admire energy more than virtue—even in an energetic paranoid, like Kinbote in *Pale Fire*, who takes all the unbleached floss of experience and weaves it into a tight, gleaming net. The French word for "plot," *trame*, also means "heft" or "weave." We are in a certain sense grateful to the paranoid who leaves no waste behind, who ties every knot. There is an energy, a force, in paranoia; the paranoid might be called a completist. He reassures us that creation follows a design, that things aren't running down through entropy.

I never met Nabokov face to face, though I exchanged phone calls and letters with him. My shrink kept encouraging me to visit him in Switzerland, on my way back from Venice, say, but I kept imagining I'd quickly dispel close up whatever good impression I might have built up long-distance. I had orchestrated a cover story of *Saturday Review* dedicated to Nabokov on the occasion of his publishing *Transparent Things* (1972). I sent Tony Armstrong-Jones (Lord Snowden) to take a portfolio of Nabokov's pictures including one dressed as Borges in a poncho. Nabokov wrote for us a short piece on "inspiration," which I illustrated with a reproduction of *Pygmalion and Galatea* by Jean-Léon Gérôme, a big bad painting from the nineteenth century that hangs in the Met, showing the infatuated sculptor embracing his creation as she turns from marble to flesh, feet last.

After much dithering I phoned Nabokov at eight in the morning from San Francisco, where I was living, speaking to him in Montreux as he was sitting down to cocktails with Alfred Appel (*The Annotated Lolita*, which didn't fare so well since Humbert is a francophone Swiss, and Appel didn't speak French and translated *le petit cadeau*—a whore's fee—literally as "the little gift"). I caught Nabokov at a good moment, apparently; he was in a jovial and expansive mood.

My boss had wanted to send a great artistic photographer such as Henri Cartier-Bresson, but I figured Nabokov would be more amused by Snowden, still married to Princess Margaret at the time and, I guessed, more polished than the austere French genius. The two men got along famously.

Then there was the delicate matter of tiny errors, typographic and even grammatical, which had crept into Nabokov's text. I had the copy set twice in print, my version and his, and sent them both by overnight express. He wired back, "Your version perfect." In the Nabokov portfolio I included rather lukewarm essays by Joyce Carol Oates, William Gass, and Joseph McElroy—and of course my own ecstatic response. A few months later I sent him galleys of *Forgetting Elena*. Nabokov sent me a note saying, "This is not for publication but my wife and I enjoyed your novel in which everything is teetering on the edge of everything." I later found this same "teetering" image in his evocation of a passenger point of view from inside a train leaving the station. I couldn't believe my good luck in gaining an endorsement from my favorite author, someone who was dismissive of Joseph Conrad, Fyodor Dostoyevsky, William Faulkner, and Balzac, even if I had to keep silent about it. Three years later Gerald Clarke, Truman Capote's biographer, interviewed Nabokov at Montreux. Although Nabokov insisted Clarke follow the ritual and submit written questions in his hotel mailbox every evening and get the answers written out every morning, Clarke became fed up with this procedure and asked the master direct questions. In an unguarded moment Nabokov revealed I was his favorite American writer. Later he attempted to convince McGraw-Hill to take a look at my new manuscript, then titled *Woman Reading Pascal*, but without success. It remains unpublished. Through the Russian scholar Simon Karlinsky, I had other echoes of Nabokov's interest in me.

Lolita is his masterpiece, of course, and it is his way of renewing the exhausted nineteenth-century tradition of the novel that analyzes the passions (*Adolphe, Anna Karenina, Madame Bovary*) by re-creating it through the eyes of a criminal pedophile, true to Nabokov's doctrine that a novel should explore not the genus nor the species but an aberrant variety. *Lolita* is romantic and funny and perverted.

My favorite book has always been *Lolita*. Maybe because I'm a Europeanized American, I am appreciative of this supreme expression by an Americanized European. The subject (pervert, nymphet) was one Nabokov tackled unsuccessfully in a novella while he still lived in Europe; the miraculous, funny, tender, terrible novel that the whole world admires became a reality only after the author had lived in the States for fifteen years. Lolita—sexy, innocent, smart but unintellectual, sporty—is the quintessence of America, just as Humbert—cultured, obsessive, suave, corrupt—is an extreme version of Continental sophistication.

But the pleasures of *Lolita* go far beyond its theme and characters. The language—mined with unobtrusive references to Arthur Rimbaud and Charles Baudelaire on the French side and to Edgar Allan Poe on the American—is itself proof of the work's mid-Atlantic status. If *Lolita* parodies everything from "Goldilocks" to *Madame Bovary*, the literary high jinks never distract from the passion coursing through its pages. *Lolita* is as cunning as a conundrum and as passionate as Jean Racine's *Phèdre*.

The image of Nabokov hunting American butterflies throughout the Far West (which is what he was doing while writing *Lolita*) is appropriate to the spirit of his great novel. He was collecting American scenes, picturesque and grotesque. He was the great lepidopterist of the spirit.

Perhaps his success parallels that of George Balanchine and Igor Stravinsky, the triumvirate of artistic genius. All three men were Russians who lived in France and admired French culture—and all three ended up in the United States. The vigor and athletic simplicity of the United States, grafted onto a European tradition of refinement and esthetic breadth, produced the three most important talents of the twentieth century.

Chapter 7

I've just been rereading *Pale Fire*, and—I'd never noticed before—it is a hilarious and sometimes tender portrait of a homosexual madman, Kinbote, who claims to have been the king of the country of Zembla but has now been deposed and is teaching in an American college (or is this a cracked fantasy by the ultimate unreliable narrator?). The whole book is a "scholarly" commentary on 999 verses by his neighbor, the venerable John Shade. The poem is actually an elegy to the poet's dead daughter, but Kinbote is convinced it is about him and his flight from his captors. For months Kinbote (without realizing what a nuisance he's become) has been stoking Shade with his own story, and now he's annotating the purloined poem to reveal its "hidden" content.

Nabokov may have been inspired by his own four-volume translation and annotation of Alexander Pushkin's *Eugene Onegin*, on which he was working simultaneously. Repeatedly in the *Onegin* notes he keeps telling the story of his own family and their lost Russian estates. It must have suddenly struck him that the self-serving scholarly annotations were funny and ripe for self-satire.

The book is also, I realize only now, the great gay comic novel. Kinbote is always drooling over some handsome lad, and as king (Charles the Beloved II), he usually has his way with them, even in a water closet: "The recent thrill of adventure had been superseded already by another sort of excitement. They locked themselves up. The tap ran unheeded. Both were in a manly state and moaning like doves."

Perhaps the funniest scene is between a putative assassin, Gradus, and a lad named Gordon. Since this is a moment completely imagined by

Kinbote (and, by any standard, not observed), the king's imagination runs wild. He dresses the comely Gordon in one clichéd gay outfit after another though the action is presumably continuous and there's no time for costume changes. At first the fifteen-year-old, tanned (or "dyed a nectarine hue by the sun"), is in a "leopard-spotted loincloth." Then he's "wreathed about the loins with ivy." A second later he's fellating "a pipe of spring water" and wiping his hands "on his black bathing trunks." Next, he's magically "striking his flanks clothed in white tennis shorts," before that image dissolves into a "Tarzan brief" that is "cast aside." Nabokov has tapped into the full wardrobe of period gay porn.

At the time he wrote *Pale Fire*, gays were portrayed in fiction and films as lonely phantoms—sad and colorless—or sometimes as instant villains. Nabokov, by contrast, depicts Kinbote as horny, entitled, screamingly absurd. There are certainly gay prisses out there who would object to poking fun at their fellow homosexuals, but for all of us others (especially now that social attitudes have so radically relaxed), we can only join in in the hilarity.

The screwy "notes," far from commenting on Shade's poem, trace out a mini-biography of Kinbote. And that biography, real or delusional, is the picture of an unrepentant homosexual, sensual, mostly guilt-free, tirelessly on the make. Only once does he see himself condemned to hell.

Kinbote, now stranded in a small American college town, takes in a "dissipated young roomer," whom he later calls "drunken, impossible, unforgettable." When a rumor springs up that Kinbote is given to a "persecution mania," he ascribes the gossip to "certain youthful instructors whose advances I'd rejected." As if . . .

One of the liberal gazettes in Zembla dubs the capital city "Uranograd." The king, when still a prince of seventeen, dances in "masques with boy-girls and girl-boys." The prince goes to "a formal heterosexual affair, rather refreshing after some previous sport." When he dances with a pretty girl, Fleur—"pretty but not repellant"—he "hardly squirmed at all when she stroked his hand or applied herself soundlessly with open lips to his cheek," nor did she "seem to mind when he abandoned her for manlier pleasures." An American medium, channeling his dead mother, fruitlessly begs him "to renounce sodomy." When he returns to his chambers, "lying all over the painted marble and piled three or four deep were his new boy pages, a whole mountain of gift boys from Troth, and Tuscany, and Albanoland."

When the Soviets take over his kingdom, he refuses to abdicate and remorselessly looks through field glasses at "lithe youths diving into the swimming pool of a fairytale sport club." Even when he's held captive, the king "kept in touch with numerous adherents, young nobles, artists, college athletes, gamblers, Black Rose Paladins, members of fencing clubs, and other men of fashion and adventure." Of his youth we learn that "in those days growing boys of high-born families wore on festive occasions—of which we had so many during our long northern spring—sleeveless jerseys, white ankle socks with black buckle shoes, and very tight, very short shorts called hotinguens."

At twelve Prince Oleg, in the "mist of the bathhouse," reveals "bold virilia contrasted harshly with his girlish grace. He was a regular faunlet." Eventually Kinbote and Oleg are allowed by the authorities "to share the same bed." Two weeks later Oleg returns. "He carried a tulip. His soft blond locks had been cut since his last visit to the palace and the young Prince thought: Yes, I knew he would be different. But when Oleg knitted his golden brows and bent close . . . the young Prince knew by the downy warmth of that crimson ear and by the vivacious nod . . . that no change had occurred in his dear bedfellow." Even as Oleg and Charles escape the castle, the king is looking at his "shapely buttocks encased in tight indigo cotton."

There are plenty of hints that Kinbote (the king, Charles) is demented or that "reality" itself is disputable. The absurd Kinbote—obsessed with his own royal story, real or invented—is fantastically unaware of John Shade's reluctance to waste time with him and especially of the scorn of Shade's wife, whom Kinbote in return loathes when he isn't condescending to her. Kinbote is the well-observed gay outsider of the past—lecherous, self-important, obsessed with fantasies of aristocracy, impervious to the subtleties of the heterosexual world around him. Kinbote would be despicable if his very earnestness, so naive, weren't so touching. His reckless "scholarship" must have been especially amusing to Nabokov (particularly to Nabokov the lepidopterist, his failure to identify even the most ordinary butterflies). But Kinbote shares Nabokov's distaste for Soviet brutes and his narrow but deep human sympathies.

I remember that at the time many gays were vexed by the satirical portrait, though now it seems perfectly acceptable. Gay critics are no longer prospecting for positive role models. What we get instead in Kinbote is a compendium of "period" gay images. The horrible exploitive photographer the Baron von Gloeden (a fake title) who shot staged pictures at the turn of the century of Sicilian boys with cracked feet, farmer tans, hunger-bloated stomachs, and coarse faces in ancient Greek togas and laurel wreaths holding papier-mâché lyres; Prussian porn and English gentlemen's proclivities for willing, paid guardsmen; the aesthetes of Oscar Wilde's day (a single tulip); a gay son of a famous womanizing king (Mad Ludwig and his royal father, lover of Lola Montes); tennis champion Bill Tilden, whose spectacular playing made him famous in the 1920s—and whose pedophilia landed him in prison; "scoutmasters with something to hide"; idyllic romances with athletes and shepherds in the style of Oxford classicist A. E. Housman, whose *Shropshire Lad* Kinbote admires above all other poems except for Tennyson's equally fruity "In Memoriam"; the sailors so sought after as "rough trade" (nonreciprocating, drunk, heterosexual bullies). It's all here, like flip cards of hot images through the ages.

Nabokov, of course, had an entomologist's delight in observing grotesqueries, but he can't resist lending Kinbote, at least in dreams, a little bit of heterosexual tenderness for his Queen Diva, living on the Riviera in exile. Nabokov read Genet's *Our Lady of the Flowers* at Edmund Wilson's urging and admired the writing but was mystified why Genet wrote about men, of all things. Even the misogynistic Kinbote thinks of Diva at night:

> This love was like an endless wringing of hands, like a blundering of the soul through an infinite maze of hopelessness and remorse. They were, in a sense, amorous dreams, for they were permeated with

tenderness, with a longing to sink his head onto her lap and sob away the monstrous past. They brimmed with the awful awareness of her being so young and so helpless. They were purer than his life. What carnal aura there was in them came not from her but from those with whom he betrayed her—prickly-chinned Phrynia, pretty Timandra with that boom under her apron—and even so the sexual scum remained somewhere far above the sunken treasure and was quite unimportant. He would see her being accosted by a misty relative so distant as to be practically featureless. She would quickly hide what she held and extend her arched hand to be kissed. He knew she had just come across a telltale object—a riding boot in his bed—establishing beyond any doubt his unfaithfulness. Sweat beaded her pale, naked forehead—but she had to listen to the prattle of a chance visitor or direct the movements of a workman with a ladder who was nodding his head and looking up as he carried it in his arms to the broken window. One might bear—a strong merciless dreamer might bear— the knowledge of her grief and pride but none could bear the sight of her automatic smile as she turned from the agony of the disclosure to the polite trivialities required of her. She would be canceling an illumination, or discussing hospital cots with the head nurse, or merely ordering breakfast for two in the sea cave—and through the everyday plainness of the talk, through the play of the charming gestures with which she always accompanied certain readymade phrases, he, the groaning dreamer, perceived the disarray of her soul and was aware that an odious, undeserved, humiliating disaster had befallen her, and that only obligations of etiquette and her staunch kindness to a guiltless third party gave her the force to smile. As one watched the light on her face, one foresaw it would fade in a moment, to be replaced— as soon as the visitor left—by that impossible little frown the dreamer could never forget. He would help her again to her feet on the same lakeside lawn, with parts of the lake fitting themselves into the spaces between the rising balusters, and presently he and she would be walking side by side along an anonymous alley, and he would feel she was looking at him out of the corner of a faint smile but when he forced himself to confront that questioning glimmer, she was no longer there. Everything had changed, everybody was happy.

This is possibly Nabokov's most lyrical tribute to a disappointed woman, but does it suit Kinbote's character? Or is it Nabokov (who cheated on his beloved Vera) expressing his own repentance for his extramarital affairs? (Luckily he's not alive, or he'd challenge me to a duel.) Or is it Nabokov peeping through a mask and making his character more sympathetic, as he does more than once with Humbert?

Nabokov had a gay brother, who died at the hand of the Nazis, and a gay uncle, who left him his fortune, which he possessed only briefly before the revolution. These relatives must have made him somewhat uneasy, since he believed homosexuality was inherited (in the past an eccentric opinion but now, in this era of "to be gay is not a choice," a fairly mainstream theory, though a more libertarian position would be: you have a right to be whatever you are, no matter the cause; even searching for a "cause" is reactionary). Nabokov had a rare capacity for imagining himself into outsiders. A paranoid outsider is a particularly good subject for a novel, since a paranoid organizes all the world's unrelated facts and random impressions around one central, focusing obsession. Kinbote sees himself as a monarch in exile threatened by an assassin, real or imagined, and he's determined to get his story out before he's killed. In all my play-acting—as the dying Jupiter, as Joan of Arc's King Charles and Hector and Boris Godunov—I, too, was a wounded or beleaguered or assassinated or mad monarch. Perhaps Nabokov had intuited something fundamental about the gay monarch, a variety of butterfly.

As it happens, perhaps, the killer is Kinbote himself and the victim is Shade, who never tells Kinbote's story except in the demented man's scholarly annotations. As the novel winds down, we discover that Shade's killer might actually be an escaped madman named Jack Grey. Of course Kinbote thinks he was the intended victim and "Jack Grey" an identity that Gradus, the would-be regicide, has assumed. Fortunately for Kinbote's delusions, Grey commits suicide before he can be interrogated. Nabokov's own father, a liberal democrat, was assassinated in 1922 in

Berlin by a misguided Russian monarchist while saving the life of the intended victim, a political rival.

Nabokov liked to play with shadow lives—"creative autobiography," we might call it. *Look at the Harlequins!* features a satanic writer who is really a heterosexual pedophile—a playful confirmation of ignorant people's worst suspicions about the author of *Lolita*. Humbert himself, like Nabokov, motors across the far reaches of the United States and teaches at a dowdy American university. *Glory* recounts the implausible return of its hero to Russia, just as *Ada* tells of a parallel universe in which Russia and America are parts of the same country. The main character, Hermann, in *Despair* imagines he's the look-alike of another man, but in fact they in no way resemble each other. This plot, too, recounts a misfired murder. Nabokov returned several times to the theme of the false doppelgänger, a parody of the despised Dostoyevsky's *The Double*, not to mention his equally scorned *Notes from Underground*.

Nabokov seemed to know that a long novel can't be devoted to an entirely hateful character, and Kinbote has many redeemable qualities, including an endearing narcissism, a strong libido, a vivid imagination, and a poetic sense, even if it's kitschy.

Even the index of *Pale Fire* is funny and gay. We're told of a cordoned-off section of the royal picture gallery that "contains the statues of Igor's 400 favorite catamites." In the entry for Kinbote himself we discover inconsequential mentions of "his boyhood in Cedarn and the little angler, a honey-skinned lad, naked except for a pair of torn dungarees, one trouser leg rolled up, frequently fed with nugget and nuts, but then school started or the weather changed." No matter that the little angler is never mentioned earlier. Kinbote also cites an entry for his loathing for a person who "makes advances and then betrays a noble and naïve heart, telling foul stories about his victim and pursuing him with brutal practical jokes." Marcel is dismissed as "the fussy, unpleasant, and not altogether plausible central character, pampered by everybody in Proust's *A la Recherche du Temps Perdu*." Under Odon, who's identified as the actor who helps the king escape, the very last index entry is "ought not to marry that blubber-lipped cinemactress, with untidy hair." Finally we're told "Uran the Last Emperor of Zembla, reigned 1798–1799; an incredibly brilliant, luxurious and cruel monarch whose whistling whip made Zembla spin like a rainbow top."

If we look at other classic authors, we can see that evil characters are not always unsympathetic; we are drawn to schemers, revenge-seekers, bad hombres, because they have strong intentions in a vapid world, piercing insights into the fog of existence, unrelenting plans in a rudderless world.

We are drawn to Balzac's Cousine Bette because she is the consummate old maid, an aging virgin, false-humble and real-arrogant, bowing and scraping to her rich, beautiful relatives and in her heart swearing vengeance on them. We don't want to be her, nor do we have anything to learn from her, but we are attracted to her dark matter, her all-engulfing will. When she learns that her pretty cousin Hortense is going to marry her protégé/beloved (a Polish sculptor she hoped to spend the rest of her life with as her son/prisoner), she has a full-scale attack: steam escapes from her eyes, it's as if all her circuits have shorted and her brain is on fire. So much energy in our listless world!

We're not drawn to good characters but to scheming ones. We are fascinated by Olive Chancellor, a feminist lesbian in Henry James's *The Bostonians*, as she struggles to win the lovely young Verena away from her handsome southern cousin Basil Ransom. Though we're supposed to be rooting for Basil as he convinces Verena to walk out on the feminist meeting and to elope with him, the last words brilliantly suggest another whole novel: " 'Ah, now I am glad!' said Verena, when they reached the street. But though she was glad, he presently discovered that, beneath her hood, she was in tears. It is to be feared that with the union, so far from brilliant, into which she was about to enter, these were not the last she was destined to shed."

Could it be that the closet-case James was on the side of the lesbian villain?

Sometimes we're inspired, or at least touched, by a moral dilemma, when a character has only two choices and both are bad. Portia, a teenager in Elizabeth Bowen's *The Death of the Heart*, must choose between marrying a much older man, Major Brutt, or continuing to live with her hostile half brother and his wife. Major Brutt is stuffy and Portia doesn't love him; her relatives dislike her, and her sister-in-law and Portia are both having an affair of sorts with the same man, the detestable, prevaricating Eddie. All of Portia's choices are bad—isn't that one definition of tragedy?

Bowen has a sharp, epigrammatic style. In this novel and in *The House in Paris*, she is way superior to Virginia Woolf and E. M. Forster, though Bowen has been relatively forgotten (Ian McEwan first pointed out to me how Woolf and Forster have unfairly eclipsed all the other excellent writers of their generation and after). Bowen is less "experimental" than Woolf; no endless efforts to approximate a state of being (albeit in Edwardian language). Bowen has crisp, thorough paragraphs introducing characters. Take the presentation of Matchett, the dignified older servant:

> She had an austere, ironical straight face, flesh padded smoothly over the strong structure of bone. Her strong, springy lusterless hair was centre-parted and drawn severely back; she wore no cap. Habitually, she walked with her eyes down and her vein-marbled eyelids were unconciliating. Her mouth, at this moment stubbornly inexpressive, still had a crease at each end from her last unwilling smile. Her expression, her attitude, were held-in and watchful. The monklike impassivity of her features made her big bust curious, out of place; it seemed some sort of structure for the bib of her apron to be fastened up to with gold pins. To her unconscious sense of inner drama, only her hands gave play; one hand seemed to support the fragile Regency pillar; the other was open fan wise, like a hand in a portrait, over her aproned hip. While she thought, or rather calculated, her eyes would move slowly under her dropped lids.

This description is bristling with movement. That crease from her last "unwilling" smile. Her hands giving play to her "unconscious sense of inner drama." Those hooded eyes "moving slowly." Was it Ezra Pound who said kinesthetic images, ones that register motion, are the most memorable? At least we can say that metaphors or descriptions that express movement are much more memorable than those that are static, as if picturing a precise moment (eyes rolling under closed lids) digs a small groove in our consciousness that a still picture cannot do.

But is a full-length portrait, even if it's kinesthetic, a bit old-fashioned? My Princeton students of creative writing seem to think so. I can understand one might want to leave the central characters a bit blurry so that the reader can fill in the blanks and more easily identify with them, but surely sharp portraiture helps with the minor actors. Is it just that getting a likeness is a lost art? Or does it stop the action flow? Or is everyone so cinematic now that they can easily supply a face and a body?

I'm not sure what readers want. I was just looking at the comments on Goodreads on Stendhal's *The Red and the Black*; one person complained it was "dated," and another disliked all the characters and their far-fetched romances. I sometimes wonder if what I consider "romance" might be dying out—*l'amour fou*, crazy love, destructive passion, crippling jealousy, extreme and violent and tragic. Scott Spencer's *Endless Love* (not either of the film adaptations) involves teenager David burning down the house of his girlfriend Jade in revenge for her father's restraining order against him. David is imprisoned; Jade marries someone else. Her life and his are sad. They've both been scorched by love.

According to the philosopher and critic Martha Nussbaum, in an essay in *Love's Knowledge*,

> stories cultivate our ability to see and care for particulars, not as representatives of the law, but as what they themselves are: to respond vigorously with senses and emotions before the new; to care deeply about chance happenings in the world, rather than to fortify ourselves against them; to wait for the outcome, and to be bewildered—to wait and float and be actively passive. We are so accustomed to the novel that we tend to forget how morally controversial a form it has been in the eyes of various sorts of religious and secular moralisms . . . questionable with very good reason: for the novel acknowledges a wonder before worldly sensuous particulars.

Nussbaum, following Richard Rorty, seems to give a prize position to the novel—not because it uncovers general truths but because it draws our attention to bright particulars. We live in a world of accidents, contingency, constant change; fiction prepares us for that. It is the only art form that places us in the mind of a perceiver. That is its great gift.

Chapter 8

I've always associated reading and writing with sex. When I was in eighth grade, fourteen years old, I would sit every afternoon for an hour in the school library across from a friend—tall, lean, freckled—who had the bruised-leaf smell of a redhead, though his hair was auburn and lushly curly. He had that scrubbed, pale, almost blue-lipped look of some boys who seem in need of rouge and lipstick, who look like actors who've just cold-creamed away their mouths and eyebrows—as in need of color as waking monkeys are in need of coffee.

It helped that he'd just had an hour of football and hadn't taken a shower. Every day he came at two o'clock direct from the playing field to the library, smelling almost rank with sweat and hormones, almost like one of those bitter herbs it's become fashionable to mix in with greens that otherwise would be too bland.

He reeked unapologetically. He always sat directly across from me at one end of the long library table. We would each pretend to read, but soon we'd clamped our fourteen-year-old legs around each other—his left leg my right leg, his right leg my left leg. He seemed like a normal, popular, athletic guy, who was also good in math and wanted to be a chemical engineer like his dad. He was going steady with a pretty blonde a foot shorter, and they would cling to each other at sock hops like drowning swimmers. Luckily most of the doo-wop songs of the period were slow, and they could grind into each other for hours. When he went to get her another cup of punch, I always looked at his crotch to see if I could detect the outlines of a wet erection. I usually could.

When we sat "reading" in the library, our legs clamped each other in a pulsing rhythm, tightening and relaxing, tightening and relaxing. I could feel the muscles in his legs, the bulging quadriceps crowning his thighs but so bulky they were spilling over to the sides. The intense herbal smell seemed to grow stronger the more eager we became.

I would scoot down in my chair and press my knee into his crotch, but he would draw back fractionally. Maybe he was afraid one of the other kids would see us, or he had his limits, as the girls back then would allow touching above the waist but not below. They might as well have worn traffic signals, green to go, amber to slow down, red to stop. Danny was mostly green or amber, and he wasted no time to get us into a crural crunch. I don't think he wanted it to go anywhere; he liked the pressure and pleasure but knew it was forbidden. When we were twelve, us guys had wrestled for hours on the lawn playing Squirrel ("Grab the nuts and run")—painful as it might have been, it was irresistible. By now we'd outgrown that, but this under-the-table thrill, just because it was unprecedented and still unidentified, was tacitly alluring.

To this day the smell of a sweating redhead male makes me think of bunched, moist underpants, the strong, pulsing vise of clamped legs, long afternoon rays of sunlight coming through half-rolled-up yellow window shades, and, across the wood table with its bordered central pad of dark leather, Danny's pale, drained face over a book, his face exhausted from sports but still game for alternating leg-squeezing. The aggressive smell of a redhead man, of weeds stewing in a hot, sunlit puddle, still intoxicates me. Like so many strong odors, it's wildly attractive, just short of being repulsive (the sadist with the stinky cigar). And part of the whole mise-en-scène is the books. Danny's eyes kept scanning in the customary direction at an unrelenting rhythm, as if he were reading. Once or twice he'd reach down to rearrange his crotch, and his bloodless lips would twitch in an acknowledging smile, but he'd never look at me. We were both playing at reading.

The difference was that I wouldn't have minded studying with him in private behind locked doors. But he'd already gone as far as—or farther than—he dared. When the sun was going down and it was getting colder and our mothers were becoming worried, I was always the one who wanted to go on playing Squirrel another half hour.

What was it like to read without reading? To see the words rushing past without registering them, a whole paragraph blurring by like an express subway hurtling so fast you can't tell whether it's the A or the C, your own hot fixation on Danny like a red letter superimposed over the pale blue illegible script of the book floating past—until you reached the end of a paragraph and couldn't honestly say anything about it except the C for "Cock" or the A for "Ass."

The mind would return to the top of the page and engage for an instant, deciphering the printed words and following the meaning, like a tug pulling a battleship—until Danny would squeeze your legs with extra force and the huge boat would pull free, drift and sink. Start all over again, discreetly underscoring the words with your fingertip and silently pronouncing the syllables, but Danny would slide an inch forward and clamp harder as if in a game—and the ship would capsize again. You were reading a dull U.S. history textbook, and you mindlessly highlighted the fugitive paragraph about the Dred Scott decision in bright yellow with its chemical smell, and superimposed on the yellow names of the Supreme Court justices. The far more urgent question: Should you follow Danny into the john, or would that spook him and spoil everything?

Books were my constant companions during those horny teenage years. I was a bookworm boring through whole stacks of public libraries. I would take a book to the lavatory and read in my closed cubicle, roosting for hours, peeking out through the doorjamb at each newcomer (rushing by too quickly to be identified) and psychoanalyzing each pair of shoes in the adjoining stall to determine if I could detect any flirtatious tapping or stance-widening worthy of a senator. The smells of bleach and urinal pads and shit were the melancholy accompaniment to my "cruising" (I didn't even know the word, since I'd not met any avowed gays yet with their coded vocabulary).

Perhaps my reading I thought of as compensating for all the hours wasted on public toilets. Maybe that's why my reading took such a serious turn toward history, linguistics, philosophy—nothing was too daunting for this serious midwestern public-library intellectual. If I ran into French dialogue among the aristocrats in an old translation of *War and Peace*, I would mutter indignantly, "For pete's sake!"; I had no patience with artificial barriers to knowledge. I admired the logical positivists such as Rudolf Carnap among philosophers because they expressed themselves clearly and confidently and swept out centuries of accumulated metaphysical cobwebs: swish, there goes Saint Thomas, swish-swish, away with Aristotle. To me the most bestial and shameful appetites were associated with the life of the mind. When I was a teen, I dreamed one night I was a convict worker sweating and laboring in the basement of a luxury hotel; we, the grizzled prisoners, weren't allowed upstairs with the lovely guests. As an adult I had a dream in which men in tuxedos sipped champagne in a room lined entirely with narrow mirrored doors; in an instant they could go through the doors into a brutal backroom given over to cruelty, blood, sex, sweat, and tears.

If I felt a wan inertia, a tepid depression during all my hours and hours "offstage" (between sexual encounters), I was electrified, face burning, blush blossoms creeping up my chest and neck, when I touched another man. Behavioral psychologists say that the most binding schedule is random reinforcement; the pigeon gets a pellet not after every third or seventh peck but at utterly unpredictable intervals. That was cruising— "random reinforcement," like slot machines. After only one more plunge of the lever, maybe three cherries will come up, or a slender, smiling young athlete might enter the library toilet.

In Cincinnati one summer when I was working as a fifteen-year-old at my father's downtown office, I ran over to the public library. A tall, slim college student in a summer suit, starched white shirt, and red-and-yellow silk rep tie walked swiftly, head lowered, to the next urinal, though the others weren't busy, unzipped—and immediately started to stare at me with an intense frown.

He was the best-looking man who'd ever shown an interest in me. And I certainly wasn't going to play hard to get. I came from a family that paid so little attention to me that I was a stutterer and had to see a speech therapist ("Just pretend you're a rag doll, you're so relaxed you're falling asleep"); whenever I'd start to speak at the dinner table, my father would glower and my cleverer older sister would interrupt. In such a world you had to light fires atop a chain of watchtowers to send a message ("The enemy is coming! The enemy is coming!"). To this day tomfoolery or irony makes me nervous—why add additional barriers to communication, already so hit-and-miss?

I turned, erect and smiling, toward my admirer—but he immediately zipped up and rushed out. I couldn't understand what had happened; what was my faux pas? When I left the restroom, I spied him standing beside a pretty girl in a pale blue dress with a white collar and long, glossy hair. He beckoned for me to come over.

Now I felt alarmed. Who were these people? Why did they want to talk to me, a shambling teen with Steve Allen black glasses and a horrible buzz cut my father had imposed on me and that threw my big ears and untanned skin into relief? I was shabby and felt ugly. The handsome man and woman were now smiling with connivance. I was afraid of them. It smelled fishy to me. Did they want to play a trick on me? Was she in on it? What was "it"? I returned to my seat and pile of books a few rows away.

And then he suddenly slid into the adjoining chair. "Why won't you join us? We think you look interesting. I'm Dan. That's Sharon. Come with us—I've got a convertible. We'll go somewhere."

"I'm Ed," I said, my mind racing. "I have to go back to work."

"Oh, take the afternoon off."

"Thanks, but I have only an hour for lunch. I work just three blocks down on Pine."

I wanted to say, "What do you have in mind?" Or, "Maybe another time." I was reluctant to shut the door and afraid to leave it open. He got up abruptly and went back to his girl. She lifted her hands, palms up, and shrugged, as if to say, "I give up."

I'd read *The Catcher in the Rye,* and though these people didn't remind me of any particular characters in that book, they seemed to have come right out of that world—East Coast, bored and privileged, too privileged to fail, whereas I felt I was just hanging on by my fingertips. They could afford to have attitudes, to make themselves conspicuous, to play little games on juvenile bystanders. I suppose I was eccentric, a nervous wreck, so graceless you couldn't tell I was a sissy, afraid of my own shadow, patiently, like a dung beetle, pushing uphill my growing ball of knowledge and culture. But it never occurred to me to question the greatness of the great, of recognized artists and thinkers, and I absorbed them all with the thirst of a desert palm. I didn't shrug or tempt strangers at the urinal just for fun. I had no sense of humor—though I knew from my reading that that was a desirable quality on the marriage market, a realization that didn't make it any more likely I'd learn to be funny. The 1950s were before the era of self-improvement. People were handsome because they were born that way, had fine eyes and strong jaws, straight noses and musical voices. Maybe if someone had a disfiguring accident, she might undergo lots of surgery, but only to get her up to speed, out of the monster category, surely not to improve on nature. Men were born tall and long-waisted and so powerful in the chest they looked as if they'd burst out of their shirts. The rest of us fit into our sharkskin suits better than those guys in their tight cords, white socks, run-down penny loafers, their formless blazers and shirts always pulled halfway out and open at the thick neck, but that the blue of the shirt matched their eyes and the red scarf mimicked their winter-rosy cheeks, or that their teeth were white, straight, and always pinging with silver stars—surely these colors and glints were God-given, not somehow . . . achieved.

If a man on the bus wore a porkpie hat, a pencil-thin mustache, and a maroon silk tie wider than it was long, he was born that way. His ugliness was genetic. That was a sort of ugliness life had drawn for him out of the hat. Boys with fluent waists, girls with resplendent hair, cheerleaders, even off-duty, who effervesced and moved in a swarm, their bracelets tinkling, their laughter rising softly and their white Oxfords unsmudged under the gray, methodically pleated skirts—that was just the way God had made them, and any usurper (awkward, her hair bouncing in long curls like metal slinkies, ambling down the stairs, lipstick on her eyetooth, her ankles bandaged with thin white socks rather than with the trendy fat white socks) was immediately identifiable and expelled.

The Catcher in the Rye was the first book (just as *Blue Denim* and *Rebel Without a Cause* were the first movies) that seemed to be about people like me and my friends. Of course I didn't really know anyone like Brandon de Wilde or James Dean (besides, Hollywood "teens" looked as if they were in their twenties to our adolescent eyes—the coordinated colors, the gripping undergarments, no pudge or acne), but they illustrated our dreams. Later, in the 1960s, rebels would find causes, but in the 1950s they were possessed by the urge to revolt, which quickly sputtered out in alienated attitudes.

This chic, tall couple at the library could have been Hollywood teens or cousins of Holden Caulfield, ever alert for "phonies," ready for spontaneous adventure, no sooner kicked out of one prep school than enrolled in another, better one. I wasn't like them. I was a neglected child. I could be depressed, quietly, privately, but I still had to get straight A's, work summer jobs, stay in line and inconspicuous. Although I returned often to the library, my exciting couple never made another appearance. I never found what they were up to. Sexual charades were my closest guess. Maybe some kind of unimaginable perversion.

My father disapproved of my reading, especially in the summertime, when I should be doing chores around his lakeside house. Reading spelled laziness, and laziness was next to sissiness. My parents were divorced, but my mother the psychologist had reported gleefully to Dad that I was "acting out," acting out with "inappropriate object choices." I begged her not to confide my secret in him, but she did it anyway, despite her promise. He never mentioned it to me but put me on a strict regime of raking pine needles: the cure for homosexuality is yard work. In *Forgetting Elena* the narrator is forced to rake needles, which feels pointless and unbearably lonely.

If I was constantly reading, I was also constantly writing. Someone gave me a rhyming dictionary in which the second half was devoted to prosody: how to write a triolet, a sestina, a canzone, a sonnet. I quickly learned to write both Petrarchan and Shakespearean sonnets (different rhyme schemes—the Shakespearean ends with a bumper-car couplet as the clincher). I was impressed by Pope's versified "essays" and soon, at fourteen, had produced a rather long one on the seasons. My eighth-grade teacher, Mrs. Kincaid, had me read it out loud to three different sections of English class: the girls doodled and the boys doubled up laughing. But I still felt special, and there and then I decided to be a writer (I'd already tried acting, composing, and painting without much success). In the eighth-grade pageant I wore a sort of tunic and sat primly like the White Rock girl with my legs to one side, which my sister later ridiculed, and I processed in and out to Schubert's "Unfinished" and said, rather loudly, "I am lit-chur" in my midwestern accent.

My erotic fantasies were all mixed up with dreams of tyrannical power, as if the sissy, after having enough sand kicked in his face, becomes the frightening strong man. I had extended fantasies about dominating whole countries, continents, the world. My whole personality, however, was gentle and cowardly, and I would scream while watching a movie where someone on screen broke a nail. I wanted to be a great general. I began a biography of Peter the Great and copied out whole pages from the standard biographies. I begged my parents to send me to Culver Military Academy in Indiana, and they did for a practice summer; I wanted to begin my military career right away. But just as gay men in my generation worshiped athletes but were bored by sports, in the same way I admired sailors, soldiers, and pilots but quickly came to detest marching, six A.M. reveilles, spit shines and hospital corners, trooping the colors across dusty, bug-infested fields, and swimming a mile (my preferred stroke was the backstroke). We were always on the move, either training or on nature hikes, where we learned to identify banal midwestern plants (goldenrod and Queen Anne's lace). Never a moment to curl up with a book. After six weeks I developed a high fever and strep throat, and my mother had to drive down from Chicago to fetch me out of the infirmary. So ended my dreams of world conquest.

My delusions of grandeur migrated to the Greek gods; I read Edith Hamilton's mythology and tried to memorize the different Greek and Roman names of the same deity. I had moments when I believed I was Zeus and could control the thunder by shaking my hand in a certain way (three sets of three bolts). I dreamed of my own death, my mother and sister weeping beside my tomb, their stupefaction when I rose from the grave. Now they were sorry they hadn't been nicer to me—nicer or at least awestruck.

When I was still in grade school, I became friends with Fred and Marilyn; he owned the local bookstore in Evanston, Illinois, and she worked there. If I couldn't be Napoleon, at least I could be the bewitching little genius. Marilyn wore peasant blouses and too much perfume. Fred was severely ascetic and wore sandals. They were amused by me and decided I should learn German from a Northwestern professor so that I could read Hermann Hesse in the original (he was just beginning to be translated). Accordingly I went twice a week to Dr. Meno Spann's apartment to take my lessons. I attended a puppet show of a pre-Goethe *Faust* that Spann devised (he played all the parts and produced all the voices). He'd made the hand puppets, with their large heads of painted, chiseled wood. His Faust was a Renaissance scholar, based on Marlowe's play, which was the source of Goethe's poem. I quickly became infatuated with him and insisted my mother invite him to dinner (maybe he should marry her, I thought, but her dinner was not copious enough for him and she must have bored him, though she put on her best dress and drank many highballs and babbled pleasantly). I loved his tallness, his culture, and his masculinity; in his living room there were photos of him in a swimsuit on the beach, holding a woman aloft on one hand. Just recently I learned that he was married five times, each wife having divorced him after just a year or two of marriage. At the time, like Bluebeard, he never mentioned his wives. He wrote a textbook of beginning German for Americans and a study of Kafka. He devised a system of exercise, which he followed all during his long life. His Hungarian mother was an actress.

I made no progress in German, even though I was so motivated; perhaps I was a dumb kid after all, or average, not the little genius my mother pretended I was. On alternating days she questioned all my abilities, and I felt my self-esteem either exalted or dashed; perhaps that's why I read my reviews to this day with dread in my heart. Was I talented or was I an idiot? This fear never made me cautious. Even in boarding school I was already writing about homosexuality (my first novel, *The Tower Window*, in which the teen hero becomes gay after a girl rejects him) or nymphomania (my second book, *Mrs. Morrigan*). That second work made my classmates titter, and when I read a bit out loud, even my teacher, whom we called the Wombat, shook his doughy hand as if he'd touched something hot and smacked his dentured, boneless mouth. Their shock and laughter incensed me; I'd portrayed a serious psychological condition, nymphomania, and all they could do was treat it as pornography. In all my sixty-some years of writing I've never written to scandalize or arouse, though people have often been horrified or titillated by my books. *Mrs. Morrigan*, in fact, was about a middle-aged, middle-class midwestern woman who sleeps around with dangerous, even homicidal riffraff after her husband rejects her. In my mind rejection immediately precipitated sexual hysteria. Because my mother was a psychologist, I tried to take a "scientific" approach to sex, which had already become my great theme in all its many forms.

Once I was ill at the school infirmary for several days and read *Wuthering Heights* with a total immersion of spirit and mind. I can't remember what I had, but it was contagious and I was isolated—which was perfect for reading a classic with rapture. Clean sheets. One window. Meals served in bed. I could picture Heathcliff with startling clarity. I thought he was as sexy as a gypsy.

Now, being an experienced writer, I might read *Wuthering Heights* with an eye to its clumsy construction (all those Chinese boxes, one inside another) or its inconsistent point of view, but back then I read with the same uncritical delight with which I still listen to music. It helps not to "professionalize" an art to remain pervious to it. Our boys' school, Cranbrook, outside Detroit, was a parody of the Gothic style, with arches and turrets and gargoyles and a red brick tower—a perfect setting for reading the ur-Gothic novel!

When I was sixteen and at home during the summer, I started taking the L from Evanston to downtown Chicago, where I discovered another good bookshop tucked in between an art-movie house showing foreign films and a narrow, expensive coffee shop serving espresso. This was the 1950s. The bookshop was on Rush Street, the heart of the nightclub district, thronged with rowdy drunks, mostly wide in the beam and red in the face. I couldn't go to a bar, straight or gay, but no one could stop me from "shopping" in a bookstore. I felt at home among the books—and turned on.

The bookstore owner was a pockmarked, somber Texan—and a gay man, I soon discovered. I would spend hours chatting with him, too hot in my overcoat, my feet tired from standing. His shop glittered before my eyes, though only the size of a modest storefront. That was before the era when bookstores sold cute coffee mugs, stuffed animals, and calendars of Impressionist paintings; there was nothing but *Fear and Trembling* by Søren Kierkegaard, Joseph Campbell's *The Hero with a Thousand Faces*, and a translation of Thomas Mann's *Dr. Faustus*. No travel books, no glossy picture books on the houses of the stars, no do-it-yourself astrology guides. In the 1950s high culture was forbiddingly high, if not widespread. I was fascinated by the owner not because I found him attractive but because I knew he was gay. I told him I was looking for a rich older lover, and he said, "They go for each other—why would a millionaire want you, a simple girl of the people?"

He enjoyed switching genders, which took me a while to get used to. Then I thought it was exhilaratingly funny, a token that I was a gay insider. He told me that European men like to "brown" (anal intercourse), whereas we Americans were famous for blowing men ("No, silly, you suck, not blow. We're known for it all over the world. Those Europeans were glad to see us arrive after World War II"). I learned that most homosexuals were passive or "femme." Only a few were "butch." Best to pay a "real" (that is, heterosexual) man rather than "bump pussies" with another faggot. If a man was "trade," he might let you suck him, especially if he was drunk enough ("All holes look good to a stiff dick")—though he might beat you up later. He told me he'd been beaten up often by drunk sailors—it wasn't so bad, all part of the game, could be kinda sexy. He had a lover who was a married man, a cop, to whom he gave money and who spanked him.

The vogue book in 1956 was Colin Wilson's *The Outsider*, which he'd written at age twenty-four while living on Hampstead Heath in a sleeping bag. It was a look at Jean-Paul Sartre's *Nausea*, Dostoyevsky's *Notes from Underground*, Rilke's *Malte Laurids Brigge*, Knut Hamsun's *Hunger*—all the tormented, isolated, existentialist misfits (I thought, glamorously, of myself as one). I can remember when the box of that book arrived and my friend, the bookstore owner, tore it open with glee, saying "I'll sell it out in a week!" We started reading random paragraphs out loud to each other: "Oh my God, this is so smart!" we'd exclaim.

Learning to be gay felt not unrelated to learning to be cultured. I forget everything now, but then I was gifted with nearly total recall; I remembered book titles, names of publishers, names of opera singers, names of operas. I was never a systematic, methodical reader. I didn't read all of Aristotle but just the *Nicomachean Ethics* and the *Poetics*. Sometimes I felt I was registered in Cocktail Party 101; I wanted to be urbane more than erudite. Of course my idea of urbanity was based on a comprehensive general knowledge (excluding science) that I'd never encountered in real life except in books (and from Chicago's cultural radio station, WFMT, which would program competing versions of *La forza del destino* during the dinner hour, or someone reciting from Pound's *Cantos*. I liked the modulated, well-bred tones of the male announcers; I tried to picture these civilized young men). My pornography at the time was black-and-white photos of male ballet dancers in tights. I studied their crotches but could detect no bumps beneath the dance belts. The powerful legs and graceful hands and heads tipped back all bewitched me.

At the bookshop I met an older but golden-haired harpist who was outraged I'd never seen him on television playing his instrument. His walls were covered with large photos of the Moscow-born dancer André Eglevsky, who he claimed with lots of batting of his gilt eyelashes had been his lover, though now I wonder, since Eglevsky had been married and had a grown dancer-daughter. Eglevsky had appeared in several movies, including Charlie Chaplin's *Limelight*. He lived in New York and danced with Balanchine. Why, exactly, would he be lovers with an overweight harpist in Chicago who reeked of patchouli, though he seemed pretty nice?

Because I was always seeing psychoanalysts, trying to go straight, I spent a lot of time with women—and even slept with them. While I was an undergrad at the University of Michigan, I wrote many things, hovered over by three different women. One was Ann Hall, a chubby heiress from Fort Wayne who was the true bohemian. A painter of big, slashing abstractions, she lived in a whole house, a little one she rented. She doted on me, listened to every word an instant after I'd written it, cooked hearty meals, and lent me her VW to drive the hundred-mile round trip once a week to Detroit to see my shrink. Privately, putting my Freudian goals to one side, I thought that women spoiled men and made them weak and egotistical; I preferred the "realism," even coldness, of other men—it was less corrupting. I slept with her a few times, once when she was having her period (I think she was impressed that that didn't dim my ardor—or at least it added to my beatnik cred). She thought everything I wrote was splendid, and I could count on her to grunt with approval every time I turned a page (though she didn't get my jokes and never laughed but blinked confusedly). Our all-nighters were fueled with white wine, heavy food, and her adoration as we both closed one eye drunkenly and approached the blank page or canvas.

A second girl was a bucktoothed free spirit with unruly hair and a beautiful body who had something like a man's frank interest in sex. She was called Suzy. She had a startlingly inappropriate laugh. She was very smart. We would sit in the basement of the house I shared, under a great unfurled red sail covering the ceiling, and both write, high on amphetamines. My low self-esteem (then as now) made me write short, but speed fed an unaccustomed logorrhea. I wrote a long-winded play about a black woman (the maid) and a black man (the gardener) who gradually take over the household of whites and rule it, before they self-destruct. It won the University of Michigan's Hopwood Award, named after a successful boulevard playwright, Avery Hopwood, who was the most highly paid writer for the stage during the Jazz Age (*Getting Gertie's Garter, The Demi-Virgin*). He was always writing something "naughty," though he was gay. He drowned in the sea on the Riviera, leaving his fortune to the University of Michigan.

My prize was announced in the *New York Times*, which led to my getting an agent, Sylvia Herscher at William Morris, who eventually sold it to Ashley Feinstein; he directed it in 1964 off-Broadway, starring Cicely

Tyson and Billy Dee Williams. The play received some good notices but ran only a month. It was a very warm May, and no one felt like going indoors when it was still hot and light outside. Ashley was completely under the spell of his mentor, Arthur Laurents (who wrote the book for *Gypsy* and *West Side Story*); Laurents breezed by one day, insisting that all the props (mirror, comb, toothbrush) should look like toy props and should be three times larger than in reality.

In my provincial university, Eugène Ionesco and the Theater of the Absurd seemed utterly up-to-date, and I adopted some of these absurdist mannerisms. The most soul-scorching moment of my literary life occurred during one preview in New York when an apparently seasoned playwright a few years older than me sat behind me and voiced all of his criticism to his date ("Oh, how dimwitted! He failed that test!"). During the intermission friends came up to me to congratulate me; after the interval my critic whispered nothing to his companion—I almost regretted it. He was intelligent and his remarks were apt, whereas the audience was usually stacked with investors, or bewildered old people who'd been handed out free tickets at their nursing home, or friends. No one said the truth, and everyone faked enthusiasm.

I didn't—and don't—have a strong enough character to weather the trials of the theater. I'd had my old-fashioned "absurdist" vision of my play, but now that I'd arrived in New York, I didn't know how to defend it. Arthur Laurents had had so many hits, and Ashley had been his assistant—surely they knew better than I how to make a play a hit.

We did everything in the usual way. My agent prompted me to send flowers to Cicely. We all waited for the reviews at Sardi's. When they came in, lukewarm for the most part, I just prayed the evening would soon be over. I was thought of as "winning" and "sociable," but I didn't like social life, which I considered an enormous strain. I was terrified of making a gaffe, perhaps due to my upbringing in the Midwest. Something about me (nothing I intended) suggested to other blue-bloods that I was one of them, but in fact I didn't know how to dress well, nor did I have enough money for clothes. And I didn't even know how to hold myself at table. I was so afraid of being dull that I was often outrageous (I also drank too much)—dull is better than shocking in polite society.

The best review of my play was from an English critic in *Theatre Arts* (which soon went out of business). Here's the Proustian part; when I met this critic, Alan Pryce-Jones, years later in Newport, I told him how sustaining his review had been for me as a young writer (he'd written that it was one of the two best plays of the season, along with Murray Schisgal's *Luv*). He said, "I have absolutely no memory of that."

The third woman who encouraged my writing at the University of Michigan was Jean Waugh, an accomplished short story writer in her own right. She helped me edit and type my short stories for the Hopwood by preparing me cold curry soup with dill and fresh slices of apple in it and by playing me vintage recordings from the 1930s of Georges Thill singing Italian opera in French (*La Bohème*: "Que cette main est froide"). I'd sleep on her daybed and awake to fragrant hot tea and Thill's seamless, sparkling, urgent voice with its rich, bare baritone tones, impeccable diction, and ringing high notes in the spinto (romantic tenor) style. Jean was black and was the fantasized original for the heroine in my play *The Blueboy in Black*. The character was devious and vengeful, but I had misread Jean, who was kindness itself. I suppose if I'd been black, I would have been enraged; being marginalized as gay already made me angry. What Jean and I had in common was that we both passed, she as white and I as straight, as I still do where people don't know me. She was so fair-skinned that her own daughter didn't seem to know her mother was black (Jean's husband was white). Jean told me in college that many of her relatives passed, though they always panicked in the 1940s and '50s when they were pregnant. What if the baby came out black? Then they'd have to move out of their white neighborhood and give up their white friends. I suppose that the only comparable thing for me would have been a visit at my fraternity house by a very queeny, camp friend.

Was I betraying Jean by portraying her as an evil schemer? I've been accused of betraying or undermining the people around me. It's true that I've always had problems with people in authority. Was I, as a king/god/general, meant to submit to other people? Throughout the years I always tried to undermine my boss, no matter who he was, even if I came to like him later when he was no longer my boss. Whereas I was a benign monarch (in plays, in childhood games), as a boss myself, I was a true Iago as an underdog.

Of course most of my critics have interpreted my dark desires and deeds in my books more charitably. Generally they've said the narrator in *A Boy's Own Story*, who betrays a teacher who has befriended him and even had sex with him, was taking his first step into the world of adulthood, as if this action were a sign (maybe a lamentable sign) of independence and maturity. Betrayal as maturity? It's amazing how much writers can get away with.

If *A Boy's Own Story* was about treachery, *Caracole* was traitorous in itself. I wrote it after I moved to Paris in 1983. At the time I said that it read like the nightmare of a grad student in comparative literature the night before his orals. So much of world literature was jumbled together— Stendhal, the life of Madame de Staël, Casanova's memoirs, minor works about Venice or by Venetians I read in a family library in the Palazzo Barbaro. The book was divided into three parts inspired by Roland Barthes and Michel Foucault: uncoded, coded, and decoded, as if I could represent an Edenic state before society imposed its rules on the individual, followed by the years of education in which someone (Gabriel) acquired a knowledge of the world, finally leading to a period when that person shed all of his acquired manners, beliefs, and attitudes. It was based on my nephew, Keith, who deeply resented it because I mentioned his bad skin. I had made him a Stendhalian hero—a Fabrizio, I thought—and all he could focus on was the acne I described.

Julien Gracq's *The Opposing Shore* might be read as a glorious, superior antecedent to *Caracole*, though I hadn't read it before writing my novel and can claim it only as a distant spiritual cousin. If Borges could talk about Kafka and his precursors (Robert Browning was one), then I could just as easily discuss my unsuspected literary cousins who only turned out to be "influences" in retrospect. When I finally read *The Opposing Shore*, I had the eerie feeling that I was writing it—or that some purer, more luminous person I knew intimately or had been in a previous or parallel life was writing it. Apparently the withdrawn Gracq, a high school geography teacher, was inspired to write it during the *drôle de guerre*—the "phony war," before Germany attacked France in World War II—and the first part of it he wrote as a prisoner of war. I also had been drawn to the subject of a superior nation defeated and ruled by an inferior one, though for me it was a subject I lived through metaphorically, anagogically, rather than experientially.

Later, in *My Lives*, an autobiography, I wrote about "my master," the last man who broke my heart. He had sex with me once in a while, whenever he could get away from his possessive lover; he sometimes came by in his jogging shorts and T-shirt and quietly and quickly unwrapped his sublime body. I always paid him a trivial sum ($100), because I thought it would make him keep coming back for more. He liked to rough me up, and he kept coming back.

He did until he fell in love with a sadist all his own ("Today's trade is tomorrow's competition," as we used to say). He stopped seeing me—and I completely fell apart. I'd wept like that in my twenties over Jim Ruddy, who went mad, and in my forties over Keith McDermott, who was never attracted to me. But now in my sixties here I was crying all the time, even on the train, even in front of my students. I wrote about my master as faithfully and honestly as I could, and I even read the chapter out loud to him for his approval, which he gave me at the time. Later he felt I'd "used" him, but by then it was too late; the book was already published. Another revenge. Another treachery.

Had I taken my revenge on him, or merely tried to control the situation by writing about it? When my French lover died of AIDS in Morocco, I'd written about him on the plane back to Paris, afraid I'd become hysterical otherwise and be put off the flight.

In this case, with my master, I'd written openly about how we sneaked around his then lover, and I talked about the few transgressive things we'd done sexually. I had the right to be frank about my own behavior, didn't I—but did I have the right to reveal his, though I concealed his name?

Janet Malcolm has described in *The Journalist and the Murderer* the lopsided relationship between writer and subject. Even when the subject has agreed to be written about, and, in my case, to the content, there is still a moral ambiguity at work. As Malcolm specifies, the ambiguity "lies not in its texts but in the relationships out of which they arise." As she goes on to explain, even the goodness of the good characters is as much a writerly invention as the evil of the bad characters. The writer is completely in charge, even if the subject hopes to manipulate the writer and to gain something from the exchange.

The writer has the last laugh; even if (as in my case) he is funny at his own expense and self-abnegating, his is still the governing point of view. He is the one who selects details and suppresses others, and he is the one who holds himself up for admiration as fiercely honest and, say, admirably sexual. For if there is a relationship between the writer and the subject, there is also a constantly shifting and growing rapport between writer and reader. There is a whole German literary school of criticism called reader-response theory, founded by Wolfgang Iser, in which the writer constructs an implied reader. Some writers pretend to be indifferent to the reception of their work, but I am constantly modeling in my mind an effigy of the reader—based on how readings go over, what real critics or Amazon readers say. Sometimes it's obvious that certain readers are hostile or uncomprehending and they can be ignored, but most call for some response, especially in matters of clarity. For instance, at the end of *Jack Holmes and His Friend*, some very clever readers have imagined that it's the straight friend who's become infected with AIDS—which never occurred to me. I keep trying to find the passage that misled them in order to eliminate it.

In *Inside a Pearl: My Years in Paris*, I think I managed to alienate all my English writer friends, which seems a pity. Part of the problem is that admiring verbal portraits are dull; they must be a little bit shocking or scandalous to open the reader's eyes and leap off the page. Kindness and generosity are usually soporific.

Could it be that prose is dull if it loses its bite? It could be an artifact of vivid style that it's always nuanced and aggressive. Or it could be that our innate nastiness always comes out on the page. Then again I've been praised for being compassionate as often as I've been damned for being "critical," as southerners say.

Sex and literature. Once I was being banged so noisily for so long that the landlady, who lived downstairs, came up at three A.M. to complain. My resourceful roommate said I was piling books. The next day I sent the landlady a bouquet with a note that said, "Sorry for the noise, you'll be pleased to know Books has moved on."

Chapter 9

My books are in such disorder that often I have to buy a title twice because I can't find it on my shelves. A friend alphabetized the books two years ago, but now once again they're in huge, teetering piles. Nor does it help that there's a row of books behind another on every shelf. We keep another pile beside the door for those rejected books destined for charity shops.

There are books on every surface and in both bedrooms. In one of the bathrooms there's a bookcase. I'm reminded of Samuel Pepys's complaint that he had stacks of books on every chair. Once in Truman Capote's apartment I saw nothing but the author's own books. I thought that the height of narcissism. But now I've learned it's vulgar and misleading to judge a writer by his library, as if it's a key to his mind. More often, he has given away to friends the books he really loves and has loaded his shelves with those sent by publishers or authors looking for a blurb or a review—most of which he's never glanced at.

Of course my books are of little value. My friend Stephen Orgel, for instance, a Shakespeare scholar at Stanford, owns hundreds of ancient books—sometimes the unique example of an Elizabethan title. I've been to some of the world's great libraries: the Bibliothèque Mazarine in Paris, next door to the French Academy, which owns an illuminated Latin Bible of the eleventh century with prefaces written by Saint Jerome, a 1664 collection of Molière's plays, a library of Italian works published in Paris during the Renaissance, Pope Leo's letters from the tenth century, and heretical books in all languages, as well as a corpus on coats of arms. Or the Trinity College Library in Dublin, which possesses the Book of

Kells, Bishop Berkeley's library, and many ancient manuscripts—some six million volumes total (it's the Irish equivalent to the U.S. Library of Congress).

I remember the Abbey Library at Einsiedeln, a Benedictine abbey in Switzerland surrounded by snow-covered mountains, consecrated by a resurrected and peripatetic Jesus Christ himself in 948 A.D. I remember visiting the abbey church, a Baroque candy box, but what really impressed me was the white-and-pale-blue library, Baroque if austere, in which the only spots of color were the books themselves, some 250,000 of them. The library was so cold we could see our breath; I'm a nonbeliever, but it all felt spiritual and conducive to the most rigorous exegesis. I was especially fascinated by an ancient Bible written in Greek, Latin, Aramaic, and Hebrew, each huge page divided into four squares. The Benedictine monks, fewer than one hundred now, are kept busy in September listening to the confessions of nearly a million pilgrims on their way to Santiago de Compostela in Spain.

I spent an unhappy month in Genoa, a sad town full of unemployed people and occasionally dangerous thieves. The few gems there are the Mussolini office tower, Columbus's birthplace, and the Via Garibaldi, a stretch of Renaissance palaces that looks like the Grand Canal in Venice minus the water and stretched out straight. Through friends I met an aristocratic couple who inhabited a nearby palace. Before the delicious, lively dinner the mistress of the house (herself an architect) showed me the large eighteenth-century library her husband had inherited. It had been assembled by an ancestor whose goal was to collect the last illuminated manuscript of a title and its first printed version. Like most collectors, he didn't actually read the books once he'd bought them. The illuminated manuscripts were pristine, as if colored and gilded only the previous day. We wore white gloves to handle the books—but they were the sort of books no one ever touches now! The original collector contacted agents throughout Europe to scout out manuscripts and incunabula for him. He had the eccentric if amusing idea of arranging all his books by color. A modern grad student had to categorize them alphabetically and digitally in order to locate them on a computer ("Purple, second row down, third from left"). The elder brother, who'd inherited the title, took the family palace with its extraordinary art collection, whereas the younger brother moved to a palace around the corner where the library, founded in 1760, is housed in two rooms beautifully designed by his architect wife. The younger brother seems to have had tax-evasion problems and was wearing an ankle monitor during dinner. He was bored with me until I mentioned I'd met the pretender to the Brazilian throne, one of his childhood friends (he grew up in Rio).

My friend J. D. McClatchy, the poet and editor of the *Yale Review*, has a splendid library of fine bindings and the key works of poetry of our tradition.

When I look around my dog-eared library, I see few volumes of value except the original edition of Jean Genet's *Querelle*, published in a limited print run of 528 copies, "not for sale," edited by Paul Morihien, who owned the local bookstore in the Palais Royal. The novel had illustrations by Jean Cocteau ("unsigned") of well-hung sailors printed on big creamy pages. Gallimard, France's premier publisher, soon brought it out in Genet's *Complete Works* without pictures. Probably the explicit Cocteau line drawings drew the attention of the censors, for Genet was given a prison sentence and a fine, neither of which were exacted. It's a large, beautiful book in a box. It was given to me by the French photographer Ariane Lopez-Huici, one of my dearest friends and the niece of Arturo Lopez, Paris's biggest party giver in the 1950s.

I have a sumptuous first edition of Pierre Loti's *Madame Chrysanthème*, complete with raised art nouveau flowers on the cover, which I found in a book market in Avignon. This was the novel (as well as the short story by the American John Luther Long) that inspired the Broadway play by David Belasco, which Puccini adapted into *Madama Butterfly*.

If I look just at the books on my dining room table, under my nose I find Denis Diderot's *Paradoxe sur le comédien* and the first volume of Colette's *Oeuvres*, in Gallimard's Pléiade series (the equivalent of the American Library, except furnished with scholarly notes, variants, chronologies, and authoritative introductions), containing among other things the naughty schoolgirl Claudine series and Colette's show-biz memoir,

La Vagabonde, about the period when she left her husband and had to support herself as a mime (often nude), performing in the houses of the very people she'd known socially earlier as a respectable married woman. Under the *Oeuvres*, I spot *Alma Venus* by the Catalan poet Pere Gimferrer, translated by my friend Adrian West.

Next I see a lyrical translation by another close friend, Paul Eprile, of Jean Giono's first novel, *Hill* (*Colline* in the original French). Recently I wrote a note to accompany Paul's translation of Giono's *Melville*, which quickly evolved into a novel that has nothing to do with the historical neurasthenic and queer-leaning Herman Melville and everything to do with Giono himself.

Giono was deeply influenced by American writers. In this he was not alone; American literature was very popular with European writers and intellectuals after World War II, who, disgusted with their own strife-torn culture, looked instead toward the New World. D. H. Lawrence devoted chapters in his *Classic Studies in American Literature* to Nathaniel Hawthorne, Poe, and Melville (in whom, indeed, he is credited with leading the movement to revive interest); Cesare Pavese, the great Italian novelist, wrote his thesis on Walt Whitman, supported himself during the Mussolini years by writing essays about American authors, and translated Melville's *Moby-Dick*; and Sartre wrote a very influential essay on Faulkner.

Giono first discovered Walt Whitman in French, reading his biography by Léon Bazalgette in 1924; he later studied "the American Homer" in English. He loved Whitman's all-embracing egalitarianism and his pantheism, and the first part of Giono's œuvre obviously owes a debt to this passionate revolutionary figure. In *Hill*, his first novel, Giono tried to illustrate two very Whitmanian truths: "The first of these truths is that there are people simple and nude; the other is that this earth fleeced [*entoisonnée*] with woods . . . this living earth, exists without literature." He decided to show the peasants of his region of Provence in all their particularity—and also to show the beauty and terror of nature in its raw state, stripped of its classical allusions (his juvenile poems had been full of Virgilian references). In these two regards he was like his contemporary the Swiss novelist C. F. Ramuz, today best known for his collaboration with Stravinsky, *L'Histoire d'un soldat*, but celebrated in the past for novels of man versus nature like *When the Mountain Fell*. Like Ramuz, Giono recorded the real speech of the ordinary people around him (without, in Giono's case, resorting to Provençal, associated with a literary movement he disapproved of) and wrote about the natural world in simple, elevated prose mostly denuded of figurative speech.

Cutting down on metaphor and simile (he could never altogether forego them) must have been painful for Giono, so naturally gifted with that kind of eloquence. As Aristotle suggests in *The Rhetoric*, metaphor is one of the greatest ornaments of writing but also the one no one can learn: "Metaphor especially has clarity and sweetness and strangeness, and its use cannot be learned from anyone else." The "clarity and sweetness and strangeness" of Giono's writing, especially in his more generous, mature style, owes everything to its poetic strategies, as many other readers and writers (Gide in France and the American Henry Miller) were quick to notice. *Hill* created a sensation when it was published; it soon led to other remarkable books.

In all these early novels, Giono deals with the people of his town—Manosque, in the Haute-Provence—and of the neighboring villages, though he shouldn't be dismissed as a regionalist, any more than Faulkner should. He is aware of—but doesn't dote on—the eccentricities of his part of the world. Except for trips to Italy and to Paris, and to other destinations in Europe, he seldom traveled except in his armchair. Widely read—in the classics, the great Russians, the nineteenth- and twentieth-century Americans, French fiction and poetry—he was always emphasizing the universal aspect of his characters' experience, the exhilaration of being an animal, and the tragedy of being human. Although he had dropped out of school early to contribute to his family's earnings, he was an ambitious autodidact who knew classical music and great painting (from reproductions); I was fortunate enough to visit his very impressive library. I only mention his wide and deep culture because even the French often dismiss him (without reading him) as a "primitive" or "Provençal colorist."

Hill has a *Desire Under the Elms* quality about it (Giono knew the work of Eugene O'Neill) in that it is about violence and love among poor farmers. *Regain* ("Second Growth" or "Aftermath," which turns out to be an agricultural term) is about a remote village that has slowly dwindled in population until it is down to just two inhabitants, an old witch from Piedmont, Mamèche, who lost her husband under a landslide and her son when he nibbled hemlock, and Panturle, a rough giant of a man who is a part-time poacher. The village comes back to life when Panturle mates with Arsule, a traveling performer—there is a happy ending. The writing is obviously the work of a man who understands nature and agriculture: "Those who have already made the trip two or three times notice [that the road is getting higher and higher] because at a given moment there are no more vegetable fields, then because the wheat stalks are getting shorter and shorter, then because you're traveling under the first chestnut trees, then because you're passing at a ford torrents of grass-colored water shining like oil, then because at last there appears the blue stem of the Vachère clock tower and that, that is the boundary." Only someone who truly knows the countryside notices that the wheat gets shorter the higher the terrain.

Giono fought as an ordinary soldier, starting in 1916, and saw battle near Verdun. In 1918 his eyelids were burned with mustard gas, though his lungs were unaffected. His company suffered huge losses. The experience made him an uncompromising pacifist, even later during the Spanish Civil War and World War II. He earned the undying hatred of French Communists for not endorsing the war that the Soviet Union was waging against Germany, eventually being imprisoned for "defeatism." His powerful antiwar novel *Le Grand Troupeau* ("The Big Herd") shows the horrors of the front but also the hardships of the home front—the untended (or confiscated) livestock, the loneliness, the physical demands of running a farm without men, or only with feeble old men. At the beginning of the novel all of the neglected sheep in the district have run away and banded together in one endless, hungry, dirty herd; the air is filled with an odor of "wool, sweat and trampled earth."

Giono's details are always well-found. Fish are dying in the stream, flies are everywhere, stray birds are "sputtering like oil in a frying pan," and the sun is "like a dead person." Big mountain bees, live or dead, are trapped in the errant sheep's fleece. "The foal has stopped nursing, he is drunk. He trembles on his hoofs. A thread of milk flows from his muzzle." The ram has been injured: "All of his wool below, soaked with blood, uncurled, heavy, was hanging down like moss under a fountain." A young woman, abandoned by her new husband who's gone off to war, has to feed the horses: "Every time that she would go to open the barn door, she would be embraced by fresh hay, this odor that made her temples ring like the basin of a fountain, this odor of hay and horse, this odor of thick life that grated against her skin like a stone."

A young soldier arrives back in the village while the family is improvising a memorial ceremony for a friend, one of the fallen. He looks around and thinks that he could stay at home and not return to battle if he were a lamp—if he "were this lamp . . . the tree, this table, the sow, I could stay. If I were the dog, I could stay. If I were the dog . . ." The accumulation of these details constitutes a burning indictment of war.

The second great American Giono discovered, in the 1930s, was Melville, whose *Moby-Dick* he translated with the help of two friends. The translation is accurate, but Melville's strange turns of phrase—as elusive as Shakespeare's—cannot be reproduced (almost all translations flatten out the quirks). When Melville, for instance, writes "The devils also, add the uncanonical Rabbins, indulged in mundane amours," it doesn't sound exactly like "Ajoutent les Rabbins, peu canoniques, les demons se livrèrent à des amours terrestres." Is there any way to capture Melville's biblical-Shakespearean prose in French? "La plus petite chose peut avoir une signification" doesn't really capture the diction of "the veriest trifles capriciously carry meanings" any more than "la joie démoniaque des vagues" renders "the madness and gladness of the demoniac waves." But translating Melville was a labor of love for Giono, who for years read him in the open fields and completed his translation—the first in French, and still the standard one—while in prison for his pacifism.

The third American who directly influenced Giono was Faulkner, whose books—in this case read in translation—expanded his concept of the novel. He began to experiment with multiple narrators, not necessarily coherent; he created his own "Provence," just as Faulkner invented his Yoknapatawpha County; finally, he dealt with incest and covered several generations of the same family. After reading *Sartoris*, Giono began to write about dynasties—the tragic fate of the Costes, for instance, in *Le Moulin de Pologne*, or the endless struggle between the two brothers in *Deux Cavaliers de L'Orage*.

If Giono learned these thematic and structural possibilities from Faulkner, he managed to avoid the American author's verbal, seemingly drunken absurdities, such as this, from *Absalom, Absalom*, one of his best books: "That aptitude and eagerness of the Anglo-Saxon for complete mystical acceptance of immolated sticks and stones." Every page of Faulkner is littered with phrases like "the augmenting and defunctive twilight," or "author and victim too of a thousand homicides and a thousand copulations and divorcements." Or this sort of rant: "He couldn't say that, you see—this man, this youth scarcely twenty, who had turned his back upon all that he knew, to cast his lot with the single friend whom, even as they rode away that night, he must have known, as he knew that what his father had told him was true, that he was doomed and destined to kill. He must have known that just as he knew that his hope was vain, what hope and what for he could not have said; what hope and dream of change in Bon or in the situation, what dream that he could someday wake from and find it had been a dream, as in the injured man's fever dream the dear suffering arm or leg is strong and sound and only the well ones sick." These passages, by the way, are from successive pages of *Absalom, Absalom* chosen at random.

Just as, Nabokov used to say, Dostoevsky's wretched, journalistic prose was cleaned up and dignified in translation, Faulkner's prestige in France (the French revived his fortunes and campaigned for the Nobel) may owe something to his expert translator, Maurice Coindreau, a French professor at Princeton. Coindreau's decision, for instance, not to try to translate Dilsey's "Negro dialect" rescued one of Faulkner's most sympathetic characters from interminable—and untranslatable— folkloric nonsense.

Unlike Faulkner, Giono never says anything hard to picture or that makes only approximate sense. His approach is always much more linear and chronological than that of Faulkner, with his traps, his "intelligent disorder." But Giono often introduced into this stew his own brand of rapturous nature descriptions, his eccentrics, who owe more to observed village "characters" than to American Gothic ravings, his irony and comedy, and his always rational, calibrated style spiced with vivid metaphors.

The mysteriously named *Le Moulin de Pologne* ("The Polish Mill"— the name of an actual farm near Manosque; Casanova, a writer whom Giono read, lived for a while in France at a farm called the Petite Pologne) is Faulknerian in the best sense. On the first page the narrator refers to himself as "us" (*nous*), and we are often reminded that he speaks for the community (in French the use of *on* or "one" is often translated by the passive voice or by "we").

The novel *Melville*, originally intended as a preface to his translation of *Moby-Dick*, was a turning point for Giono, marking a transition between his Pan cycle (including the recently translated *Hill*), works that highlighted his native Provençal landscape, and his Hussard cycle, in which he invested his extraordinary energies in fashioning unforgettable characters. As he said in a later interview, "In the preceding novels, nature was in the foreground, the character in the background . . . I called 'chronicles' the whole series of novels which put humanity before nature." The most famous of these chronicles is *The Horseman on the Roof*, which in 1995 the French turned into one of their best historical films, starring Juliette Binoche and Olivier Martinez.

Of course literary things are never that simple. The two cycles overlap; for instance, the characters in the early books are already very strong, and the Provençal landscape plays a major role in Giono's chronicles as well. In the foreground of *Horseman on the Roof* may be Giono's very Stendhalian young Italian hero, Angelo, but directly behind him is the flourishing landscape of his Provence, never lusher than as a background for the devastating cholera pandemic of 1832.

There were some similarities between Melville and Giono. Melville, as a fierce egalitarian, was against flogging and the severe penalties (Billy Budd is executed) so prevalent on the high seas; Giono was a pacifist. When he wrote *Melville* he'd just emerged from prison for the crime of pacifism. He would be briefly imprisoned later, during the war, for "collaboration" with the fascists. Actually his biggest "collaboration" was the reprinting of an old photo without his permission in a collaborationist magazine. The real problem was that in the mid-1930s he'd broken definitively with the Stalinists; a Moscow-directed French Communist writers' union kept Giono from being published in France from right after the war until 1947.

Both Giono and Melville had overbearing mothers. Both were precocious boys. Both had to drop out of school when their fathers died, and both as young men, oddly enough, had to go to work in a bank. Giono wrote several folkloric novels, which he felt he could manufacture like little buns, just as Melville wrote his maritime adventure stories (*Typee, Redburn, Omoo, White Jacket*), which seemed to him almost formulaic (*Mardi* is an exception). Shortly after the war Giono began his Angelo cycle and wrote an unrelated book, his enigmatic, granitic *Un Roi sans divertissement* ("A King without Distraction"). It was certainly a more ambitious novel than anything he'd penned previously.

Giono had also at this point in his life fallen in love with a married woman, Blanche Meyer, with whom he had an affair for the next thirty-five years. Her given name reappears in the surname of her literary double Adelina White, the heroine of *Melville*. They had a voluminous correspondence. Though they both lived in the same Provençal town of Manosque, they had to be extremely careful about seeing each other. Between 1939 and 1969 Giono wrote her more than a thousand letters and cards; they are now housed at Yale's Beinecke Library, but many of them are sealed until a future date. Her letters were burned. She went on to write a tell-nothing memoir about him. Somewhat as F. Scott Fitzgerald used Zelda's letters, Giono apparently ascribed many passages from Blanche's letters to Adelina.

Melville, it seems, was quite different from Giono's portrait. He was infatuated with Hawthorne, who was fifteen years older. For nearly two years the two authors saw each other often and talked deep into the night. Hawthorne's wife remarked that Melville wanted more from Hawthorne than he could give. Nevertheless, it was an inspiring period for both men, who felt that the conventional novel of the day had become too narrow a form. During that period Hawthorne wrote *The Scarlet Letter* and Melville wrote *Moby-Dick*, which he dedicated to Hawthorne. When Hawthorne wrote Melville a letter praising *Moby-Dick* (which may be, in the eyes of many critics, the greatest American novel ever written), Melville said, "Knowing you persuades me more than the Bible of our immortality."

Melville, far from the expansive, self-confident man Giono portrays, was in fact touchy, taciturn, and shy. Giono was the one with the big personality, and "Melville," the character, is his alter ego. In point of fact, Giono wasn't as much interested in the historic Melville as in the text and the big, manly Whitmanian figures of the New World. Like many Europeans, after the war Giono was fed up with the timidity of much Continental prose, or with its erudition.

Melville's bisexuality is evident everywhere in *Moby-Dick*. In one passage Ishmael is rubbing the knots out of big vats of whale sperm: "Squeeze! squeeze! squeeze! All the morning long; I squeezed that sperm till I myself almost melted into it; I squeezed that sperm until a strange sort of insanity came over me; and I found myself unwittingly squeezing my co-laborers' hands in it, mistaking their hands for the gentle globules. Such an abounding, affectionate, friendly, loving feeling did this avocation beget; that at last I was continually squeezing their hands, and looking up into their eyes sentimentally; as much as to say,—Oh! My dear fellow beings . . . Come; let us squeeze hands all round; nay, let us squeeze ourselves into each other; let us squeeze ourselves universally into the very milk and sperm of kindness. Would that I could keep squeezing that sperm forever."

If Melville can invoke both the female (mother whales nursing their babies underwater) and the male principles through the guise of whales, Giono's "Melville" summons up the whole universe while out riding in a carriage and discoursing with Adelina, in the book's most stunning passages: "So now Herman started to talk about the world that lay before them. He rolled up the sky, from one edge to the other, as though it were made of colored silk. And, for a brief moment, there was no more sky. Then, after an interval of four hoof-beats, at a gallop he rolled the sky open again, but now it had turned into a huge skin, tightly enclosing earth's arteries and veins."

He invokes the smell of rain: "He sustained everything else; only he lowered the register, as if he were lifting off, ever so slightly, the pressure from the pedal of a big, cathedral organ." Giono's Melville has the power to summon all of nature, like Prospero. It's a strange, erotico-mystic-botanical form of courtship. Prospero? No, like God. Giono, who lost his faith at the end of his childhood, does not hesitate to deify himself ("She could plainly feel that he was granting her his own world"). Even though their romance is chaste (in the book), we can feel her body; when she removes her hoops and gathers up the excess silk around her childlike body, we can see and touch her.

Both Melville and Giono were pantheists, or animists, if that means they intuited a god in every tree and a goddess in every lake. Melville, like Emily Dickinson, was discovered only in the mid-twentieth century; Giono has yet to be fully appreciated.

———————

Under Giono's *Hill* is Frederic Tuten's novel *The Green Hour*, a heterosexual love story set in Paris. Once I received from the *New York Times Book Review* a Tuten novel to review without recognizing that the characters were all named after those in Thomas Mann's *The Magic Mountain* (which I'd never read). Almost as wince-making is an editorial I ghostwrote for the new owners of *Saturday Review*. I made two serious mistakes: I misattributed (I think) T. E. Hulme's comment that Romanticism was "spilt religion," and I referred to the southern novelist Walker Percy as "Percy Walker." That was in the early 1970s, long before Google; the new owners were excoriated as "philistines" by enraged readers. It was all my fault.

Next in the pile is Nabokov's *Speak, Memory*. I had my class in memoir at Princeton read the second chapter; they were unimpressed. They liked the language but deplored the lack of feeling (I must say I've come to agree with them). The first person I ever heard express such a heretical view was the great Russian novelist Nina Berberova, who disliked all that doting on a vanished aristocratic past.

Then there are two books being read by my husband, Michael Carroll: Wolfgang Koeppen's *Death in Rome*, about postwar Germans in Italy, including a former Nazi, and *The Noonday Demon: An Atlas of Depression* by Andrew Solomon (Michael has a bipolar young lover with a beautiful body and often a mood that is dangerously depressed).

Then *How to Survive a Plague*, the definitive book on the social history of AIDS by David France, which I will blurb; and gosh—so many others!

And yet like most old people, I spend time watching TV news rather than reading. What are we old folks hoping to see and learn from the little screen? That the world is in decline, as we suspect? Or that our opinion (vote) is still relevant? Or is it for that overview we seek in conversation with contemporaries (though we rarely obtain it) that will make sense of everything, add it all up to a huge, rounded-off sum?

Reading, of course, is a melancholy project. You don't smile at the characters' witticisms as I find myself idiotically smiling back at my favorite TV newscasters. I do sometimes smile while reading—Henry Green makes me smile with his batty, I'm-so-helpless ladies who are champion strategists; Colette makes me smile with her rosy, lush bedroom interiors, all lace and embroidered linen, against which a naked young man, black when contre-jour, prances about like a thin, fit devil, wearing a heavy necklace of thirty-nine pearls. Elizabeth Bowen makes me smile with her ruthless, rich heroine Eva Trout, driving her powerful Jaguar and living in a tacky, rotting house named Cathay on the bleak coast of England.

Speaking of bleak coastal England, I love that novel by W. G. Sebald in which he's in some ghastly English resort eating a bad fish and looking out at the shingle in the rain. Really horrible scenes always make me laugh. The grisly operation in *The Makioka Sisters*; Tolstoy's battle scenes and wounds.

Books, unlike movies, give us the thoughts of the characters. That's why books are so essential: we live inside our heads. With a movie, unless there's an unidiomatic voice-over, we must ascribe reactions and perceptions to the beautiful faces on the screen. That's why the sentiments in films are so banal, literally so black-and-white (except in Ingmar Bergman's *Wild Strawberries*, possibly). A film as morally subtle ("Who on earth is the good guy?") as a Chekhov story or as nuanced as *The Good Soldier* would confuse, even enrage us. We can only ascribe cliché feelings to actors that are *déjà vécu* or unambiguous; violence or horniness or craziness read loud and clear, but whimsy or boredom or sleepiness cannot be immediately flagged, though novels can depict those and every other shade of feeling. It is less taxing to identify raw emotions than fifty or one hundred shades of gray.

Film, with its gliding, focusing, or panoramic camerawork and its constantly signaling score or sound effects, knows how to lull us or terrify us or soften us up for a big, resolving clinch and kiss, but subtler emotions are indecipherable or undetectable. Again, it's more satisfying to live in the realm of shoot-outs or chase scenes on-screen than to read about the peeping and twittering of a Henry James character wondering if our motives are pure enough—and deciding not to disembark at Le Havre after all.

The television is warm to the touch. It's good company. The full, detailed, and vivid picture instantly wells up; the canned laughter and grinning MC tell you you're watching something funny; Rachel Maddow—a stranger you know better than your own sister in far-off Chicago—looks right at you and confides something alarming or amusing about a Nevada congressman. It's all instantly gratifying, unlike the endless gray columns of unillustrated print in a book—surely the least beguiling medium in the world, the one easiest to resist and the slowest to warm up, even if in the long run (the very long run) fiction maps out our sensibilities with the greatest detail and accuracy. An old person, trust me, is tired of himself and usually prefers a car chase to more introspection, bright, simple truths right out of the "tube" to the grisaille of a good novel. And then literary novelists can be so demanding! Do you really want to accompany two talkative politicians for a 600-page stroll across Paris (*The Horrors of Love* by Jean Dutourd)? Or to read an equally long comparison of baseball to our national political history? If someone invites you to a new film, you wrinkle your nose like a cat sussing out an unfamiliar brand of tuna, anticipating pleasure, but if your friend gives you volume 2 of his memoirs, you purr audibly but privately feel irritated by the imposition, and he finds it unread beside your bed a year later. Books are a forty-hour demand of your time.

No wonder so many people read mysteries and Washington legal thrillers on the plane; I always want to snatch them out of their hands and substitute *War and Peace*. My intolerance of popular fiction is tyrannical, but if I end up with a suspense story by mistake, by John Banville or Georges Simenon or Richard Flanagan, say, I'm utterly engrossed and praise it immoderately, not knowing I'm responding to the unfamiliar genre and not necessarily to this particular book.

There's a section of one bookcase devoted to my own books in various editions and translations and to the three or four books about me (*Understanding Edmund White* is one title). The most recent arrivals, the ones that don't go directly to the discard pile, are stacked in great, teetering piles on the floor. Every once in a while I spot a shelved title two or three years old that I resolve to banish to the discards. There are several shelves devoted to Proust and books about Proust. Maybe one-fifth of my books are in French (I sometimes pretend I can read Italian and Spanish, but only with a well-thumbed dictionary).

I don't feel obliged to study the classics. My first translator in Paris (he was also a novelist and essayist and editor), Gilles Barbedette, was always reading Racine or Homer or Shakespeare or Blaise Pascal—and he seemed to find those classics nourishing. He dutifully kept a commonplace book into which he copied Great Passages from Great Authors. I almost thought he was posing for his portrait for the French Academy, current or posthumous. Unlike me, he believed in the whole sacralized vocation of Absorbing Culture and Making Art. For me, fiction is the new poetry—a coterie pursuit read only by other adepts. I never complain about low sales figures or lack of fame; it strikes me as only natural that what we like is just for the initiated, the "happy few." I don't question Gilles's sincerity or deep knowledge, and sometimes I think I should have followed his example of consulting only the blue-chip writers (mainly of the past, since time alone can vouchsafe for true quality). But I suspected those waters had been fished out. My library reflects my taste for the exotic, the minor, the unheralded, the neglected, or the still controversial new. Mixed in with poems by Thom Gunn and a bad biography of Robert Mapplethorpe are novels by Stacey D'Erasmo, Rachel Kushner, and Carson McCullers. People interested in putting together a very restricted canon of great books don't really like reading; true readers, among whom I have the impertinence to include myself, are always sniffing out more and more titles. Reading is a hobby that never grows stale— and an unpunished vice.

Chapter 10

I like most writers. John Irving is one of my best friends, and one of the few I've made late in life. We have mainly an e-mail relationship and give each other reports on our progress with our respective novels. His big Dickensian novels, with their high-wattage brilliance and playfully inventive plots, have made him justifiably world-famous, but he never avoids difficult subjects or courts low public favor. From the very beginning he has drawn verbal portraits of trans people and homosexuals, of orphans and abortionists, of immigrants and working people. He is a very dear man, rugged and affectionate. A few years back he received a richly deserved prize from a queer literary group as a "straight friend" of gays.

I know the cliché is that writers are twisted, bitter, resentful people, always cutting their less clever friends down to size—but on the contrary, I find writers are the best company, almost never dull, unusually broad-minded. The few dull writers I know teach on provincial American campuses. They've passed so many years each being the Big Man on Campus, universally respected by their humbler colleagues, that they've failed to pick up any social polish. Worse, they've learned the tedious suburban manly arts of talking about sports scores or the real estate market and imagining that is interesting. Because of an inferior milieu they don't know how to talk fiction or poetry in a way that might interest an actress or an admiral; they can't discuss their work in a general conversation.

Writers who must swim in the biggest ponds (New York, London, Berlin, Paris), though, have had the arrogance bleached out of them—and they are often killingly funny. A. M. Homes is always in a good mood, though she reports the occasional depression. I love to eavesdrop on her when she's teaching; she always has something droll and illuminating to say. Her novels are shocking. In the first chapter a husband kills his wife—and we still have three hundred pages to go! Salman Rushdie can keep a whole table laughing with his mordant social and political barbs.

Peter Carey is outrageous in a very Australian way, imputing evil excesses to mild-mannered me and taking so much piss out of me he leaves me bone-dry. He has an eldritch, taunting, heckling manner that almost disguises his sweetness; he can be very sentimental over his friends and gets tears in his eyes when he says something tender. He's a humble man, though on some level he must know he's a genius. If you mention to him (sincerely) what a great writer he is, this two-time Booker winner, he folds his tents out of shyness and slips away across the night desert. I told him that an Australian friend of mine who met him said that people back home regard him as being like Emerson. He immediately responded, "Roy Emerson?", naming the tennis player.

In my novel *Fanny* I described a cross-Atlantic passage in the 1820s. I researched the scene at the British Library for weeks—and still wrote about the same event in a stiffer, less convincing way than Peter did in his novel *Parrot and Olivier in America*, which I read soon afterward. He's grown over the years; *The Chemistry of Tears* is so much fuller and felt than the early *Oscar and Lucinda*, wondrous as that national epic might be, with its crystal cathedral floating up an Australian River.

Peter never writes autobiographically, but his life peeks out from the holes in the scenery. For instance, one of his sons, while Peter and his wife were going through a difficult divorce, lost interest in everything—everything except Japanese manga. Accordingly Peter and his son traveled to Japan and met some of the top manga artists, and Peter wrote a nonfiction book about it. *The Chemistry of Tears* is about, among other things, a Victorian father who dotes on his dying son and keeps him alive by commissioning ever more intriguing inventions for him to marvel at—ultimately a majestic, mechanical swan. This novel is a tribute to a father's love for his son, not a common theme in fiction, though ubiquitous in life. Cormac McCarthy's *The Road* is another example.

I asked several writers if they were inspired when they wrote, and Peter replied: "Really, truly, I just write. I type badly. I misspell continually. I dredge through the silt lying at the bottom of my mind. I sketch. I repeat, over and over. I find stuff. I climb on it and fall off it. None of this could be called inspiration, more like wading in the flooded basement of my mind. It gets clearer on the second day."

Michael Ondaatje is one of my favorite writers, both as a creator and a man. Maybe because he is a Sri Lankan Canadian, he doesn't feel the pressure to repeat his successes. He writes whatever interests him; sometimes his work reels in millions (of dollars) and sometimes hundreds.

I wonder how we're friends, since I can neither read his handwriting nor understand him when he speaks (or rather mumbles). Luckily his books transmit clear, intelligent reports from his mind. And his Midwest American wife, Linda, is such a kind, gracious, and practical presence, totally transparent and eloquent. When my young French lover Hubert Sorin was dying of AIDS, he abandoned his work as an architect and turned himself into a cartoonist. Linda and Michael published some of his first cartoons in their quarterly *Brick*, even though the dialogues were so prickly and unsparingly satirical and bitter that they alienated more than a few readers, who canceled their subscriptions. At that point I began writing little harmless texts about our daily life in Paris for Hubert to illustrate. They ended up in a book we did together, *Our Paris*, something he was so pleased to see into print before he died. I was so grateful that Michael and Linda had let him continue working.

David McConnell—dear friend, ex-lover, and neighbor—is writing a double biography of a death-row prisoner he's known and interviewed extensively and of himself, a privileged coupon-puncher from Shaker Heights. We generalize about the top 1 percent in America and about the third of our citizens who live below the poverty belt, but David has put flesh on these bones. His prisoner never had a chance, condemned by chaotic, abusive, alcoholic parents to an existence of want and exploitation.

David, by contrast, grew up rich and sheltered with assorted parents and grandparents in a leafy Cleveland suburb of big houses on even bigger lots, a world that could afford soft voices, indirection, and self-deprecation. Though he was kicked out of boarding school more than once, they were always the best schools in the States.

David and I read to each other what we're working on. He goes gentle with me and I with him. I've heard of graduate creative writing classes where the criticism gets very tough, but I've never been exposed to that sort of malice. In the late 1970s and early 1980s I belonged to a gay writers' group, the Violet Quill, which for a while we considered calling the All-Praise Club. We were attempting to get gay lit (not Gaelic) off the ground in spite of great resistance from editors. We needed affirmation, not hostile criticism. The moment—a decade after Stonewall, the starting point of gay liberation—was propitious. Suddenly there were good serious gay reviewing organisms, there were gay bookshops, and there were even a few good gay book editors. Later, when gay lit didn't take off or cross over, the publications and bookstores flamed out and the editors lost their jobs. Now, finally, in the second decade of the twenty-first century, gay fiction and poetry have entered the foreground once again, partly due to a new crop of gay editors and especially due to excellent gay writers (Garth Greenwell, Paul Lisicky, Hanya Yanagihara, Ocean Vuong).

Rick Whitaker is the soul of generosity. He admires fellow writers. He admires avant-garde composers, whom he presents at the Italian Academy's jewel box of a theater at Columbia University. He's an unexpected combination of the whipped dog and the manly man, dignified, reserved, but with a slight flaw in his eye, as if he's afraid you might be about to turn on him. He had a ghastly childhood (his abusive stepfather was actually named Butch), but he's turned himself into a loving, erudite adult—something he's created all on his own and out of thin air.

Rick would be a great Maecenas if he were rich—and if he had enough energy left over from his own ingenious, spectacular writing. He appreciates the people around him—not all of them (for he's very discerning), but those who meet his high standards. He has a deep and wide knowledge not only of music and fiction but also of film and poetry and good food. He likes to bring people together and watch them discover each other. He's the perfect house guest (off by himself during the day, reading and writing and hiking, fun and excited over dinner as you barrel off in a car to the next village over). He takes nothing for granted, not a moment of his lovely if impoverished life. If freedom is the ultimate luxury, then he is rich indeed.

Rick likes the avant-garde in music, film, and fiction, which makes him a lone, almost unique figure in our disabused world. I used to think New Yorkers invented trends and foisted them off on a gullible nation but weren't themselves susceptible to them. That describes many of my friends, but not Rick. He roots out the most difficult films and scores, and his own fiction is militantly experimental, as if we were still living on the crest of something instead of in its wake.

Rick has an adopted gay son; he got him out of the foster child system precisely because he was gay and had aged out and the social worker thought they'd be a good match. In the 1970s my fifteen-year-old nephew, Keith, came to live with me and was soon joined by his even younger Mexican girlfriend, Laura, whom he'd met in the mental hospital. My nephew was strange—he moved like a robot, and he was so little socialized he seemed hard of hearing and would lean into a conversation if he realized he'd been asked a question. He was painfully polite with me but brutal and mocking with others. He'd beat Laura, and she'd cheat on him with much older men in the neighborhood.

Keith had a talent for reading and writing. He wrote two books that were published and praised, both about me. But he had delusions of grandeur and wasn't content with a prominent review in the *New York Times Book Review* (which said he was a better writer than his uncle) and ten thousand sales for *The Boy with the Thorn in His Side*. Maybe because he didn't live in the literary milieu, he didn't know how unusual that degree of success was for a debut. He blamed me, as the subject, for relegating him to the gay shelf in bookstores. I also wrote an article about him in *Bomb*, purely to promote him, but he took it ironically and thought I was subtly badmouthing him. In the novel called *The Farewell Symphony*, I again wrote about him—but again he hated my portrayal of him. There was no way I could win.

Years passed. Keith lived with an older Finnish woman in Providence, Rhode Island. He became more and more withdrawn. Apparently he seldom ventured out of the house. He made a meager living doing proofreading for New York editors. He met an old friend who reignited his dreams of becoming a rock musician, though now he was approaching fifty. Nothing came of this fantasy. His proofreading work started drying up. His girlfriend spoke of leaving him and moving back to Finland. He killed himself. A while later, his old ex-girlfriend, Laura, killed herself.

Rick's son, David, when he reached his early twenties, wouldn't work and wouldn't pay rent. Rick kicked him out. Eventually everything worked out, and father and son are now on a good footing, but I was deeply worried that Rick was about to go through the same hell I'd known. Rick was worried, too, but determined to take a firm stand with his son.

Will Carnes is in his mid-twenties and, unusual for an American his age, reads all the time. Like Rousseau, he reads as he walks. He reads philosophy, history, fiction, poetry, and not only occasionally but all of them all the time. He underlines. He's remarkably handsome but would just as soon stay in as go out with another A-list lad on a Grindr date. People twice or three times his age are astonished by the depth and breadth of his reading. He's even stopped working so he can read full-time. I keep hoping he'll start writing, but I'm afraid he's inhibited by the exquisite taste he's honed in just a few years. Proust says somewhere that you must make yourself stupid in order to write. Paul Valéry remarked that he could never be a novelist because he could never bring himself to put down on paper "The Marquise went out at 5 o'clock" (which Baron Edmond de Rothschild's wife Nadine cleverly twisted into the title of her 1984 memoir *La baronne rentre à cinq heures* ("The Baroness Will Return at Five"). The impossibility of committing a banal line of narration must have stopped many an intellectual from writing fiction. Is that why the young Borges never wrote a novel but just those brain-teasing short stories? Why Roland Barthes only dared to consider writing a novel in middle age? He chose to write long fiction after his mother's death, just like Proust, who started his novel by re-creating a philosophical conversation he might have had one morning with his mother.

Just this morning Will wrote me an e-mail saying he was working his way through minor and unfinished books by D. H. Lawrence, *Mr. Noon* and *Aaron's Rod* ("They're all so breathtaking and weird, it's hard to believe how great even his minor works and leftovers are").

Although Will can be harsh and dismissive, especially when he's been drinking, with me he's usually quiet and well-mannered. Since I'm the age of everyone's grandfather, I probably inspire different emotions in everyone than younger people do. Have I mentioned he's shockingly handsome? I'm also the person who doesn't want anything. I'm not looking for a job or money or sex, or not much of it. I just want companionship, and even for that I have a wide selection to choose from—and don't mind being alone in the interim. I'm fond of many people, not more.

Don't be misled because I mention only men. I have many women writer friends. Every January I stay in Key West with Alison Lurie, whom I adore. She's so wise and funny and independent. She knows exactly how to be a successful old person. She swims every day, goes for long walks alone, conducts a mild (not intense) social life, and doesn't seem to mind that now she's less famous than she was in the 1970s ("I've had my moment—now it's the turn of younger people"). She still writes reviews for the *New York Review of Books*, remains curious, and reads all the time. And knits potholders while watching TV.

If Alison writes a book-length essay about architecture, she doesn't start with Roland Barthes, as the rest of us would. She conjures up her own completely original thoughts: she is an original. She's always reading something. She's an expert in children's literature. Her husband adores her and is proud of her; she is on good terms with her own sons. She seems to have been an atheist since birth, certainly rational, and the idea of aromatherapy, say, makes her laugh loud and long. When her kindly, forbearing husband is away, she's capable of malice; then she catches herself and says, "Edward wouldn't approve."

Joyce Carol Oates is one of my dearest friends. She's kind and funny (a rare combination), surprisingly competitive, a very loyal friend, a tower of artistic strength. I've known very rich people who try to be sympathetic about the financial woes of ordinary people; Joyce must feel the same sort of good-natured but slightly uncomprehending sympathy with people who have writer's block. As everyone knows, she is an artesian well of creativity, but her work in all its majestic strength and abundance seldom reflects her shy sense of humor—she is a gentle tease—and her almost old-fashioned sense of propriety. She pretends to be scandalized by an off-color remark in real life, but her characters are ax murderers and rapists.

Lord Chesterfield thought that every "great man" harbored a secret ambition. His advice to his natural son was to praise a man immediately and without reservation for his entire œuvre and then find his secret ambition. In Joyce's case one would laud her hundred-plus books (including the poems, plays, thrillers, and children's books) and then swear that in gaining a great writer, the world lost a great athlete, for Joyce is a runner and once played basketball, and after we went to see Alvin Ailey she was often seen dancing in the corridors at school. I've spotted her running in the corridors as well, as if jolts of energy were spilling off her frail body. She can't swim; you need some fat on your body to stay afloat.

Joyce has always been like a big sister to me. She made my coming to Princeton such a joy. I'm sure she's the one who championed my teaching there in the first place, and once I'd arrived, she introduced me to everyone at little dinners she arranged. She was always including me in public readings she gave and suggesting me for prizes. She and her late husband, Ray, published us and our friends in the *Ontario Review*. People imagine she works all the time, but she has quite a busy social life. She often gives dinners and parties and keeps up with a host of friends. I remember for years she and Gloria Vanderbilt exchanged daily faxes (remember faxes?), and Gloria dressed Joyce in Miyake. On top of it all, Joyce writes long reviews for the *New York Review of Books* and keeps up the correspondence of a minister of state.

Joyce almost never writes anything identifiably autobiographical, and yet I can picture a teenage girl in upstate New York crossing an empty, wintry lot, clutching her schoolbooks to her chest. She is running away from an escaped convict—this part isn't so clear. I saw a one-man play of hers about Jeffrey Dahmer called *Zombie*. It was very upsetting, maybe because we could all imagine drilling holes in a young man's head so he wouldn't leave us. She thinks most violent criminals are suffering from brain damage, which sounds right.

Joyce never wastes a moment, and she can accomplish any task in a matter of minutes—we used to choose candidates for a fellowship together. If she has written well, she rewards herself by vacuuming the house.

Ann Beattie is a good girl, respectful of her elders, always ready to serve on a committee, an excellent cook. She keeps her nails as long as a Chinese mandarin of the ancien régime and types with them at a furious rate. She's intermittently productive—not constantly like Oates. She can be stuck for a long time and then turn out a book in a few weeks, clacking those nails on the keys. She is a great complainer ("Oh, Greece!" "Oh, Spain!"), but she has the most acute sense of humor and can find something funny in each of her European misadventures. I like to read to her, and she's sometimes willing to read to me. I'm always amazed how much information, how many details, she is able to wedge into the marquetry of her plots. She seems to feed off the very air around her, she has such a capacity for keeping up to date and assembling the most abstruse information.

How do all these writer-readers affect one's own efforts? They provide an audience of discerning and usually generous readers—sometimes in person, if they submit to being read to, more often after they've read a current or past book. If they're sophisticated and sensitive and quick to grasp something, their mere presence raises the bar: don't be so obvious/ slow-witted/long-winded/overemphatic, I tell myself after spending time with them. Speed and lightness are two of the great qualities of a mature style, and compassion—or at least a searching understanding—is the most radiant aspect of a moral vision. We like writers who can see the world around them, who don't attribute impossible motives or responses to their characters, who can keep a balance between action and introspection, whose style is relaxed and flowing and conversational; in fiction we want the people to do things that are fresh but representational, that are "in character" but unexpected. I suppose above all we like fiction that is bold and new, either in form or in content or both, but that at the same time adheres to the rules it has set for itself. John Banville writes fiction of this sort, both polished and startling.

And the complete opposite might also be true. I took only one fiction workshop in college, and I made note of all the teacher's "rules" and thought how much fun it would be to break every one of them. That's why it's so hard to teach creative writing: for every rule, one can imagine an outstanding exception, and the more one knows, the less one can say with confidence. At the beginning of the semester I'm tongue-tied.

In college I also studied with Kenneth Rowe, who'd been Arthur Miller's teacher. He'd had very precise notions as to how a play must be constructed and pronounced the words "major dramatic question," "rising action," and "wavelike motion" with authority. The rumor went around that Eugène Ionesco had written an entire play in defiance of Rowe's rules, but I haven't been able to verify that. Not that Rowe wasn't flexible and resourceful in applying his principles. I wrote a play, *The Blueboy in Black*, that won a prize and was eventually staged in New York. Dr. Rowe put his finger right on the structural flaw in the play; no matter how well it was cast, directed, played, it would always be weak exactly there. Now it's been lost—*tant mieux*!

For me writing is a performance art. I remember a book by Richard Poirier called *The Performing Self*. I'm not sure what it was about, but I choose to think it means the writer's a sort of high-wire artist.

We're always modeling the wax figure of the Ideal Reader, revising it, shaping it. For me she tolerates whimsy and divagations, is happy to learn a new word, wants to be entertained and edified, is capable of getting lost in a book, can tolerate a cliché. I used to say Mrs. Nabokov was my ideal reader: cultured, European, not American, not gay, not able to catch casual allusions to American products or TV personalities. A sort of filter against anything too topical, too parochial. And then Europeans like her, I realized, were not too impressed with a careful reproduction of American suburban life or nostalgia or infidelities, the coffee-cup realism of our material life. It's foolish (and reactionary) to talk about "universality" in fiction, but we can argue for what's representative, fully rendered, documented from the ground up. I point out to my students how nothing in

Jane Austen, written two hundred years ago, needs to be footnoted, whereas all their brand names will have to be explained in fifty years—fine if you're a social historian, but distracting if you're a casual reader. I can recall the closing words in one chapter of Carl Van Vechten's forgettable 1929 novel *Parties*, when a countess heading for a night in Harlem throws her pearls over her shoulder and says the vogue phrase of the day, "And how!" That must've made quite the impression back then.

The Ideal Reader is not impervious to strong emotions, but the writer must earn them. Poetic props (harps, roses) should not be stand-ins for beauty, just as a sentimental subject (the death of a child) should not be an automatic bid for tears. Baudelaire was right to find beauty in the mud; we admire the transformative powers of the artist who, in a metaphor, compares two things that are different in size, use, and kind—the wider the stretch, the better. (Cocteau compares gangrene to ivy covering a marble pediment, and James Jones describes pain: "Like with cold water until you finally get up your nerve to take yourself in hand. Then you take a deep breath and dive in and let yourself sink down it clear to the bottom. And after you had been down inside pain a while you found that like with cold water it is not really as cold as you thought it was when your muscles were cringing themselves away from the outside edge of it as you moved around it trying to get up your nerve. He knew pain.")

The Ideal Reader may be moral but not moralistic, interested in what is good or fair but not shocked by evil, and certainly not by promiscuity or perversion or any victimless crime. The reader, it seems, is the definition of a good person, although she is characterized by her receptivity, not her actions. The Ideal Reader is not too commonsensical; by taking the piss out of everything experimental or difficult the English, for instance, missed out on most of the great visual art of the twentieth century. The English never had a major Cubist show, for instance, until 1983—with disastrous consequences for much of British art. The Brits turn up their noses at Robert Wilson; he's only staged one opera at Covent Garden, in 2003, and presented only one play in Manchester. Yet he is our greatest, most visionary director. And Balanchine, the best choreographer of the twentieth or any century, is not exactly a household name in England.

During the AIDS crisis of the 1980s my Ideal Reader changed from Mrs. Nabokov to another American gay man, maybe a bit younger than me. Living in Paris, I felt out of the loop, cut off from Gay Men's Health Crisis (which I'd helped to found) or Act Up (which I'd missed out on altogether). I was diagnosed as positive in 1985; little did I know that I was a "slow progresser" and would live on and on. At that time I wanted to share my hopes and fears with men like myself. I wrote a book of AIDS short stories, *Skinned Alive* (Adam Mars-Jones contributed over half the stories), and *The Farewell Symphony*, a novel that ended with the AIDS catastrophe.

With this change of reader I was on more intimate terms—I was a brother or uncle if not a lover. I could write unashamedly, at length and in detail, about gay sex, for instance, whereas when I still had in mind an older straight woman I felt I was straining her patience when I rhapsodized about cocks and balls. Romance, possibly, but not sweaty, hairy sex with gaping orifices.

Once the reader became a male, there was always the possibility of seducing him—a seduction based on truth-telling, not omission or flattering lighting. If fiction, as I've said, is a dialogue in which one person does all the talking, it should be at least an honest monologue, and full disclosure should be the seduction method. And yes, the world is full of gerontophiles.

Writers come in as many colors as their books do. Together they form a useful and agreeable milieu. How many good writers can you name who emerged all alone and not as part of a movement? Under Louis XIV half a dozen writers came up at the same time. In England the Romantic poets all knew each other. Surely there are social and economic forces behind this artistic flourishing (the emergence of the middle-class reader and the lending library, the confidence of a world power), but alliances and competition among writers also play a role.

Boris Kochno, Sergei Diaghilev's secretary, once said to me that individual friends may come and go, but nothing is more important than the milieu. If so, then all these writer friends represent the milieu, the admiring or disapproving chorus that never speaks with a single voice but with overlapping and contradictory opinions. What we want is not a consensus but a rousing intensification of response, a feeling that someone out there is getting even our subtlest comments or jokes.

Each of us has to be as great as Tolstoy or Flaubert—as great-hearted, as thoughtful, as sensitive to every signal, as passionate—or else we wouldn't understand Anna Karenina or Madame Bovary. We must re-create within ourselves Vronsky's horror when he sees his favorite horse being put down or Anna's desperate happiness when she pushes past every obstacle and servant and embraces her son once again. If we couldn't feel those things, then we wouldn't get those scenes. If Tolstoy is greater than we are, it's only because he's steadier and surer and more able to stay on point. But the dramas he sets in motion in our inner theaters are our tragedies, not his. He may be playing the instrument, but the strings that are plucked are ours.

To be sure, the score sounds different every time it's played. As we get older and more experienced, the timbre deepens, the volume grows, the ornamentation becomes denser. We never read the same book twice. But each time it is our book, locked in our innermost heart as we move and change through time.

Chapter 11

My young husband, Michael Carroll, works harder at his craft than anyone I know. When writers say in their *Paris Review* interviews that they work eight to ten hours a day, I always think, "What rubbish!" and picture them rereading their pages or sharpening pencils. I at least would rather chitchat or cook than write, and I can't sit still more than half an hour. Often I fall down a Wikipedia rabbit hole. I write longhand at the dining room table and hope for an interruption—a call, an e-mail, or a visit. For that reason I get most done away from New York.

But Michael writes every day in a deserted bar during the extremely unpopular happy hour from four to nine, away from the Internet—the Unhappy Hours, as I call them. He goes through three or four drafts. He never reads to other people from a work-in-progress, though I'm constantly buttonholing victims. Poor Marilyn, who preferred ideas to narrative and was offended or bored by my endless sex scenes, sacrificed years of her life listening to me. I'd love to hear Michael's writing, but he's thrown off, I suspect, by people's comments.

He works very slowly, doesn't word-edit (as I do) but redrafts an entire chapter or story (as D. H. Lawrence did). Nabokov, incidentally, built up his novels card by index card but then wrote through the whole thing again rapidly, "with a wet brush," benefiting from both patient accretion and spontaneity, or at least its semblance.

Michael hates culture, abhors the theater, is allergic to ballet and opera, dislikes museums; maybe he's opposed to my generation (he's twenty-five years younger) of ravenous American culture vultures. Certainly he is against people who, like me, are preparing for God's great quiz show in the sky, the eschatological twenty questions that, if properly answered, will gain us admission to paradise, where we can all coo over great performances with other esthetes and erudites. It may seem paradoxical that given his philistinism he spends all his working hours making art with monastic zeal, but Michael, I guess, needs to preserve his street cred, though you couldn't locate his street on any known map. He hated my snobbish, condescending friends in Paris, who insisted he learn French and give a standing ovation to every Handel opera. He's proud to say he's descended from resentful Scotch-Irish stock, those small farmers in Tennessee too poor to own slaves, who specialized in schadenfreude and revenge, who were "down to earth" and disliked folks who "put on airs," as if, like Antaeus, they lost strength when no longer in touch with the hardscrabble dirt.

Despite being a borderline atheist, Michael has a nearly encyclopedic knowledge of the history of Christianity and is especially at home and at ease with Calvinism, the bleak determinism of his impoverished ancestors. Like them he laughs at Catholic gewgaws and popish ceremony, though he can discuss the Trinity and the Immaculate Conception with a real appetite and glittering eyes. It's all unfathomable, his militant iconoclasm and hunger for religion, his distaste for the very word *spirituality* and love for theology, this immersion in the history of the most obscure cults and a strong conviction that religion of all sorts is the enemy of equality and enlightenment.

My blasé airs and cosmopolitan good manners irritate him, the way I constantly rustle my ruff to prove that I belong to the cultural elite. He wants to be a real person and to write about real people; his characters can be eccentric, though only in a strangely self-invented and not in a campy, familiar way. The other day Joyce Carol Oates observed, "Michael is a real person." His favorite writer is Richard Yates. Like his characters, his conversational style is more disruptive than conciliatory. I never swear, not out of prudery but from fear of offending, though Michael is capable of invoking "Jesus fucked his mother in the ass" to a room full of matrons in Chanel. I'm always surprised how unshocked and smilingly accepting they are of his profanity. I waste so much time frowning at Michael disapprovingly or struggling to change the subject, which makes me look prissy and him look vital and natural.

I don't want to make him sound like a bully, since he can be kind and consoling and is always surprised that I don't ask any questions when Janet, say, has announced she was getting divorced. "You didn't find out why or when?" I pass off my lack of curiosity as good manners instead of the indifference and self-centeredness it actually is.

If I'm curious about people, I always want to know about their latest ideas and the latest trends and sensations and books. Michael reads not widely but deeply. He has his favorite writers—Joy Williams and John Cheever and Yates—whom he reads and rereads. He doesn't much like Faulkner (nor do I), but he is a southerner and keeps pegging away at Faulkner's novels and his biographies, much as I read and reread the inscrutable Stéphane Mallarmé. Do we think that someday these authors will make sense?

Michael has kept writing for thirty-five years with an iron determination and little encouragement. When the University of Wisconsin published his story collection *Little Reef*, the collection won the Sue Kaufman Prize for First Fiction from the American Academy of Arts and Letters. The judges included Mark Strand, Joy Williams, John Guare, Philip Levine, and Charles Wright. And yet he still couldn't find a literary agent after all that, and no publisher will read unagented manuscripts. I suppose living with me for twenty-two years has been of no help, since he doesn't show me his work, doesn't share my literary tastes, and has never connected with agents through me (though he has met writers who've given him blurbs). He claims people in the business avoid him because I'm so "powerful" (you could have fooled me) that they're afraid of offending me.

Over the last few years I've been in the hospital for about two months with two strokes and a heart attack. Michael rented a car and drove to Providence, Rhode Island, where I was hospitalized one time, and brought me back to New York. He visited me every day when I was hospitalized with my second stroke and my heart attack, in New York and an hour away in New Jersey. He arranged for friends to see me all the time, constantly updated them through e-mails about my condition, filled out the endless insurance forms . . . in fact, devoted most of his time to my care and feeding in hospital and later during my lengthy rehabilitations. He was always cheerful and seemingly optimistic. He constantly encouraged me as I made my first hesitant moves back toward writing. He's a good guy, a very good guy, a true foul-weather friend.

If I ever was, because of my age, a father figure to him, after my illnesses everything reversed. Now he's become the worried parent and I the naughty boy, staying up too late eating butter and bacon, refusing to walk around the block, shopping extravagantly online, running up huge bills at the gourmet shop across the street. Michael has to accompany me to Princeton on my teaching days, since he says I have a bad sense of balance, which more rehab could have easily corrected. I insist the window of opportunity for physical improvement has passed. Nonsense, he says.

Although he is bored by my frivolous social evenings and dinner parties, he likes to see me laugh and "sparkle" with my friends. He is the sober husband with the airhead wife.

He never buys new clothes, he trudges miles through the snow to Trader Joe's, the cheap supermarket, he insists I travel first class on planes while he sits with his knees around his chin in economy, wedged in between a crying baby and a three-hundred-pound sweating man.

Although he seldom dresses up and expresses no vanity through clothes, he does keep his skin moisturized and his hair straightened— and he looks years younger than he is. People are always astonished when they learn his age. I wonder if some day he'll let himself go, once he becomes a famous writer. He's a bit like my eternally youthful character Guy in *Our Young Man*.

No wonder he's sometimes bitter and harsh; he's been made to wait too long for some sort of minimal recognition. There are just too few slots in our English-language culture; better to be Dutch or Romanian and have three thousand readers rather than thirty thousand—or none.

Michael is small, and self-conscious about it, but he's actually adorable (and taller than I am, now that I've shrunk with age), with a slim waist, strong legs, a sweet face with dark, moody eyes—and a low, beautiful speaking voice.

I first fell in love with him over the phone. He wrote me a fan letter from Plzeň, in the Czech Republic, where he was teaching English for the Peace Corps. When we spoke, I liked his low, resonating voice with the southern burr; when he made his way to Paris, I fell for his neat, compact body and ready smile—he reminded me of myself when I was young. Absurd as that might sound, there is often a narcissistic aspect to gay love (ha! ha!). I was never that attractive—but almost.

He has the knack for schmoozing. When I leave the dining room to fetch the next course, I always hear the conversation revive, led by Michael's straightforward questions. I'm so old, so controlling, so pervasive, that people wait for me to introduce a topic, which makes everyone self-conscious. Michael is unintimidating, curious, egalitarian without thinking about it. He has a potty mouth. People chitchat easily around him. His students (mostly women) in Rome where he teaches every summer are all in love with him. Sometimes when he's tipsy he goes to the dark side and starts haranguing people, preaching his anticultural gospel. He thinks he must drink and smoke to write. I certainly used to do both, though now I do neither; I used to be stymied writing without tobacco or making love without booze.

His bookshelves are full of nonfiction about history, religion, Florida, obscure facts—and he has lots of new novels. He likes American classics. He's also read all of Fitzgerald and Ernest Hemingway. On his bedroom walls are old hand-colored pictures of Florida (maps, Indians, alligators) and prints of Prague as well as photos of friends and family.

He reminds me that in public school in northern Florida he was always in "gifted" classes taught by the transplanted Ivy League wives of Yankee businessman transferred down south; he read the Greeks and Shakespeare at fourteen. He was so bored he kept dropping out of the first few colleges he attended. He knows everything about the history of Florida, about Frederick Delius and Lynyrd Skynyrd (both Floridians). He has no tattoos or piercings or extensions, earrings or Prince Alberts. He will be in his natal state for the Resurrection. I took him along when I interviewed Elton John and David Geffen for magazines (unlike me, he knew who they were, which was convenient).

He hates something he may have invented called "capital culture," i.e., the culture of Paris, London, New York, which he sees as a uniform, nefarious racket. He will not see foreign films, only American action movies. But he becomes angry when there's too much killing in a film, which rules out most of the American things; he points out he's never seen anyone shot—he's not even seen a gun (I've seen lots of guns but only one person shot to death).

He buys flowers for me, because he knows I like them, but he's indifferent to them himself. He's very tidy but doesn't complain about my messes. He does aerobics every day; I never exercise. He cooks healthy meals and complains all the time about the waste of time. I prepare buttery, heart-attack dishes, and I welcome the waste of time (better than writing). We both retire by midnight but are still rattling around at two or three, incapable of falling asleep; we each sleep till noon if possible. He is religious about writing every day; I'm whatever is the opposite—impious?

If he gives a pizza party for twenty-five or thirty, it's effortless; I wear myself out preparing a dinner for six or eight.

Every square inch of wall space is covered with art, by friends, mostly (James Lord, Robert Mapplethorpe, Eric Amouyal, Lincoln Perry, Carol Munder). I like that, and I think he does too. We never discuss it and seldom talk about anything. I can remember when I was in my twenties I wore myself out talking everything to death, the meaning of everything, the subtleties of our relationship, the value of art in a socialist state, that sort of thing, and feelings, too—could you be both sincere and mannered, didn't true sincerity rule out all forms of style? People in their twenties were obsessed about sincerity. At least I was, and my friends too. Did we just outgrow it, and was that good or bad? In a sense we thought we were universal legislators and that we had to resolve all moral questions once and for all. Was that as true of Michael's generation as of mine? Or have we coarsened? Somewhere James Merrill addresses "the vain, flippant, unfeeling monster" he's sure to become. Has that happened to me?

My French lover Hubert, who died of AIDS, was as antisocial as Michael, though his chilliness was streaked with paranoia, whereas

Michael is just bored by *mondanités*. Hubert wanted to be perceived by others as endlessly polite and aristocratically cheerful; Michael thinks all that is a waste of time. If he likes someone, it's quite genuine. Both Hubert and Michael are mysterious—Hubert strategically, Michael just because he forgets to keep me up to speed. I often discover what he's thinking or feeling from casual remarks I overhear him making to acquaintances. Is that sort of indirection typical of most couples?

Michael and I can sit through entire meals not saying a word, more his choice than mine. If I ask a question beyond "More soup?" he gets angry and ridicules me for being a trivially polite person. Hostessy. We both had southern mothers, although his was less frilly and "social" than mine (his mother was my age). I can usually count on someone's egotism responding to my leading questions, but not in Michael's case. He is wise to all my ploys and prefers to be left alone with his thoughts after a hard day's work. He is exhausted by my all-too-predictable chitchat (even though I vary my remarks, I can't vary my reasons for making them). For him my conversational gambits are just further examples of my silly and dated idea of how civilized people should behave ("What's your favorite color?"). Michael resents any imperatives and perhaps my eighteenth-century notion of civilization itself.

I think ruefully how our friends imagined we were engaged in a fascinating lifelong debate about the technical aspects of our work and the intricacies of our social and intimate exchanges. They wouldn't have recognized these two zombies at the table, feasting on their own entrails.

To be fair, Michael was always cheering me on when after a long silence I'd start writing again. And he is always willing to do a "plot walk" with me in my attempts to excavate a story line. I trust myself in description, reflection, and portrait-making, but I feel on shaky ground about "what happens." Oddly enough, Michael has a clear and inventive sense of plot, although it's part of his method to improvise as he goes along. He revises extensively, but he doesn't like to know in advance where he's going.

Nor do I. I like horizons toward which I'm heading, as E. M. Forster puts it, but I treasure discoveries along the way, even those that lead me in an entirely new direction.

But there's something casual-seeming (never slapdash) about Michael's exquisitely crafted prose. My early training as a journalist makes my writing marmoreally smooth and seamless. It "tracks" perfectly, as journalists say, whereas Michael's prose pivots and stutters; the surface is corrugated, not facelessly polished. Perhaps some nasty person is reading this now and thinking, "Don't fret, chum. You've become artistically incoherent enough."

Michael has spent long hours editing my manuscripts, often for days on end. Especially after my two strokes and my heart attack, my writing needs extensive and careful work. He'll unscramble confusing passages, condense my longueurs, unpack my obscurities, break up long sentences, start new paragraphs. His surgery is so precise I can scarcely detect his cuts and stitches.

Marilyn and I used to plan vaguely on writing a book called *Martyrs to Art*. The idea was to show how the longing to make art can ruin a life, somewhat as Edwin Reardon suffers in George Gissing's *New Grub Street*. Now that I'm so old and feeble, my fondest hope is that Michael will succeed—whatever counts as literary "success" in today's deflated currency. Michael himself is utterly disabused and resigned about winning success in any public way, though he's written some absorbing, hard-edge, and not particularly flattering pages about me. People find me more interesting than my books. At least two writers have made me a major character—without knowing me. Maybe, without realizing it, I've become amusingly historical, like Quentin Crisp or Elizabeth Arden. Or alarmingly jolly, like Falstaff. Michael keeps writing about me in novels he abandons; his verbal portraits worry me, since a literary picture feels like the kiss-off. Nabokov, I recall, in *Speak, Memory* hesitated to write about his French nanny because he realized that once he wrote about someone, he never thought about them again.

Chapter 12

My lodestar was always Paris. In prep school I listened to Juliette Gréco records and read (or pretended to read) Madame de Sévigné's letters in French. Little did I guess that thirty years later I'd be living in the middle of the Seine on the Île Saint-Louis and be dining at the Voltaire restaurant next to Gréco's older sister and her friend (and mine) Alexis de Redé, or that over dinner at my house a French literary journalist would mention that Juliette Gréco was her lover (at the time Gréco, going on eighty, was also married to a third husband, her accompanist).

Is it better to dream of a Paris, mist and bridges, in the lonely Michigan dorm room—or actually to live there in a tiny seventeenth-century apartment across the silent, solemn street from the church of Saint-Louis-en-l'Île, with its bell tower that is *ajouré*, pierced in several places to let light, *le jour*, traverse? I just had to look that word up in French to find out what it means in English. That sounds awfully pretentious, doesn't it, but I promise that's one of the few words I know in French but not in English.

I'm not all that fluent in French. When I thumb through an English dictionary, I can guess the meaning of most nontechnical words; in a French dictionary I recognize only about a third of the entries. If I read a nineteenth-century French novel, say, I understand everything; in a contemporary French novel I recognize all but two or three words per page.

To answer my question, it's better to live in Paris than to daydream about it, as Elizabeth Bishop discovered about Brazil in her great book of poems, *Questions of Travel*:

Is it lack of imagination that makes us come
to imagine places, not just stay at home?
Or could Pascal have been not entirely right
about just sitting quietly in one's room?

Bishop leaves that as a question but gives so many enticing Brazilian details ("pink trees," "the sound of unmatched clogs walking") that they make her argument for her. James Merrill (another poet, a friend, and a friend of Bishop) seemed to be taking the other position once when he wrote a description of South American wonders and posted it from the airport before he left the States, a bravura piece proving that his imagination was superior to everyone's travel reminiscences. It's called "Peru: The Landscape Game."

Paris as it really is certainly surpassed my imaginative powers. The taste of real croissants, crusty on the shell-shaped brown outside, buttery and stringy as a lobster thorax on the inside—extra buttery if one ordered a *croissant au beurre*. The delicate fretwork of the Tour Saint-Jacques, like the pillar of the pedal harp if the strings, neck, and soundboard had been hacked away; the tower is all that is left of a medieval church that burned down. The delicate mist rising around the Île Saint-Louis, bluish pearls pierced by the silver string of a *bateau-mouche* searchlight. Brazilian transvestite prostitutes, as made-up as mass-produced cream cakes, with their soccer-player calves, as tall as clowns on their stilts or stilettos, breaking through the bush of the Bois de Boulogne. The stationery shop (now gone) where I bought my thick blue writing paper, the envelopes of a blue as intense as spring gentians. The *bouquinistes* along the Seine with their yellowed novels by Paul Morand (a reject favorite due to his prewar prominence and later regrettable Nazi sympathies); the book sheds and their tattered prints in glassine casings hanging from clothespins along a horizontal string like freshly made sausages. The eternal rain on the cobblestones of the rue Quincampoix, like wet dinosaur scales. The little shop that sells just old Jules Verne editions, gaudy as Ruritanian medals. The shop centered around a chocolate fountain, bubbling gently all night to itself, ignoring the melancholy deserted snow-covered street outside.

The brilliantly lit presence along the Seine of the Louvre, Châtelet, the Conciergerie, the Hôtel de Ville, abruptly snapped off at midnight like distinguished men blindly scrambling for the exit after the phosphorus flash dies out for the group portrait. The knocking of the steam pipes in my cozy apartment, like prisoners tapping code to each other. For me, Paris is looking out the big window on the unlit, extinct convent across the street. Or the saffron smell of Le Monde des Epices. Or the voice of the pasta shopkeeper impatiently advising each lady as she anxiously asks him how to sauce this particular shape of spaghetti or gnocchi, "Uniquement la crème fraîche, Madame," a recipe that would make a real Italian cringe. Or the haughty, hieratic conduct of shopgirls at Guerlain on the Champs-Elysées as they fill out the order slip, go to the strange inconvenience of making change, wrap up your flask with a religious attention to detail, walk you to the door, and show you out as if you were an ambassador to the Holy See. Or a tradesman.

Of course Paris is also the home of great painting and books and music—vulgar (Offenbach) and sublime (Ravel)—and every night 250 curtains go up, cabarets and operas and dance and classical and contemporary theater included. It's hard to see how the same country that produced Paul Cézanne also produced Bernard Buffet, or how César grew up in the country where Alberto Giacometti lived and worked. France has always had great writers, however, and still does; authors sound off on prime-time TV shows and the French government sends writers off on "missions" around the world, all expenses paid. Even the smallest town has a bookshop selling the complete works of established writers entombed in expensive Pléiade editions.

Nothing I know can compete with good French conversation—it's far-ranging, polite, varied, informed. Parisians are witty but never whinny at their own jokes. The more pornographic and polite they are, the higher their social standing.

If Proust was my introduction to French literature (along with Alphonse Daudet's *Tartarin de Tarascon*, which we read in high school French class), Colette was my first great passion. When she was sixteen, she sobbed to her early-thirties lover (later husband), "I think I'll die if

I'm not your mistress." I had a similarly proprietary if illicit hunger for her, though she'd recently died when I first started reading her in 1954.

In rereading Colette's *La Vagabonde*, I was struck by the high level of her insight into love and descriptions of nature. She wrote it as a mild sort of revenge novel against her ex-husband, Henry Gauthier-Villars, a journalist known as "Willy." He ran a real writing factory, with lots of collaborators he paid but didn't usually credit. The closest thing in our own day is *The Painted Bird* author Jerzy Kosinski's atelier of ghostwriters, not to mention his outright plagiarism of obscure Polish novels of the 1930s. Kosinski was too busy playing polo and kissing hands to write. I used to know one of his ghosts, a doughy man endlessly smiling and mopping his face and closing his eyes whenever he spoke.

Colette actually wrote the Claudine novels, which sold three hundred thousand copies at the time, but Willy claimed the authorship. Fed up, Colette took off with a melancholy butch lesbian, "Missy," with whom she performed as a mime on stage—until the law forbade Missy as an aristocrat (the Marquise de Morny) to take to the boards: too lowering!

La Vagabonde doesn't mention sapphism, but it does deal with the handsome, rich, idle male suitor whom the narrator eventually rejects because he opens her old wounds—and because her only idea of a woman's love for man is submission. This "noble" (if unlikely) rejection of an impeccable (and wealthy if dull) candidate is a dim echo of *La Princesse de Clèves*, a seventeenth-century classic of inexplicable self-denial written by a whole salon of noble wits headed by Madame Lafayette. It's one of the few novels written by a committee.

When I read Claude Pichois's preface to the first volume of the Pléiade edition of her collected works, I was impressed by how the brilliant Colette arose like a breaker out of the choppy sea of mostly forgotten novelists of her period. They, too, were writing about naughty girls and mustache-twirling older male millionaires; they, too, were writing about perversion and gender-bending; they, too, were writing about backstage romances and misalliances. The milieu . . .

The difference was that most of the others wrote about tawdry sex rather than tenderness—and word for word no one wrote as well as

Colette. When she's describing the suitor, she says, "To be entirely honest let me mention what I like best in him: a look that is sometimes absent and seeking, and that kind of private smile in the eyes which one sees in sensitive people who are both violent and shy." Perhaps this comes dangerously close to "the psychology of men" that Roland Barthes ridicules in Balzac (Colette's favorite author). Whereas Balzac seems to be a bit of a blowhard (if at the same time the most compelling of all storytellers), Colette is vivid and specific; I wish she wouldn't generalize about "people" and talk just about him, Dufferein-Chantel. Nevertheless, her characterization seems tailor-made.

When she strolls through the woods, it is under "a chinchilla sky," and she kicks and releases "the bitter musk of old, decayed leaves." Every page is studded with these jewels, dim jewels perhaps, but the real thing. To be clever, I used to say that Colette never wrote a bad line nor a good book—but in a sense she's always writing the same book, a very good one indeed, about a bewitched man and an insecure female lover who fears her looks will fade soon and she'll be dropped. Her writing is seldom flashy, always apt. As Anatole France (an author she probably disliked) said, "Simple style is like white light. It is complex, but its complexity is not obvious."

As though to tempt fate, in real life Colette had an affair with her sixteen-year-old stepson, which she wrote about in *The Ripening Seed*. There's always a tension between men and women in Colette—the older woman in *Seed* has a masculine smile even as she timorously takes note of her young lover's very male selfishness and arrogance and glories in them. She "smiled with the virile smile that often made her look like a handsome boy." A fifteen-year-old girl blossoms and pirouettes as a "ravishing" woman under the appreciative eye of an older Parisian man but shrinks back into wounded childishness when her jealous teen boyfriend momentarily rejects her. Men become feminine, the old become young, the fierce become gentle, straights turn queer . . . Whereas Colette seems to subscribe to Balzac's ironclad typology of human characters, in fact each person—in action real or perceived—is so unstable, so shimmering with possibility, that no type remains fixed for long. David Hume, followed by Gaston Bachelard in *Intuition of the Instant*, thought that human beings have nothing except the moment and die from second to second and are endlessly reborn; Colette might have agreed.

Love, of course, is her great subject. When a woman asks her suitor, "Don't you feel that I'm beginning to get fond of you?" he replies, "To get fond of me . . . that's just what I'm afraid of . . .; that hardly ever leads to love."

They make love, and during the "truce" afterward, she is eager to look in the mirror to "see what my new face looked like." She wonders if she is feeling love with him or is just surrendering to sensuality. She lets him spoil her with "next summer's fruits" and an arrow brooch "all bleeding with rubies." He makes love so well that she thinks of a girlfriend who said, "One couldn't do better oneself."

She visits a friend and observes her "minute dog in an old flannel shirt, a little yellow monster . . . gazing up at her with the beautiful, imploring eyes of a squirrel, under the bumpy forehead of a bonze." She hears about a dog seen in the pet shop with a spine protruding like rosary beads.

Colette's animals, especially her dogs and cats, are unforgettable. During World War II, probably to make money, she simplified all her precious Lolitas into Gigi and all her previous cats into a jealous, possessive, combative Cat who drives away a mistress, her rival.

"Just think, Margot, I shall soon be thirty-four," says Renée despairingly in *La Vagabonde*; more or less the same age as the Marschallin in *Der Rosenkavalier*, singing farewell to love forever. We gays in the 1950s used to hold funerals for each other at thirty—farewell to love! It seems Colette was endlessly, needlessly complaining about being too old, given that she was never without a lover and that her last husband, Maurice Goudeket, seventeen years her junior and a Jew, was so devoted he stayed with her as he wore his yellow star and she penned her anti-Semitic (if hauntingly beautiful) novel *Julie de Carneilhan*. He was interned for seven weeks until she pulled strings and got him out; like her neighbor Jean Cocteau she was a mild if entirely reprehensible sort of collaborator, though both she and Cocteau used their connections to save Jewish friends. The description of the aristocratic Julie leaving a besieged and dangerous Paris on horseback with her brother is one of the most memorable scenes in her œuvre.

Colette wrote about eighty books, almost of all them autobiographical. Sometimes she calls herself Claudine, sometimes Renée. Her most famous book, *Chéri*, is about an older woman, Léa, who's become rich from all her royal and plutocratic lovers and now, a cougar in deep middle age, treats herself to a headstrong young lover of twenty-five. When she realizes she's losing her looks, she marries Chéri off, cuts her hair, gains weight, and plays cards with other old ladies. Chéri's wife, innocent and naive, bores him; he realizes he's still in love with Léa. He pushes his way into her apartment and sees this crop-haired, obese old woman that Léa's become. In order to recapture *his* Léa he meets another old lady who, for a price, will let him smoke opium at her place and leaf through her yellowing clippings of Léa at the races, Léa with the king of Belgium, etc. He finally puts a bullet through his head. Colette enjoyed playing Léa on stage, year after year. *Chéri* is a sort of masterpiece. It invokes every woman's (and every gay man's) fear of aging. Léa is materialistic. She embodies what the French prize the most—she is "realistic" about looks, love, the good life, and the amusements available to each age group.

A young friend of mine who had to deal with a slightly older and very handsome lover and *his* much older lover asked me what he should do. I told him "to take the couple" and imagine he was in a Colette novel. Now, ten years later, all three men are happy and prospering.

Léa is so sensual, so rigorously "realistic," so aware of all the nuances of pleasure she can confer and enjoy, that she is a much more convincing *grande cocotte* of the Belle Époque than Proust's Odette. In fact Proust once wrote a fan letter to Colette telling her she'd achieved more in her 100-page novella *Mitsou* than he had in his thousands of pages. He's exaggerating, of course. He had a lot of genius and no talent; he botches most of his scenes by overwriting and by unwieldy interpolations. Colette, by contrast, had a narrow genius but a very deep talent, and she always tells a good story.

Colette is very careful about maintaining and monitoring her image. At one point she starts to say something unflattering about herself and abruptly admits that she's going to draw a curtain lest she repulse the young reader (male, no doubt). One sees a constant struggle in her to bear witness to the truth and to seduce, to arrange her corpulent body and frizzy hair in the right half-light—and to expose it fully to the full glare of exhibitionism and "realism." She weighed 170 pounds at one point, though she had her own home gym to stay toned. During the Depression she opened a beauty salon/day spa. Her enemies said her clients emerged looking ten years older.

Colette was a total masochist and could see a man only as a master. Mind you, he had to be worthy of her submission—not smart or rich enough, but virile, cruel, sexy, entitled enough. Someone said she knew about every kind of love but mutual.

In *The Sentimental Retreat*, the last book in which she calls herself Claudine, Colette's older, fictionalized husband has been hospitalized, and she's staying with a meek (possibly stupid) friend, Annie, who confesses that after her divorce she discovered she liked more than anything else to have sex with younger men, one after another. "If I've got this right," she tells Claudine,

> the woman today who is the least guarded, she who whimpers first and the most easily, who's the most timid, the least talkative, she who never offers her shoulder or her knee to a groping flirtatious man, she who thinks naughty thoughts the least often, you understand! She lowers her eyes, she scarcely answers, she slides her foot under her chair. She doesn't even think something might ever happen to her. Except, when someone puts his hand on her forehead to tip her backwards and sees a glimmer light up in her eye, she's lost. She falls because she is utterly unaware of herself, because she's fearful, because she's afraid of being ridiculed—yes, Claudine!—and also she desires that it should all be over quickly, so that she won't have to struggle any more, because she's confused and thinks by giving in she'll find peace and solitude immediately afterwards . . . except, it turns out that in touching sin she's understood the goal and the meaning of her life, and so . . . We're the women someone forgot to arm.

Men and women are considered opponents—and Colette greets her lovers as "dear enemies." So different from the Revolutionary epoch, when men and women consider their mates as their best friends. For instance, in their last letters, prisoners about to be guillotined during the French Revolution addressed their spouses as "dearest friend." Perhaps in those traditional Catholic and royalist families, once the frivolity of Versailles was put behind them, men and women saw their mates as God-given companions; sincere friendship became the governing metaphor for marriage rather than warfare. But most of French fiction, from *Manon Lescaut* to Proust, sees the beloved as an enemy to be defeated. Few of my students today seem to have that old military model in mind; for them, if they're not chaste, wearing "purity rings," or part of the nightly "hookup culture," they're sort of unisex pals, dressed alike, not coquettish nor seductive but just "good guys" trudging about wearing matching jeans and haircuts, some 60 percent claiming (in trendy theory if not in gritty practice) that they're "bisexual." They don't understand proud, fierce women like Carmen nor kept women with winter gardens like Odette, trained to light a man's cigar. They don't get a whore like Blanche posing as a faded southern aristocrat. They are never tempted to forgive or even understand the tormented, poetic, satanic Humbert Humbert; for them he is just a charmless "pedophile."

If Colette was one tastemaker of her period, Jean Cocteau was another. Cocteau was a controversial figure, during his life and now. He once told of someone placing a chameleon on a piece of plaid to keep it warm; one could say he was that chameleon, a friend and defender of the featherweight champion Panama Al Brown and just as intimate with Barbette, a transvestite high-wire artist from Texas. Cocteau was a poet and a sensationally successful playwright and cinema director (perhaps best known today for his masterpiece *Beauty and the Beast*). He worshiped his own long, white, nervous hands and had them frequently photographed. He was so productive that people said he was as many-handed as the Hindu god Vishnu—another idea for a picture of his hands and several fake ones.

Cocteau also had a nimble pen and a silver tongue. Whenever I have to deliver a toast or salute a friend or dash off a prefatory note, I pretend I'm Cocteau, jangling with paradoxes; all my *mots* are *bons*. He didn't live that long ago and died only in the 1960s. Several of my friends knew him, and one even gave me a letter from Cocteau as a birthday present. The definitive biography of Cocteau, by Claude Arnaud, is dedicated to me.

Cocteau loved famous friends and would even swallow their insults masochistically. Pablo Picasso was certainly his most famous friend; it was Cocteau who had convinced him to design sets for the ballet *Parade* during World War I, a step that had cemented his international reputation. Cocteau admitted that meeting Picasso was the major encounter of his life—but years later, when Picasso was safely off in Barcelona, the painter gave an indiscreet interview in Spanish, assuming it would never get back to Paris: "Cocteau is a machine for thinking. His drawings are very graceful; his literature very journalistic. If there were newspapers for intellectuals, Cocteau would serve up every day a new dish, an elegant pirouette. If he could sell his talent, we'd go throughout our lives to the drug store to buy a Cocteau pill without ever running out of his talent." Cocteau was so distressed when this interview was translated into French in *L'Intransigeant* that he thought all the young artists he was trying to impress would suddenly doubt that he'd ever been Picasso's intimate. Surprisingly, he thought these words were a real blow to his prestige. That his writings were "journalistic"! That his work was like "a new dish" or a "pill"!

Cocteau dashed off a letter to his mother: "My dear, yesterday I received the hardest blow of my life. Picasso expressed himself about me as only my worst enemies would . . . I didn't throw myself off the balcony only because of you and the Church . . . I think I'll never have the strength to come back to the city . . . Pray for me; I'm suffering atrociously."

But then he had an inspiration. The Spanish were such idiots, they could have easily confused the name of the much less important painter Francis Picabia with Picasso. Yes, he could tell everyone Picabia had said those terrible things about him. During the intermission at the opera, Cocteau's mother came swarming up to Picasso and said to the artist that she and her son had been so comforted to discover that the horrible interview hadn't been given by him, Picasso. Then she asked Picasso directly, "It wasn't you, was it?" Picasso's Russian wife, Olga, who was very fond of Cocteau, took pity on him and said, "No, it wasn't him."

Cocteau was born in the quiet wealthy Paris suburb of Maisons-Laffitte in 1889, a few hours before the Eiffel Tower, that bold symbol of modernity, was inaugurated. It was a town devoted to horse-racing. (I once rented the chateau there and gave a Halloween party there, which at the time was a novelty.) He came from a prosperous Catholic family of stockbrokers and notaries. His father committed suicide when Jean (the youngest of three children) was only eight; he didn't leave a note behind, but there are reasons to think he might have been homosexual. Cocteau was raised by his self-dramatizing mother and a German nanny; he could speak German, and right after World War I he surprised everyone by bringing out an anthology of German poetry—a palm branch extended to the enemy.

Although he went to the elite Condorcet high school, where Proust had studied as well as the Goncourt brothers and a whole regiment of celebrities, and where Jean-Paul Sartre would teach philosophy, Cocteau was an indifferent student, remarkable for his lack of application. He who would become one of the two or three most brilliant conversationalists of his day and was curious about everything, from dance to religion to painting to poetry, evidenced none of this mental agility in school.

Cocteau, however, was precocious and enterprising, and he arranged to have his poems published while he was still in his teens. His second collection was named, fatally, *The Frivolous Prince*, a name that stuck. In it we read:

> Disdainful, frivolous and slender,
> Day-dreaming and childish,
> I was born to be a prince,
> A little prince in exile.

Whereas I fancied myself an all-powerful potentate like Frederick the Great, Cocteau's imagination turned him into someone day-dreaming and childish.

Cocteau arranged to have his poems read out loud in a theater by Édouard de Max, one of the leading actors of the day, to just a few hundred intimate friends. De Max was such a notorious homosexual that, as Cocteau recalled years later, his mother's friends would say to her, "Your son knows de Max, he is lost." The extravagantly dressed de Max would motor around Paris every afternoon with Cocteau and other high school boys as passengers. Oddly enough he became the idol of an English aesthete I revere, Ronald Firbank.

Proust tried to warn Cocteau, who was two decades younger, that mixing with society people and frequenting their salons and dazzling them with his chatter would destroy his talent. Proust was shocked by how blasé the adolescent Cocteau had already become, like someone who'd nibbled on *marrons glacés* all day on New Year's Eve and had no appetite left for real food. What would tempt his counterpart in America today? To give up poetry for prose and fiction for screenwriting? I've seen many of my contemporaries go down that treacherous road—not just hacks but talented writers. They end up unhappy—sometimes *rich* and unhappy, but unhappy all the same.

During World War I Cocteau, who was judged too weak to serve in the army, went to battle anyway in a uniform designed by the leading couturier of the day, Paul Poiret; he joined an ambulance corps put together by a friend who was a fraud, a fake officer who would be the inspiration for Cocteau's insouciant war novel *Thomas the Imposter.* Cocteau must have cut quite a figure in his chic uniform and heavy makeup (the Comtesse de Chevigné, the main model for Proust's Duchesse de Guermantes, once forbade Cocteau to kiss her lapdog: "You'll get face powder on his nose!"). Why was he so courageous and merry as bombs exploded on every side? If you live in a play-acting world, maybe even bombs look like make-believe.

Cocteau smoked opium most of his life, as did many of his well-heeled friends. Colette, his celebrated and hardworking neighbor in the Palais-Royal, wrote about the smart opium set in her book *The Pure and the Impure*, though there is no evidence that she was a user. Cocteau loved to visit Colette and has left an indelible portrait of her in words and lines on the page: "Between the dust-cloud of her hair and the scarf knotted around her neck, set in that triangular face with its pointed nose and its mouth like a circumflex accent, were eyes of a lioness at the zoo who becomes the audience instead of the show, watching those who watch her, with folded paws, and a sovereign disdain." Colette also wrote memorably about Cocteau in her World War II memoir *Paris From My Window*.

Although Proust and Cocteau should have been friends (both homosexual, both fascinated by society, both famous writers, both sons of the rich bourgeoisie), Cocteau was often exasperated by the older and wiser but frailer Proust. Once Cocteau was reading a book-length poem to friends toward the end of World War I. They had assembled at ten and waited an hour for Proust, who only arrived at midnight (because of his asthma he had to wait till the dust had settled). Proust was accompanied by the handsome bisexual American Walter Berry, whom both Edith Wharton and Henry James were infatuated with. Cocteau was very anxious because he had changed his manner from the transparence and charm of his early poems to something much more "modern" and difficult, dedicated to the heroic pilot Roland Garros and influenced by the trendy work of his new friend Guillaume Apollinaire. The society ladies were puzzled and confused; nobody had seen Cocteau since the beginning of the war. He had "molted" into something new, as his friends Stravinsky and Picasso would do so often in their long careers. His long poem, called *The Cape of Good Hope*, was a flop.

It seemed that from one day to the next Cocteau had changed his graceful Symbolist style for something Futurist, celebrating steel, propellers, and war. He was reading in his new machine-gun delivery in the stifling heat of mid-August; his audience was visibly wilting. Cocteau was furious at Proust for arriving late: "Get out, Marcel, you're ruining my reading!" he shouted. There followed an exchange of letters; to a friend Proust said that even though Cocteau was a brilliant young poet, he was acting like an old narcissist ("un vieux beau")—like Montesquiou, the original model of Charlus.

Cocteau wanted above all to be avant-garde. He was very taken by the Ballets Russes and its impresario Diaghilev and star male dancer Vaslav Nijinsky. It was Diaghilev who stopped one day on the Champs-Elysées and said to him, "Astonish me!" Cocteau liked nothing more than these arbitrary, imperious orders; soon he had conceived and plotted out a ballet, *Parade*, with Picasso's sets and Erik Satie's music. Now he had his own "scandal" to rival the scandalous earlier 1913 Stravinsky-Nijinsky debut of *The Rite of Spring*, during which the audience became so violent, resorting to fisticuffs, that the stage manager had to raise the house lights.

One of the young soldiers at his poetry reading who refused to praise Cocteau—and who walked out on his recitation—was André Breton, who eventually became the "pope" of surrealism. He and his friends despised Cocteau, partly because they were hostile to all homosexuals and partly because they disliked his particular brand of classical references and high-class kitsch. Cocteau was very Right Bank, with his titled ladies and couturiers and opium dreams; the surrealists were an odd mix of communism and Freudianism and Left Bank bohemianism. Until the surrealists sputtered out after World War II (Breton sat out the war in New York), they were a constant thorn in Cocteau's side.

Cocteau was a master of the autobiographical essay; his essays are at once wonderfully intimate and revealing and deeply philosophical. *Opium*, a journal kept during a detoxification cure, contains this memorable entry: "Picasso said that the smell of opium is the least stupid smell in the world. You could compare it only to the smell of a circus or of a seaport." Cocteau wrote *Opium* during a hospitalization in 1928, and it is scarcely a denunciation of the drug and its "euphoria superior to health." More practically, he tells us the first sign of getting off opium is a return of sexuality as well as yawning, sneezing, and the production of snot and tears. He also tells us that everything one does in life if one is not smoking is headed toward death, has to do with dying or death, whereas opium addiction is something else, a way of getting off the "train" that's death-bound. Cocteau drew constantly while writing the book; "Writing," he said, "for me is to draw, to tie the lines together in such a way as to turn them into writing or to untie them so that the writing becomes drawing."

In 1919 he met a brilliant young novelist, the fifteen-year-old Raymond Radiguet. Just as the nineteenth-century encounter between Paul Verlaine and the teenage Rimbaud changed the life and the poetry of the older, married Verlaine, in the same way Cocteau fell half in love with the myopic boy, who (like Rimbaud) was the dominant partner, both artistically and psychologically. Despite Radiguet's inconvenient heterosexuality, he was willing to sleep (just sleep) with the infatuated Cocteau, and it is no accident that Cocteau's most inspired collection of poetry, *Plain Song*, is about lying, pensive and awake, next to the sleeping beloved. Radiguet once bragged in his diary that he never "refused" himself to anyone. He couldn't help it, could he, if his body didn't happen to respond to a man?

The intellectual union between a prodigy and an experienced Parisian fifteen years his senior was very productive, one of the richest collaborations in history, claims Cocteau's biographer, Claude Arnaud. Both writers decided to submit to the influence of novels of the distant past that observed with restraint the workings of the passions—*La Princesse de Clèves*, *Les Liaisons dangereuses*, and *Adolphe*. Radiguet produced the impeccable *The Devil in the Flesh*, and Cocteau eventually wrote his tragedy about brother-sister love, *Les Enfants Terribles* (sometimes translated as *The Holy Terrors*).

Despite his literary success, Radiguet drank a bottle of whiskey and of gin every day; he contracted typhoid fever and died at age twenty, leaving behind 900 pages of fiction, including the unfinished *Count d'Orgel's Ball*, which Cocteau trimmed by 9 percent and spruced up with his natural gift for epigrams. Coco Chanel and the great patron of the ballet, Misia Sert, arranged a funeral all in white, the color consecrated to dead newborns and children. White coffin, white suit, white horses. For years afterward Cocteau was inconsolable; jeering enemies called him *le veuf sur le toit* ("the widower on the roof"), after Le Bœuf sur le Toit (the Ox on the Roof), the hot spot where Cocteau's crowd dined and drank.

Cocteau's memoir *The Difficulty of Being* has memorable pages on his eccentricities as well as his style: "I attach no importance to what people call style and by which they like to think they can recognize an author. I want people to recognize my ideas or, better, my way of doing things. I want to make myself understood in the briefest way possible. I've noticed that when a story doesn't connect with the mind it's because it can be read too rapidly, the slope is too slippery. That's why in this book I contort my style." He wrote this book in the late 1940s, after directing his successful movie *Beauty and the Beast*, under dreadful wartime and postwar deprivations and while suffering from a painful skin disease. The title is an echo of the eighteenth-century philosopher Bernard de Fontenelle's remark to his doctor when he was dying at nearly a hundred, "I'm feeling a certain difficulty of being." He draws verbal portraits of famous friends and also, like Montaigne, dissects himself, even his looks: "I've always had my hair growing every which way, my teeth and the hairs of my beard as well. It must be that my nerves and my whole soul grow that way too. That's why I'm so hard to figure out for people who go all in one way and can scarcely conceive of a colic. That's what upsets those people who can't cure me of my mythological leprosy. They don't know by which end to grab me."

A glance at a chronology of Cocteau's life reveals how hard he worked and how constantly and in how many media. For instance, he spent the month of February 1938 in Montargis with his lover, the movie star Jean Marais; there he wrote in eight days the play *Les Parents terribles* (it was produced in 1995 on Broadway as *Indiscretions*, starring Jude Law, Kathleen Turner, Eileen Atkins, and Cynthia Nixon). The following September he wrote a long poem dedicated to Jean Marais. On November 14 *Les Parents* premiered; forbidden at its original theater (it deals with mother-son incest), it was a triumph when it opened at a second theater. The play was published in 1939—and that's just one year.

In 1940 Cocteau not only wrote a play, *Sacred Monsters*, but also a one-act curtain raiser, *The Handsome Indifferent Man*, a revised version of *The Human Voice*. This time the woman, who is pleading with her lover not to leave her, is talking directly to him, not on the phone as in the original. And now the role was assumed by Edith Piaf. Cocteau went for another opium detox and published a new book of poems and *Sacred Monsters*. The next year he wrote *The Typewriter*, a play, and a verse drama based on *Tristan and Isolde* and published two collections of poetry. When he couldn't write, he drew.

Cocteau had always wanted to write a novel about homosexuals, but he decided to wait until his mother's death. She died in 1943, and he'd already been "scooped" by yet another of his discoveries, the thief and jailbird Jean Genet, who was already publishing *Our Lady of the Flowers*, a masterful account of Divine, one of the first drag queens in literature. Cocteau could console himself with *Le Livre blanc*, a rather tame gay book he had already published anonymously in the 1920s; but to the degree the story was mild, the illustrations (added two years later in a second edition) were sulfurous—and acknowledged by Cocteau as his own work. "People have said that *The White Notebook* was my work. I suppose that's the reason why you have asked me to illustrate it and for which I have accepted," Cocteau coyly wrote in an open letter to the publisher.

Cocteau was a great impresario of talents, the soul of generosity, capable of sponsoring younger, usually male talents. He was a man of excess—a nonstop talker, a passionate Catholic convert, a drug addict, a devoted friend who was often lonely. He played footsie with the Nazis during the war, but only because the French fascist collaborators (of the Céline sort) were so hostile to him and his lover Jean Marais, throwing ink on the actor during a performance of *Britannicus* and beating up the two of them one night on the Champs-Elysées. To win them some protection in high places, Cocteau wrote a positive essay about Hitler's favorite sculptor, Arno Breker, who was having an exhibit at the Orangerie. To be fair, Cocteau had known Breker since the sculptor studied in Paris in the 1920s, and he, Cocteau, chose to be buried twenty years after the war under a statue by Breker. But many left-wing French friends condemned Cocteau for praising the favorite of Hitler, who'd imprisoned and slaughtered so many of their friends.

If Cocteau was notoriously criticized by André Gide, the surrealists, and Catholics like François Mauriac (particularly after Cocteau abandoned his spectacular conversion to the Church to return to boys and opium), he and his longtime lover Jean Marais were idolized by the public, especially after Marais starred in a glossy wartime film *The Eternal Return*, a semimythical update of *Tristan and Isolde* for which Cocteau wrote the script. Hordes of teenage girls lingered in the courtyard of the Palais-Royal, hoping to get a glimpse of the movie star or even of their dog Moujik. In fact, Cocteau and Marais were the first well-known gay couple in the world, though Cocteau was reluctant to pronounce the dreaded word "homosexual."

Cocteau knew Sarah Bernhardt, the leading actress of the 1890s, as well as Andy Warhol in the 1950s (Andy was a fervent admirer of this early genius of self-promotion). His life was long and fruitful. He is perhaps most highly regarded today for his movie *La Belle et La Bête*, his screenplay for and narration of *Les Enfants terribles*, his book-length poem *Plain Song*, and his *Portraits-Souvenir*. Like Colette, he never wrote a bad line—an excellence that was honored when he was made, improbably, a member of the august French Academy, just as she was the first woman received into the Belgian Academy. The beloved, hard-living singing legend Edith Piaf died just before Cocteau—just long enough for him to fire off his homage in carefully selected words before he expired.

France is still tyrannized, as it was in Cocteau's day, by the tradition of the new. The only problem is that no one is sure what is new enough or where to seek it out. Subsidized arts, such as dance or theater, can be rigorously avant-garde. Something like painting or sculpture or video art or performance art, which is often promoted by a gallery and in any event needs only a handful of rich collectors, can continue to be experimental. But as for fiction, which is expected to earn money and pay for itself, the New is usually remaindered; look at the Nouveau Roman.

The only incontestably avant-garde novelist in France today is Pierre Guyotat. He is an exact contemporary of mine.

Pierre Guyotat was born in January 1940. He has written a wonderfully detailed recent book, *Formation*, that concentrates on his childhood and adolescence, including his first attempts to write poetry. The books that Guyotat wrote in the 1960s and '70s were startling, considered obscene and were often subject to censorship. *Tomb for 500,000 Soldiers* was inspired by his service as a soldier during the Algerian War. It is hallucinated rather than recounted, and it dwells obsessively on prostitution, torture, and slavery, and on dogs, soldiers, and generals. Although Guyotat in his early twenties went to Algeria willingly as a soldier, he soon enough sided with the Algerians against the French and was imprisoned and eventually sent back to France. In the dark, crowded canvas of his novel, concupiscent priests, hungry rats, terrified soldiers, and exploited children all make their appearance.

When Guyotat's novels of this period were condemned and censored by the government, they were defended by Pier Paolo Pasolini, Roland Barthes, Jean Genet, Michel Foucault, and Jacques Derrida, among others. Barthes wrote the preface to the following novel, *Eden, Eden, Eden*; it was censored in France for a period of eleven years. It is one long sentence, and again it takes place in Algeria. The language is dense, compacted.

When I first encountered Guyotat in the 1980s, he was giving performances at the Centre Georges Pompidou. Sometimes he would read from a prepared text, but sometimes he would improvise, even for very long periods. Occasionally he would speak and write in a language of his own devising. He was mesmerizing, and one felt one was in the presence of a priest or even a god, the great god Baal. Guyotat was often compared to Jean Genet or the Marquis de Sade or Rimbaud—to transgressive writers, in any case.

While working on a long, ambitious book called quite simply *Le Livre*, and on an accompanying text, *Histoires de Samora Machel*, Guyotat became ill. This is the period charted by *Coma*, which was published originally in 2006. In that book the author is always working outdoors, often in bad health, driving himself to create. He travels across southern France and Corsica, often staying with friends and relatives. Travel, as the English critic Stephen Barber has written, "generates a mobile, mutating text with which the reader is always on slippery, displaced ground." The writer has terrifying hallucinations, including one of hordes of dogs attacking him, which can be pushed back only by cries ripped out of his body.

Guyotat's œuvre is one of the most original and powerful of the twentieth and twenty-first centuries; it is too vast and varied to summarize. Whereas *Eden* and *Tomb for 500,000 Soldiers* are written in a dense, fragmentary style, *Coma* and his more recent books, *Formation* and *Arrière-Fond*, are full of characters who return and realistic episodes that take place at dated periods. These recent books of memory seem a departure from the totally imagined works of the 1960s and '70s.

The violence of Guyotat's youth is reflected in the mythology of his books. As a child he saw six of his close relatives arrested as *résistants* and sent to German camps; he was raped at school by several boys and circumcised at age twelve; his mother was ill with cancer for years, and he had a loving but conflicted relationship with his father. He's only interested in what could be called the "generative" aspects of his body—those that might generate art.

Guyotat dictated *Arrière-Fond* (titled *In the Deep* in English), and thus it enjoys a degree of clarity and momentum lacking in some of his recent works, such as *Progénitures 1 et 2*. At first glance it feels like an autobiography of a trip he took across the English Channel from the end of June to the end of August 1955, when he was fifteen years old. That it was dictated shouldn't leave the impression that it is careless or conversational, no more than the fact that Henry James dictated his last three novels should suggest they were somehow light; they are, in fact, James's most searching and dense novels.

Upon closer examination, Guyotat's book (is it a novel? a memoir?) feels like a source for his personal mythology and practices. Don't search these pages looking for "period" memories of postwar Britain, or for carefully shaded portraits of English eccentrics. Although there are stories and characters here that no doubt have their equivalents in real experience and that the scrupulous biographer should not neglect, nevertheless part of the pleasure and adventure of reading *Arrière-Fond* is seeking to determine what is fact and what is fiction. It's not as if Guyotat is misleading us; it's rather that the wall between event and fantasy is very low, and what interests him is locating the sources of his lifelong obsessions.

All of Guyotat's themes—slavery, prostitution, the tender love of the mother, the fearful love of the father, the pungency of odors, the rule of God and his suffering Son, the eternal present of history, the rapport between masturbation and writing (the "branlée avec texte")—are introduced here. Does he write with his sperm? It's not quite clear. What is clear is that masturbation is the great source of his imagination.

This is not masturbation of the usual sort. It is not done for pleasure, or pleasure alone. The masturbator does not respond to writings or pictures that are erotic, nor to replayed sexy memories. In fact, the narrator creates new fantasies, which may be linked to memories of real people, but that take on an independent existence and destiny.

Proust has been part of my life all my life, and I have nothing new to say about him. I'm reading Paul Morand's *Journal inutile*, in which he claims

Proust never made it into the intimate circles of the aristocrats he writes about, that he met the chic at large salons but seldom at dinners for six people or eight. That might be loosely confirmed by a story the Princesse de Caraman-Chimay told me: that one day her great-grandfather (a model for the Duc de Guermantes) found his butler sobbing. "Why are you crying?" "Because Monsieur Proust died. He used to quiz me about your dinners, who came, who said what, and tip me handsomely." If Proust had actually been at those gatherings, would he have had to depend on the *commérages d'un concierge?*

I've only written directly about the high life (a British phrase the French imported early in the twentieth century according to Morand— one wonders how they pronounced it: "Ig Liff"?) in Paris in my memoir *Inside a Pearl*, where I dropped a lot of names. "But I don't know those names," my very worldly agent complained. The English Channel is one of the *widest* bodies of water in the world. Like Proust only in that minor regard, I was seldom on intimate terms with the movers and shakers of the day, though I met them all.

I really liked Ben Taylor's little biography of Proust. Unlike me he plowed through all twenty-some volumes of the correspondence and culled the most sensual, the showiest roses. His book appeared in Yale's Jewish Lives series. I wrote an e-mail to Ben: "Poor Proust, I made him gay and you made him a Jew." I was in fact criticized in print for calling Proust queer, the idea being that such a universal author couldn't possibly be homosexual, and anyway he was just a masturbator, according to one expert. Certainly Proust was very closeted and once fought a duel with another queen for alluding to his affair with Lucien Daudet to the effect that Lucien's father, the famous novelist Alphonse Daudet, would now have to blurb Proust's book, since Proust had become so intimate with his son. When a newspaper listed Proust as one of the best "Hebraic" authors, he strenuously objected, insisting he was born and raised Catholic. Indeed he was raised as a Catholic, but his mother (née Weill) was Jewish, and Proust would leave stones on the graves of his maternal grandparents. Once, though he remained mute during an anti-Semitic soirée, he bravely wrote the host next day that he couldn't participate in the talk, since his mother was Jewish. The odd thing is that Alphonse

Daudet, whose salon Proust eagerly attended, was a leading anti-Semite. Daudet paid for the publication of Édouard Drumont's two-volume, 1,200-page *La France juive* (1886), a bestseller that went through two hundred editions by 1914, the bible of anti-Semitism until *The Protocols of the Elders of Zion* was published in 1901. *La France juive* spawned other books in imitation, such as *Jewish Austria* and *Jewish Russia*. *Jewish France* claimed that the Jews had killed Christ, that the Rothschild bank had deliberately triggered the crash of 1882, that Jews had a stranglehold on the economy, that the two religions, Christian and Jewish, were fundamentally opposed, and so on. Of course the *Protocols*, which is still cited by bigots and was quoted in *Mein Kampf*, went one better in pretending to be the record of a meeting of Jewish elders plotting to destroy Christianity. In the beginning of *Cities of the Plain*, Proust develops the parallelism between assimilated Jews and masculine homosexuals, the "cursed races" who pass but live in dread of being outed. Proust was writing these pages during World War I, when many of the prejudices of the earlier Dreyfus affair reappeared.

———

Mine was probably the last American generation that took France seriously. We wanted to learn the language, the fashions, the heritage. We learned to cook French from Julia Child, to think French from Michel Foucault, to dress French in whatever stylish Parisian way we could afford.

But we knew that we were ending a long, glorious tradition of Americans in France, starting with Gouverneur Morris, Thomas Jefferson, and Ben Franklin and going up through the hordes of American painters, composers, and writers who lived in Paris for a few years throughout the nineteenth and early twentieth centuries.

Ostensibly the period from after the Civil War in the United States is one of cast-iron Gothic and pressed tin ceilings, of linoleum and elevated trains, of greed and political corruption on an unprecedented scale. It's a period that has been labeled derisively the Gilded Age, the Tragic Era, and the Brown Decades.

But in a quiet, sometimes unperceived way America was being born as a great artistic nation. Melville wrote *Moby-Dick* in 1851, though few people read it, and soon he essentially gave up writing. Emily Dickinson was turning out her cryptic, sublime poems that sounded like church hymns but were the testament of a doubter—and almost no one knew of her work. Thomas Eakins, our greatest painter, was living in disgrace in Philadelphia after he was fired from the art school where he taught for allowing an undraped male model to pose for a mixed class of men and women students. Walt Whitman was strenuously denying his homosexuality after writing the Calamus poems, the best gay verse in the language. Mark Twain was underestimated by his fans; Henry James was largely ignored by his countrymen and preferred to live in England (he even became a British citizen). America was, alas, a country of great eccentrics and great prudes, of great writers and few readers.

Chapter 13

Writers are constantly reading and being inspired by earlier writers—what the critic Harold Bloom calls "the anxiety of influence," though imitation can be a calm and happy procedure as well. Almost no one detects influence anyway; when I worry that something I've written sounds like a blatant pastiche of Chekhov, no one has ever pointed that out; is it because my own style is so distinctive that it camouflages its sources? Or is it that few critics are sensitive to the diction or strategies or tone characteristic of a particular writer? When I point out one of these elements, an academic critic will say, "Only a real writer would single that out."

As I've said, one of my favorite writers is Jean Giono, who midway through his career discovered Stendhal and *The Charterhouse of Parma* and invented his character Angelo, a young Italian aristocrat not unlike Stendhal's Fabrice: the same youthful beauty and energy and courage, the same devotion to high ideals, the same wit, the same almost aesthetic determination never to behave churlishly.

In 1840 Balzac wrote a long essay in praise of Stendhal, placing him in an older eighteenth-century classical tradition based on character and action, whereas he saw himself as a Romantic more given to scene-painting. This essay is unusual for its generosity; few writers praise their contemporaries. Balzac even admits that Stendhal's battle scenes (such as the stunning Waterloo scenes at the beginning of *Charterhouse*, when the confused Fabrice is not even certain that he really is at Waterloo) are superior to his own; Tolstoy must have adored that Waterloo scene, too, since he based his Borodino battle scenes, in all their confusion, on

Stendhal's Waterloo (it's no accident that the real-life accounts of these two history-making battles are the most contradictory of the period). This new way of treating warfare, not as an opportunity for acquiring glory but as an occasion for blood, cowardice, betrayal, and total mystery, became the standard. Stendhal, after all, had been in Napoleon's army during the retreat from Moscow and knew about war firsthand.

Giono was so clearly imitating Stendhal that his friends talked him out of publishing *Angelo*, his first stab at this theme. Giono's own father was Italian, but a village cobbler, not a rebellious aristocrat. By the time Giono wrote *Horseman on the Roof*, he had fully transplanted his renegade Italian to the Provence of the 1830s, in the midst of a cholera plague. When I visited Giono's household library, I found many books from the nineteenth century on medicine and disease, his reference works.

My point is that writers are inspired by earlier books and by earlier literary techniques. Stendhal may use dialogue, action, and only abstract adjectives ("tender" is a favorite, "gay" is another), what Balzac called his classic side. Giono adds lushly precise descriptions to the stew, as if classicism (action) and Romanticism (description) finally came together in him.

Balzac, an often tedious and inexact stylist himself, reproaches Stendhal for being a sloppy writer and encourages him to look to François-René de Chateaubriand, who apparently revised his memoirs many times to remove all infelicities. I'm not sensitive enough to the French language to be able to detect Stendhal's stylistic flaws (Balzac's are more obvious), but I do recall that Stendhal dictated his book in fifty-some days, which explains its forward momentum and dash and forgives its repetitions and plot glitches.

Balzac suggests that Stendhal's understanding of court intrigue is so sophisticated that only career diplomats and heads of state can read him, "the happy few": "The *Charterhouse* can find its readers only among the 1,200 or 1,500 people who are at the head of Europe." Certainly with age and an experience of the world the reader finds more and more to appreciate in Stendhal, as in Proust.

Proust himself wrote a whole volume of pastiches of past authors—to exorcise their influence, he said, but more likely to express his high literary spirits. A true newspaper story about a man who invents a machine to produce false diamonds gets written up by Proust in the manner of nine authors, including Balzac, the Goncourt brothers, and Saint-Simon. All this before *A la Recherche*, though there he also included a Goncourt pastiche. Wasn't it Nabokov who thought pastiche was life and parody death? Whatever—we ourselves can say that parody mocks, but pastiche honors a text.

Everything from *Don Quixote* to *Lolita* is a pastiche, if that means retelling a tale with particular attention to stylistic tics. These influences, less anxious than grateful, are what have inspired all the great works of imagination we have. I once wrote an essay arguing that *Lolita* was a rewrite of Pushkin's *Eugene Onegin*, and "scholars" have elaborated that idea.

I'm enough of a believer in realism, almost as a scientific pursuit, to say that the inspiration afforded to works of art is only half the act of creation. The other half is a direct copy of nature as understood in any particular epoch (nature, either internal or external, subjective or objective), aspects of consciousness or of the world around us that have never previously been described. Flaubert must be the first to have described the blue and black colors at the back of an extinct fireplace in summer, say. Was Proust the first to pinpoint the impossibility of communicating with the beloved? "Sometimes we mobilize all our spiritual forces in a glittering array in order to bring our influence to bear on other human beings who, we may well know, are situated outside ourselves where we can never reach them." Was Petrarch the first person ever to climb a mountain for the view? Was Saint Augustine the first person ever to read without moving his lips? Was Casanova the last person to close the shutters of his carriage as he rode through the Alps so he wouldn't have to look at these appalling excrescences of nature? Did the troubadour invent hopeless, passionate romantic love? Who first fasted for a week? Who first stayed up all night to dance? Was Homer the first to notice the wine-dark sea? And what time of day would that have been when the sea took on that color? Was Foucault right that fisting was the only practice that the twentieth century added to the sexual armamentarium? Was Benjamin Disraeli's father the last human being in history who read everything?

My husband is one of those people (the majority?) who believes human nature never changes, that nothing is new under the sun. I prefer to think it does change, and radically, since I'm loosely speaking a Marxist and believe in history, not in a human essence. Well, yes, there may be certain inherent reactions, like sucking, fearing snakes, and seeking with the eyes the maximum contrast in light and shadow (that's why a baby's eyes go to the corner of the ceiling or search out a human face, with its tightly inscribed planes in a small circle, its great nave of a nose). But it does seem most behavior is malleable.

Take male homosexuality. In ancient Greece, adult men became patrons/lovers/teachers of beardless boys, practiced frottage between the thighs, and if the youth got an erection, he was considered a slut. Louis XIV's homosexual brother held an all-male shadow court, but he had to make his men sign a pledge there'd be no backsliding toward women. In the Meiji period in Japan homosexual men were not considered sufficiently refined for heterosexuality; gay men (brutes mostly from the South) were condemned to finding solace in each other's muscular arms.

Or take pedophilia. Genji thinks nothing of raising a little girl to be his ideal mate. Romeo's Juliet was thirteen, and he seems to have been twenty. Beatrice was eight and Dante nine when they met. Jerry Lee Lewis married his third wife, his cousin Myra Gale Brown, in 1957 when she was thirteen and he twenty-two (altogether he married seven times).

And then childhood itself has changed. Children were once considered small, inferior adults, not particularly innocent, and were dressed in abbreviated versions of adult clothes. Children gave long sermons on Golgotha in Latin when they were six or seven. When a French king was engaged to be married at age six and awakened by courtiers at midnight, who demanded what was the queen's delight, he raised his nightshirt and pointed to his tiny penis. A good laugh was had by all.

By this token—the malleability of the human—then we'd expect the wax statue of the Ideal Reader to melt and be reconfigured along with the times. Tolstoy, for instance, despises the smug, aristocratic Russian reader, but he knows he must appeal to him, or at least reassure him that he, Tolstoy, knows how to order oysters and address royalty. Lionel Trilling's 1947 novel *The Middle of the Journey* offends our feminist sensibilities because of the way it treats women as pretty little irritable things; maybe it will be readable in fifty years, when it's clearly something of the past:

> "She's cheap Village, cheap Provincetown, quaint tearoom. She did run a tearoom once, as a matter of fact."
> "It's not exactly a penitentiary offence." But Arthur liked to see his wife pitched high and angry.

James Salter, who is one of my favorite writers and was a dear friend, in his excellent 1975 novel *Light Years* has his two heterosexual couples tittering over Sartre's title *Saint Genet*, as if it were automatically risible to call this famous fag a saint. It's just light banter, but educated, sophisticated people wouldn't joke like that today.

I remember a wholesome young woman student of mine in boots and jeans when we read Tennessee Williams's *Streetcar Named Desire*. She was utterly baffled by the character of Blanche Dubois and her "feminine wiles," her alcoholic, flirtatious ways. "Why on earth is she acting like that?" was her question, more puzzled than indignant.

Maybe "texts" get worn out. I once debated with Alan Sinfield, a professor in England, who argued that even classics like Shakespeare's plays lose their appeal or relevance over time. Or maybe he was just saying, as Foucault might have said, that works of literature are "constructed" by cultural materialism and can't be separated from their political context—just the opposite view from all our "humanists" who think the classics are eternal.

I've written very few bad reviews, but those I've turned out have usually been against novels that pretend to be historical but get everything wrong. I attacked Alison Fell, the Scottish poet, for a novel she wrote that was set in medieval Japan; she filled it with very modern feminists rushing about and ensured my wrath. (In the end I felt terrible about it, since as a consequence, as I was told, her publisher canceled her American book tour.) I ended up being nicer to a novel about Haussmann, the man who rebuilt Paris in the nineteenth century, but I really disliked it because I thought the writer wasted the subject of this fascinating man by inventing an irrelevant fantasy of his own about him. I suppose it's the same reasoning that makes me resent a production of Stravinsky's opera *The Rake's Progress* set in a California high-security prison today. I can't help thinking that this might be the only production of this great work some members of the audience will ever see; why must it be so eccentric and counterintuitive? (And why should the Italo Calvino/Luciano Berio opera *La vera storia* be set in a Nazi concentration camp, except that Nazis are so chic?) I suppose one could justify revivifying a production of *Così fan tutte* in Salzburg when it's performed for the thousandth time (though for some children in the audience it will be the first). Why must *La Bohème* be set in the 1930s? I guess no director except Franco Zeffirelli ever got famous for historical accuracy; *La Traviata* in Auschwitz is definitely the way to go. Writers like Beryl Bainbridge and Penelope Fitzgerald are all the more impressive because of their faithfulness to the period.

Chapter 14

There are two kinds of novelists, the terse and the prolix. Penelope Fitzgerald never writes long, but her novels feel full and lived. Prolix novelists seem to be making up their characters and plots as they go along, almost as if they go into a kind of autohypnosis or trance state, lulled into the preconscious by the warmth of their laptops. They write the same thing three times in a row, perhaps to reach speed readers. Or for emphasis? For dimwits?

By contrast a terse novelist (not necessarily one who underwrites) like Fitzgerald spends a lot of downtime researching and daydreaming about her characters, or so one deduces. She knows what they would do in any situation. If it's a historical novel, she knows where they shop, what they eat, and how the laundry gets done. In *The Beginning of Spring*, which takes place among an English family in prerevolutionary Moscow, Fitzgerald (according to her excellent biographer, Hermione Lee) studied a turn-of-the-century Baedeker for Moscow and read memoirs written by English expats in Russia from that period. Since the family she wrote about were printers, Fitzgerald researched printing methods of the place and period, both outmoded and ultramodern, though she claimed she invented everything about printing (not true). Her characters aren't stereotypes, but they're not chosen at random either. There are no "flat characters" in E. M. Forster's sense. All of them are rounded, have quirks and a backstory. For instance there's a strange English bachelor named Selwyn who works at the printing press. He's a Tolstoyan, a bad poet, a vegetarian, a man given to sudden stops in the road, when he throws his head back to look at the stars. His poems, *Birch Tree Thoughts*, are unintentionally hilarious:

> "Doest feel the cold, sister Birch?"
> "No, brother snow,
> I feel it not."
> "What? Not?"
> "No, not!"

Perhaps because she'd begun by writing well-researched biographies (Edward Burne-Jones; her father, the editor of *Punch*, and his three brothers), Fitzgerald was used to copious documentation. She visited Russia only once for two weeks on an organized tour, but she obviously took notes. She knew how the trains worked in the dying days of the tsars, what it was like to live under the constant threat of anarchic violence, how Moscow felt like a village in the morning as livestock was herded through the streets, how workers exchanged their leather shoes for felt slippers at the printing press, how people made decisions by tossing a coin (tsar or eagle), how a merchant of the period might serve four liqueurs (currant-leaf, plum, cherry, and birch-sap). But if she was a born researcher, she was also an educated Englishwoman—that is, modest and self-deprecating, learned but not pedantic. Whereas some historical novelists dump all their notes on the page, Fitzgerald gives you just the telling if odd detail—little true facts, *les petits faits vrais*. Whereas some historical novelists trick out their long-dead subjects in modern feelings and period drag, Fitzgerald is an archaeologist of the sentiments. For instance, *The Blue Flower*, her last and greatest novel, takes place in Germany in the late eighteenth century, at the height of German Romanticism. The main character, who will become the German mystical Romantic poet Novalis, falls suddenly, almost magically in love with Sophie, a twelve-year-old girl, a commoner (he's an aristocrat, and marriage across class lines is frowned on).

Although Fitzgerald for some reason didn't like to be linked with Beryl Bainbridge, they both wrote short books that are evocative of the period (the Crimean war in Bainbridge's *Master Geordie*, for instance). Fitzgerald captures in *The Blue Flower* the extreme piety and formality of the Hardenbergs (Novalis was a pen name). Their rare invitations were "so formally expressed, that they seemed less of a celebration than a register of slowly passing time, like mortality itself." There is a visit from Goethe, who makes definitive pronouncements on everything (as we know he did from Johann Peter Eckermann's *Conversations with Goethe*). The characters all get "the" added to their first names ("The Bernhard," "Der Bernhard"), as people still put it affectionately in German—just as Italians say "La Callas" out of respect, even awe. Again there are no minor characters; they're all fully rendered. There's Sophie's stepfather, the generous joking Herr Rockenthien. There's old Freiherr von Hardenberg, who always knows exactly what he wants to do next and is so pious that he requires the entire family to assemble at the end of the year and give a moral accounting of themselves. The typical shoddy historical novelist would have forgotten how important religion was, a constant affair in everyone's life at that time. Even the educated Novalis, who studied with the great Friedrich Schlegel, is religious in a mystical way (he sees Sophie as his "Sophia," Wisdom). Fritz (or Novalis) sees the spiritual everywhere: "It was by now the very late afternoon, pale blue above clear yellow, with the burning clarity of the northern skies, growing more and more transparent, as though to end in revelation."

Fitzgerald herself was religious and attended church every Sunday. She was born in a bishop's palace into the Knox family and wrote a book about the Knox brothers. She may have been born in grandeur, but her husband was an alcoholic who drank up every penny, was convicted for stealing checks, and lost his job. Eventually she lived with him and their three children on a houseboat on the Thames in a chic part of London; the boat sank twice, and her family was homeless for a while, then given public housing. To make ends meet, she taught in two private schools, tutoring posh girls, including the actress Helena Bonham Carter.

She was, as Henry James would have wanted, someone on whom nothing was wasted. I met her once for lunch in York with Julian Barnes; perhaps she was visiting her biographer, Hermione Lee, who taught there for twenty years until she moved on to Oxford. I recall distinctly her sweetness, the ordinariness of a "jam-making grandmother," as Julian said, though just below the surface was a brusqueness that didn't suffer fools lightly (maybe I was that fool). I remember offering her some water, and she said, "I never touch the stuff!" going back to her whiskey neat. We Americans want so badly to be liked wherever we go and by whomever we meet that we can't imagine being brusque with anyone. Maybe it's because we move so often that if we don't befriend everyone instantly, we'll end up alone. The English, however, move only once—to London—just as the French relocate only once, to Paris. People can afford to be (and are advised to be) standoffish in those capital cities because they'll be stuck with their new "friends" for the rest of their lives. Fitzgerald wasn't exactly cold but cool, given to small talk with Julian about mutual acquaintances, uninterested in me.

When I met her, I didn't realize how heroic she was, raising three children almost on her own and leading them toward important careers, facing down the disapproving with scatty, illogical upper-middle-class chirping, working long hours teaching and reviewing, beginning to write only close to sixty, accumulating hundreds of background notes on everything, knowledge she modestly tucked into the little corners of her novels. She thought it was vulgar to talk about money, never had an agent, and got paid laughably small advances even after she won the Booker. She was not a popular prizewinner, since critics spoke of her as a "light" novelist devoid of deep moral lessons (thank God!). When she was poor and homeless, she and the children would go into white-napery restaurants, hold the menus, and sop up the bread and olive oil—then storm out as if offended by something. That's how they survived. She was always, it seems, sure of herself; after all, she was a Knox.

She learned Russian and the usual European languages. Her children complained later that she'd often been cross and seldom embraced them. Perhaps she had spent all her inner resources.

The modesty, even shyness, and indirection I remarked in her personality were certainly characteristics of Fitzgerald's style. In *The Beginning of Spring*, for instance, the English printer in Moscow is deserted by his

English wife at the start of the book. We never know why. She runs off with their children, whom she sends back unaccompanied to their father from some provincial stopover. We don't know why. Much later we learn that she did so because she'd expected to meet up with Selwyn the Tolstoyan poet—the most nerdish specimen whom we could ever suspect of being anyone's love object. Selwyn has had scruples about running off with his boss's (and friend's) wife. Just as inexplicably as she left at the beginning of the book, she returns at the end—but in the meanwhile her husband has had the first great sexual passion of his life with the children's Russian governess (possibly a spy for the government). Fitzgerald loved to stage her novels in periods full of promise but also uncertainty (the Napoleonic Wars in *The Blue Flower*, the prerevolutionary Russian rumblings in *The Beginning of Spring*). It seems absurd to mention my own work in this exalted context, but I set *Fanny* in the 1820s, the optimistic moment in America between the triumphalism of the revolution and the despair of the Civil War, and *Hotel de Dream* comes in the 1890s, at the dawn of America's destiny as a great power (and the beginning of modernism in art and scientific relativism and agnosticism in morality).

In Fitzgerald's *Innocence*, about a penniless Tuscan noble family in the 1950s, her love of *petits faits vrais* is everywhere present but not conspicuous. Guests pour out their own wine "in the Italian manner." There is a scheme afoot for the elderly to take care of infants—the "toothless" with the "toothless." As in *The Beginning of Spring*, for the protagonists it's love at first sight. A doctor from the south of Italy (Salvatore) falls in love instantaneously with the heiress of the penniless Tuscan family— and the heiress falls in love with the doctor, too. This fairy-tale element coexists with meticulously documented reality, as in Chekhov. (The poet and critic Howard Moss observed that Chekhov's stories were part fairy tale and part newspaper article—a good definition of some fiction at its best.)

If Fitzgerald didn't start writing until late, another favorite English author, Henry Green, gave up early. A rich industrialist with socialist tendencies, at least at first, Green's real name was Henry Yorke. Between

1926 and 1952 he produced nine novels, and then he stopped altogether until his death in 1973 at the age of sixty-eight—two decades of silence.

When I was a teen in Illinois in the 1950s, I used to wander through the open stacks of the Evanston Public Library, a stately Andrew Carnegie building. Whoever has not known the pleasures of open stacks—with their erotically charged corridors, usually empty, occasionally frequented by the odd stranger, their shelves weighted with all the printed treasures of the world—is like a music lover who's never owned a CD. As a child (I must have started visiting libraries when I was ten or eleven), I was attracted to books in beautiful editions, preferably in series. It was so hard to find unaided the "good books." With no older guides, how did one find the books worth reading? I remember distinctly when I discovered the Modern Library, with its signature hardcover design and its book jackets, which contained on the inside flap, next to the book itself, a list of all the other titles published in the series. My maternal grandparents lived in a West Texas ghost town with a ragged banner flapping over the main street, declaring "Ranger, the Oil Capital of America." Despite the chickens pecking in the backyard and the dusty grape arbor blistering in the sun, they owned the Harvard Classics—otherwise known as Dr. Eliot's Five-Foot Shelf—a bona fide collection of excellence, including Charles Dana's *Two Years Before the Mast*, Longfellow's translation of Dante, and lots of Emerson.

But in the Evanston Public Library I discovered Henry Green's stylishly slim novels with their gerund titles like *Loving, Doting,* and *Concluding.* I liked reading them because they looked modern or at least recent, and they had lots of dialogue and white spaces. Nothing much seemed to happen that I could detect. Green's intense irony and satire about hypocrisy went right over my head. Children are not alert to irony, and the good adult burghers of Chicago whom I knew seldom resorted to it. It was as if a whole bandwidth of light was imperceptible to my optic nerves.

My favorite Green novel, then and now, *Nothing,* I've reread often, and each time I've grown up or become jaded just a little bit more and pick up on whole new levels of cattiness, strategic artifice, and stylish double-talk. Even though I initially esteemed Green for his apparent simplicity,

I keep coming back to him for his intricacy. *Nothing* is the story of John Pomfret, a widower of forty-eight, who had a youthful affair with Jane Weatherby, now a widow. John has a pretty younger mistress, Liz Jennings, whom he takes out to lunch at a grand hotel looking out on Hyde Park—and then off to bed! He also has a grown daughter, Mary, who has a dreary government job where she works with—and flirts with—Jane Weatherby's dim son Philip, who seems to feel attached only to "family" in the form of distant and spiteful relatives. Jane has a younger daughter, Penelope, still at home, who is constantly on the edge of a nervous breakdown, or so her mother likes to think.

The comedy is that the parents are egocentric monsters who live in luxury and are maneuvering to get back together and marry. Their pawns are their children, who barely scrape by on their low wages. Rather intemperately Philip, at a party for his twenty-first birthday, announces that he plans to marry Mary. But then gossips start murmuring that the marriage will actually be incest—that John is Philip's real father, his and Jane's love child, and that Philip is Mary's half brother.

The novel begins with a mock wedding between John and Penelope, Jane's little girl. The child takes it seriously, however, and develops a major neurosis over it—unless we're to think Jane is using her daughter as emotional blackmail in her elaborate game of seducing John.

If the book begins with a mock wedding, it ends with John and Jane's decision to marry for real. Jane seemed to think nothing of sending Penelope off to boarding school, even at her young age; all the psychiatric fussing over Pen has just been tactical.

Everything is sly and droll. All the characters speak with breathless, scatty inconsequence, almost always saying the opposite of what they mean—the women are especially infected with this Mayfair vocabulary: "Sweet," "Jolly decent," "You are sweet to be so sad," etc. Jane improbably says to her son that many young women are eating their hearts out over him (he's much too dull for that): "In a little sweat of excitement in their frocks!" After she instructs her son, she relaxes in the tub: "She settled back, like a giant peacock after a dust bath, sighing."

Philip and his Mary take turns buying each other drinks at a sordid pub; they are shocked by their parents' lasciviousness, and he denounces them: "They're wicked, darling!" he exclaimed. "They've had two frightful wars they've done nothing about except fight it and they're rotten to the core." Almost no punctuation, lack of grammatical parallelism, run-on sentences, illogical leaps—it all adds to the humor and spontaneity. John, who appears to be terminally lazy, is always wailing, "This endless work work work . . ."

John's mistress Liz likes to tipple, and her dialogue is particularly woozy. She's jealous and wary of John's and Jane's rapprochement:

"Take John now. There are times I could shake him, just shake him. You know what they were once supposed to mean to one another and never will, again those two, well as if that wasn't enough he's always going back. He won't admit if you ask him but he's got an idea that once he's had anything in his life he's only to lift his voice to get that back once more and dear Jane's too sweet to let him see."

"Wonderful woman Jane."

"Isn't she?" Miss Jennings sighed. She drank down a full glass of wine. "Too sweet and wonderful. Sometimes . . ."

That "Sometimes" is devastating. And Liz's pronouncement that once an affair is over, it's over for good is just wishful thinking. Jane and John are slowly, constantly clawing their way back toward each other, no matter what harm they might do to their children and their friends.

In his *Paris Review* interview with Terry Southern, Henry Green admitted that *Nothing* was a very "hard" (as opposed to a soft) novel because it was about the upper class. He also talked about the importance of making a novel "live," in which case it was good for the next five hundred years. He felt that nothing innovative in the novel had been done since Henry Fielding. Terry Southern's questions are so intrusive and long-winded that it's hard to sort out what Green is saying, but he seems to be in favor of a novel in which the author is as unobtrusive as possible.

But on the contrary, Green's characters speak in such an artificial, sometimes hard-to-follow dialect (it helps to say his lines out loud) that in many ways he's created a world as artificial and "author-manipulated" as

Ronald Firbank's or Ivy Compton-Burnett's—or Virginia Woolf's *The Waves*, in which the characters all talk alike and are indistinguishable, whether young or old. Or as Jane Weatherby says in *Nothing*, "Good heavens, I simply never mean anything yet all my life I've got into such frightful trouble with my tongue."

Green claims in his interview that he never drew up a plan for a novel but simply invented it as it went along. But since so many elements repeat, develop, and are linked, he had to carry it all in his head, which he declared was ready to burst by the time he got to the end. Certainly in *Nothing* he must link up poor, saintly little Penelope's numerous "mentions" (she's almost always offstage) or Liz Jennings's dawning awareness that she's losing John to Jane—and her scheme to start up with Richard Abbott, Jane's old admirer.

Although Green's editorial comments on his characters are always minimal, they are as apt and colorful as a snake in an Easter basket: the mannish, plain-spoken Elaine Winder "smacked their backs and generally behaved as if she were on a kill."

The whole book is full of an almost whispered snobbism, the most killing kind. When John Pomfret complains about his future son-in-law's suits, he calls them "artistic." When Jane imagines that her Italian servant, Isabella, must prefer men in Italy to those in England, John says, "You wouldn't want a fat man about the house always singing opera." When Philip tells his mother that he doesn't want to marry Mary after all, Jane cries gaily, "Oh dear, but isn't it going to be rather exciting and dreadful." When people really blurt out what they mean, it's doubly shocking, as when Jane virtually orders John to stop seeing his mistress Liz: "Because when I say what I do about Liz I don't really mean anything, only that she's such a horrid beast who simply oughtn't to be alive."

Such outbursts, however, are rare. Usually everything stays within the same tonality of language and effect. There's a lovely and untranslatable French word that applies here: *camaïeu*, which refers to a variety of close shades of color (pearl gray, steel gray, dove gray). We can say Green never strays far from his *camaïeu*, his narrow tonality of lethal silliness.

His two aged lovers at long last have decided to marry (she proposes), and John Pomfret, dozing comfortably, when asked by Jane if he wants anything, murmurs, "Nothing . . . nothing . . ." As for drowsy Jane, in a rare authorial comment, Green has told us there are "three great furnaces quiescent in her lovely head just showing through eyeholes to warn a man, if warning were needed, that she could be very much awake, did entirely love him, was molten metal within her bones within the cool back of her skull which under its living weight of hair was deeply, deeply known by his fingers." There is something surprising in every word; if you put your hand over the second or third part of that passage you'd never guess the next words.

Why did Green stop writing? Boredom and drink, no doubt, though I should reread Jeremy Treglown's excellent biography to find out (that's one of the problems—and joys—of old age: every time you read a book it's the first).

As we've seen with Fitzgerald, a few authors get their start late. One is Henri-Pierre Roché, who in his seventies wrote his first novel, *Jules et Jim*, based on his bohemian adventures fifty years earlier (it's my favorite François Truffaut film and Jeanne Moreau's best role). I suppose Roché had had such a pleasurable life so full of excitement (he was the one who introduced Gertrude Stein to Picasso), he felt no need to write until he'd outlived everyone and enjoyed nothing but evoking the past.

Another older writer was an American dead ringer for Green called W. M. Spackman, who was highly praised by John Updike and Stanley Elkin. It wasn't until he was seventy-three that he wrote *An Armful of Warm Girl* (1978), a charming novel in which the dialogue sounds like Green's—the same unpunctuated, fluty, scatterbrained sentences. I wrote the introduction to his 1980 novel *A Presence with Secrets*, a "corrected" version of Henry James's *The Ambassadors*—Spackman felt James had misunderstood the complex Franco-American social reality of his book. "In James," he said, "all is unconsidered paradox and confusion of the will—a constant self-exhortation to 'dramatize, dramatize!' yet a devotion to a way of writing that slows the action to a crawl and inundates the plot with the bilge of irrelevances; an infatuation with mechanical melo-drama of the well-made Boulevard play, yet an unwillingness to work out his scenes à faire to the full; over anxiety about his audience, yet delusions of what it consisted of and blindness to what his lamentable anxiety implied; creativity confounded with the merest scrabble of industrious-ness; above all, the arrogance of a settled way."

Spackman knew the classics and even wrote a book of essays, *On the Decay of Humanism* (1997), in which I first took notice of Ovid's *Heroides* (16 B.C.). Spackman claims that the whole European novel that analyzes the passions, from *La Princesse de Clèves* to Proust, stemmed from these letters in verse attributed to wronged heroines in myth or history, everyone from Dido to Phaedra.

All three members of the Spackman fan club—Laurie Colwin (*Happy All the Time*), Ann Arensberg (*Sister Wolf*), and I—took the train to have lunch with him in Princeton in the late 1970s or early 1980s. He was an old-fashioned gentleman (born in 1905) who lived in a proper brick house with the proper sitting room (sherry) and dining room (chipped beef in cream). His wife was a rather sinister Lebanese heavy-duty nurse, Laurice, who for years had taken care of the Madwoman in the Attic, Spackman's first wife, a debutante who'd run off the rails. Spackman himself was charming and inconsequential until he disintegrated into alcoholic incoherence and belligerence, and we fans beat a hasty retreat.

Ronald Firbank was a coterie favorite of my twenties, now mostly forgotten, though Richard Canning is bringing out a biography that will remind readers of his importance. Firbank was a writer's writer, admired by E. M. Forster, the Sitwells, and W. H. Auden, who said of him, "A person who dislikes Firbank's novels may, for all I know, possess some admirable quality but I do not wish ever to see him again."

People have always been interested in this strange, lonely, wildly gifted aesthete's personality. There have been two full-length biographies of him, one by Brigid Brophy and one by Miriam Benkovitz, an American bibliographer who always struck me as an elephant in pursuit of a butterfly. Firbank started publishing his odd tales quite young and, like the young Proust, subsidized his own books. He rarely ate, though he drank a lot; once he ignored an elaborate meal prepared in his honor and consumed only a single pea. He was pathologically restless and always writhing about anxiously. When the painter Augustus John handed him a precious Tanagra figurine for him to study while posing, he immediately dropped it and smashed it and declared, "There!" as if destroying it had been his intention all along.

He loved the theater and ballet and was always attending the most acclaimed or avant-garde productions (he wrote a play, *The Princess Zoubaroff*, in which all the young men go off on a trip together around the world, leaving their wives behind to form a holy order of nuns). He and his sister inherited a fortune from his father; she spent her money on designer frocks, which she never wore more than once (now housed in the Victoria and Albert Museum as a perfect year-by-year collection of Edwardian fashion). He spent his money on incessant travel, to Spain, Portugal (where he rented a palace for a season), and North Africa. In Tunisia at a hotel after a drunken, solitary lunch, he dozed off in the lobby while watching in the fountain one rose petal pursue another, which gave him the idea of a lesbian crush between the British Ambassadress and the Queen of the Land of Dates in *The Flower Beneath the Foot*.

He was always in delicate health, which saved him from service in the army during World War I (Proust was not so lucky, despite his asthma— nonetheless life in the barracks was one of the happiest periods in Proust's life). As Osbert Sitwell says, "Virtuosity and style were for him the chief merits of literature," though he displayed more style than virtuosity.

Firbank's range was rather narrow, which leads readers to either adore him or detest him. Mind you, his range was no narrower than Jane Austen's, but whereas she explored the "universal" themes of courtship, money, and filial piety, he devoted himself merely to varieties of camp. He was one of the three great gigglers in literary history—the others being Proust and Kafka—and would laugh so hard at his own absurdities he was incapable of reading his work out loud to friends.

In *The Flower Beneath the Foot* he makes delicate fun of snobbism, court etiquette, and social climbing. Mrs. Wetme, a café proprietor, is determined to be properly introduced into society and is using her considerable wealth to persuade the bankrupt Duchess of Varne to sponsor her. The Crown Prince, His Weariness, is infatuated with a girl beneath his station, but his mother, Her Dreaminess the Queen, is backing the suit of an English Royal Princess.

A pet project of the queen's is an archaeological dig "among the ruins of Chedorlahomor, a faubourg of Sodom." Participating in the dig is the Hon. "Eddy" Monteith (the absurd portrait of one of Firbank's real-life enemies), a man who shouts "Basta" to his Neapolitan servant, with all the brilliant glibness of the Berlitz school.

Apparently Firbank would stroll about and jot lines on slips of paper and put them in his pocket, words or phrases that amused him or suggested twists on his daffy plots. Thus the visiting black Queen of the Land of Dates is intrigued by the very idea of plates; as she holds one up admiringly, she declares, "I'm forever spoilt for shells." A lady courtier announces that her favorite Shakespeare play is *Julia Sees Her*. We listen in on a girl's (and future saint's) prayer, "Let me always look young never more than sixteen or seventeen . . . and keep me ever free from the malicious scandal of the Court. Amen." Sometimes he just notates a strange conjunction of words ("the blue doom of summer"). Sometimes the comedy is almost infantile, as when one elderly royal spends all her time and effort constructing public conveniences ("my new pipi") and contemplates erecting one for animals: "Her hobby was designing, for the use of the public, sanitary, but artistic, places of necessity on a novel system of ventilation." How he must have relished punctuating that sentence!

We can see the fossils of a privileged childhood (his father built trains): a servant is criticized for not recognizing the various bells rung in a great house ("When will you learn your bells?"). Or a girl is "blooded"—her face smeared with the dead animal's blood—after her first foxhunt. A gossip rag is called *The Jaw-Waw's Journal*.

There is a kind of cheerful, noncreepy androgyny everywhere. A shopkeeper named Bashir calls in an Armenian clerk when he gets busy. As he says in his broken way of speaking, "More attached to him am I than a branch of Jessamine is about a vine." This is a musical recapitulation of an earlier bisexual statement by the Queen of the Land of Dates, "It is the land of the Jessamine flower, the little amorous Jessamine flower . . . that twines itself to the right-hand, at others to the left, just according to its caprices!" The Hon. "Eddy" Monteith has published a book of juvenilia including poems titled "Doigts Obscènes" and "They Call Me Lily!!" *Whipping* and *birching* are exciting words in a naughty way. Men are treated as lovable "despots" or "procurers of delights" or "those adorable humbugs." The English governess, who is teaching the royal children to imitate her Cockney accent, speaks in *h*-free sentences and confesses, "I never could resist a man!" We can picture the lonely, cracked Firbank constantly giggling to himself. Every woman in his work has had a lesbian adventure; every man is darting a burning side glance at a comely choirboy. The Cardinal spots "a pale youth, all mouchoir and waist." The central romance is between the black Queen and Her Excellency Lady Something.

As in Auden's poem "Musée des Beaux-Arts," something magical is always happening in our peripheral vision. When the Royal Date couple enter in native dress, "there was some slight confusion as to which was the gentleman and which the lady of the two." If *The Flower Beneath the Foot* is royal camp, *Concerning the Eccentricities of Cardinal Pirelli*, Firbank's last book, is Catholic camp. A Spanish cardinal is observed by a Vatican spy baptizing a duchess's police dog in white crème de menthe. Almost nothing happens except that the pope decides to prosecute and the cardinal dies of heart failure, presumably, while chasing a choirboy through the cathedral.

Firbank, apparently, tried to join the Swiss Guard at the Vatican and was rejected. He had a rather queenly taste for revenge and decided to mock the church that had rejected him. Another cardinal is identifiable because of "old, out-at-heel hose." The pope has the "head of an elderly lady's maid." A prominent woman wants a church to "make 'a little Christian' of her blue chow." Homosexuality—or rather pedophilia—is observable at every corner. Boys are called "the lesser delights." An older choirboy receives a cigarette case as fee for singing "Say it with Edelweiss" at a society wedding. A priest is seated "beneath a somber study of the

Magdalen waylaying our Lord." Cardinal Pirelli, when he goes into town, disguises himself as a matron ("disliking to forgo altogether the militant bravura of a skirt"). That's my favorite line—the ultimate gender-bending impertinence. "Vanity once had proved all but fatal [to the cardinal]: 'I remember it was the night I wore ringlets and was called "my queen."' " A statue of the Madonna is declared "one of the worst and most expensively dressed little saints in the world." The cardinal himself has a vision of Saint Teresa of Avila after his sixth cocktail.

There are delightful ruptures in Firbank's style. Although the tone of *The Flower Beneath the Foot* is resolutely ahistorical and out of a fairy tale, every once in a while it is broken by a shockingly contemporary note—someone points out, between the convent and the Column of Justice, "the automobile club." Or the queen murmurs with a grimace to her physician, "Not Johnnie, doctor"; "For a glass of Johnnie Walker at bed-time was the great doctor's favorite receipt." A woman is declared "the one intellectual in town." In *Prancing Nigger* (the American title; Firbank's original title was *Sorrow in Sunlight*) Mrs. Miami Mouth is a social climber who moves to the capital to advance her standing, but, as she confesses after a concert, "Dat music ob Wagner, it gib me the wretches." Cuna-Cuna, the capital, is known as "little city of cocktails."

In all Firbank's novels the camp and plain silliness alternate with passages of pure lyricism, usually in the description of nature: "Swans in sunlight. A little fishing boat with coral sails. A lake all gray and green. Beatitude intense. Consummate calm. It was nice to be at the Summer Palace after all." Firbank might almost have been an imagist poet with his haiku-like glimpses of paradise.

He himself was so lonely and ignored that more than once he has himself appear as an author everyone's buzzing about. A man with the jolly face and poodles passes by a bookstore: "Have you *Valmouth* by Ronald Firbank or *Inclinations* by the same author?"

"Neither. I'm sorry—both are out!"

Everything is ruled by fashion—fiction, art ("The Last Supper at two tables!"), love, neighborhoods, even diseases (everyone has the same chic ailment in *The Flower Beneath the Foot*). Fashion by its very arbitrariness and the absoluteness of its rule is well accommodated to Firbank's world—"iron caprice," one might say, except the atmosphere of his books is light, giddy, iridescent.

Firbank's imagination is so ubiquitous and thorough that he often produces a paragraph such as this one:

> Through the open window a bee droned in on the blue air of evening. Closing his eyes he fell to considering whether the bee of one country would understand the remarks of that of another. The effect of the soil of a nation, had it consequences upon its flora? Were plants influenced at their roots? People sometimes spoke (and especially ladies) of the language of flowers . . . The pollen therefore of an English rose would probably vary, not inconsiderably, from that of a French, and the bee born and bred at home . . . would be at a loss to understand (it clearly followed) the conversation of one born and bred, here, abroad. A bee's idiom varied then, as did man's. And he wondered, this being proved the case, where the best bees' accents were generally acquired.

Joyce Carol Oates once said that the best writers write sentences that do more than one thing at once. Certainly in this passage Firbank draws on snobbism ("the best bees' accents"), philosophers' insubstantiated double-talk ("this being proved the case"), apology, English exclusivism ("abroad"), a parallelism with sign language (no universal symbols), Goethe's—and Maurice Barrès and Gertrude Stein's—idea of native soil being the best ("the effect of the soil of a nation"), and pseudoscience ("the language of flowers").

Other writers, especially the ones you admire, can steer you to good books. The great Chinese-American novelist Yiyun Li guided me to Rebecca West and her autobiographical novel *The Fountain Overflows* (West is lousy with titles). Yiyun moved to America in 1996 and immediately, at age twenty-four, began to work her way through the Western canon, which had been closed to her till then. She discovered Chekhov. She discovered Alice Munro. Her own writing, considered attractively old-fashioned, gained immediate recognition; she's been published in the

New Yorker and nominated for all the prizes. I'm happy to say she's replacing me at Princeton now that I've retired. When we met we discovered we liked all the same books—and mainly for the beauty of the writing. Many people like books because they're suspenseful or scary or touching or inspirational or because one admires the characters as if they were real people. Maybe it's only writers who like the writing.

I'd always associated Rebecca West with her big book on Yugoslavia, her long affair with H. G. Wells, and her dismaying feud with their son Anthony West, who'd written about her as the Mother from Hell. So I was delighted to read *The Fountain Overflows*, a family novel about an eccentric English family in which the father is a gifted political polemicist who, alas, is also a compulsive gambler; the mother, a Scottish concert pianist, once praised by Brahms, has retired to raise her family. Her twin daughters become her piano pupils. A third daughter, the oldest child, is a pretty girl and an incompetent violinist who manages to bewitch her plain, lesbian teacher. Then there's the youngest child, Richard Quin, a genuinely magical child named after an uncle who died young. Richard Quin is also destined to die young in World War I, so retrospectively it makes sense that he neglects his studies and befriends the entire world.

People like to say about domestic dramas that "nothing much happens," though in West's book there are repeated bankruptcies and a dun constantly at the door; the father vanishes, and the pretty, talentless violinist is denounced by a famous performer. The children play with imaginary horses in the stable, poltergeists destroy the house of friends until the ghosts are exorcised, a rich Jew (Mr. Morpurgo) becomes enchanted with the entire impoverished family, another friend kills her husband, the mother finally admits that her Gainsboroughs are not copies but the real thing—and on and on. These characters are as endearing as the little old ladies in Mrs. Gaskell's *Cranford* and as fierce and colorful as the people in *Vanity Fair*. Why do readers dismiss the same dramas they themselves might live through as "Nothing happens"? What constitutes "something"? A war? Murder? A duel?

The sequel, *This Real Night* (another dud title), is equally brilliant, though people say it was assembled by editors posthumously. One of the children says, "All grown-ups feel that children ought to be brought up as merry peasants." The bohemian children regard marriage as an outdated if "glorious rite of a sacrificial nature." West paints a picture of the "unity" of English life before World War I:

> At times I come on shreds of this unity still clinging to the earth. Driving through a village on a Sunday afternoon, I pass a cricket match on the green, and the silver gleam of the white flannels under the golden sun, the ball in flight, the monosyllable of the ball on the bat. The flowerbed of the spectators, the Red Dragon on the inn sign, the eternal perfection of delight. But now such sights come rarely, and at that period, I do assure you they were the connective tissue that held the whole of life together.

The figurative language is usually rapid and unflashy and compressed, as it is in Elizabeth Bowen, and just as original: "I was overcome by an abstract sense of grief, something like the moan of shingle dragging back to sea between breakers." She observes "that men find a special pleasure in rejecting women, and will contrive to do it even to women who have not been offered to them." Birds land on telegraph wires like musical notes, "as close-pressed demi-semi-quavers." Music itself "is a missionary effort to colonize earth for imperialistic heaven." Mist covers the houses of Parliament "so they looked evanescent and eternal," a beautiful oxymoron, as accurate as it is clever. If the goal of a good style is to keep readers on their toes with a minimum of fuss, reviving dead metaphors without using the violence of stylistic defibrillation, then Rebecca West is an incomparable writer.

Why is she not better known today? Possibly because she was a leftist anticommunist, a friend of Emma Goldman, the first Westerner to blow the whistle on the Soviet Union. Young people do not know that in the whole European and American artistic and intellectual world, the worst thing you could be was anticommunist. André Gide was roundly denounced by French intellectuals for his *Return from the USSR* (1936), in which he expressed his bitter disappointment with communism. As late as 1981 Susan Sontag was pelted by the American left for equating communism and fascism; she was (absurdly) accused of supporting the newly elected Reagan. By the same token Jean Giono was rejected by the Communists, who controlled the press, and forbidden to print his books for several years after World War II. Only someone who has studied the fate of writers recognizes that politics can play an enormous role in determining reputations.

Chapter 15

Nearly everything about Curzio Malaparte—who wrote *Kaputt* and *The Skin*, two of the most memorable books about World War II—was bogus, starting with his name. He was born in the town of Prato in Tuscany in 1898, the son of an irascible German (and Protestant) father, Erwin Suckert, and a Tuscan mother. Originally the future writer was dubbed Kurt Erich, but quickly that difficult Teutonic name was italianized into Curzio. When he was in his twenties and already the author of a few published works, he decided to change his last name from Suckert to Malaparte because that sounded more Italian (in that way he was like Ettore Schmitz, who became Italo Svevo). Malaparte was also obviously an allusion to Bonaparte, the dark side of the good. If he is not a famous writer today, it's all because of politics.

Although after World War II Malaparte was adroit in claiming that he had been a victim of the Fascists, in fact he had joined the party as early as 1922, shortly before the March on Rome, and had been an eager journalistic supporter and cultural mainstay of the regime until Mussolini put him under house arrest and sent him to the island of Lipari off the coast of Sicily in 1933. Later he would claim that he'd been arrested because he had opposed Mussolini, but in fact he never publicly criticized the dictator. No, he'd been arrested because he'd slandered a high government minister, the ace pilot Italo Balbo, saying that Balbo had become so physically and morally plump that he would have been a suitable minister under the nineteenth-century bourgeois French king Louis-Philippe. As soon as these words, scribbled on the back of a postcard, were inevitably brought to Balbo's attention by state censors, Malaparte was arrested and sentenced to five years of relegation (eventually the sentence was reduced to several months). Mussolini loved to play cat-and-mouse with his followers, punishing them before restoring them to favor.

Malaparte's active complicity with Mussolini was fairly constant and had started much earlier, in 1924–25, when the dictatorship was first declared. Giacomo Matteotti, a socialist deputy who was vocal in his denunciations of fascism, had been kidnapped and murdered. Mussolini (either correctly or incorrectly) was blamed for the assassination—and many Fascists abandoned the party, outraged by the illegal, high-handed violence. Despite this forceful attack on his regime by members of his own party, Mussolini, supported by the king of Italy, now usurped parliamentary power and declared himself the sole ruler of the country. Malaparte, in a cool act of opportunism, testified in court on behalf of Mussolini at this crucial junction of his career. The writer probably expected "Muss" (as he called him) to be grateful, but if so he failed to understand how short the dictator's memory could be.

Of course after the war Malaparte rewrote his role in this historical crisis, the most important one in Mussolini's career, so that he came out as an innocent opponent of the regime. No wonder that Malaparte came to be known as "Don Camaleón" (later the title of one of his books). At various points in his long career he became a playwright, a novelist, a polemicist, a journalist, and the editor of the leading newspaper *La Stampa*, the youngest in the paper's history; he criticized Hitler initially but later endorsed him, sympathized with Stalinism, made a pilgrimage to Mao's China and praised it, attacked the bourgeoisie of Tuscany—and ended up joining the Catholic Church. In fact that was the most fascist thing about him—his admiration for brute power in whatever form it took. Otherwise he did not subscribe to right-wing nostalgia for the past or a veneration for the altar and throne, nor was he an anti-Semite or racist. He was in favor of unions and belonged to the labor wing of the Fascist Party.

Malaparte was not unlike other literary buccaneers who came to prominence between the wars—Louis-Ferdinand Céline, for instance, or André Malraux or Pierre Drieu de la Rochelle or Louis Aragon. But there were differences as well. Céline and Drieu were both anti-Semites and right-wing partisans; Malraux was so mercurial and such a liar and poseur that it was hard to say what he stood for, though he started off stealing antiquities and ended up being Charles de Gaulle's minister of culture. Malaparte knew some of these men and was certainly aware of the others, since he was a Francophile, gained prominence in France when he had trouble getting his work past the Italian censors, and lived for extended periods in Paris. To this day he is better known in France than in his native Italy. He supervised the translations of his own books into French and drove his translators wild with his revisions; his best friends were Marianne and Daniel Halévy, an intelligent, well-connected Parisian Jewish couple who remained loyal to him throughout his stormy life.

An excellent recent biography of Malaparte was written by an Italian in French, which in itself is emblematic of the great novelist's wide appeal. The author, Maurizio Serra, was the Italian ambassador to UNESCO in Paris and also an astute author fascinated by European figures of the first half of the twentieth century who, like Malaparte, are difficult to categorize or summarize. One of his recent books is *Les Frères séparés: Drieu La Rochelle, Aragon, Malraux face à l'histoire*, which examines these multifaceted personalities (to paraphrase Serra's words): Drieu, the dandy, with one foot in fascism and the other in mysticism; Aragon, the surrealist converted to communism who reverted in old age back to the libertinage of his youth and went from worshiping his wife to being a flamboyant homosexual; and Malraux, the youthful revolutionary who ended up a government minister in a double-breasted suit. Drieu may have committed suicide as the war was winding down partly because he feared reprisals for his participation in French fascism, but Aragon and Malraux were survivors who managed to prevail no matter what regime was in power. They were more successful versions of what Malaparte aspired to be.

With one difference: though all three were brilliant writers, none had the literary panache of Malaparte, the ability to create emblematic scenes, unforgettable visual tableaux, haunting moments of political horror that bypass historical exposition and scene-setting and condense all the tensions of the epoch. Which leads me back to his two masterpieces, *Kaputt* and *The Skin*.

It's not quite clear whether these books are novels or works of nonfiction. There is a narrator named Malaparte in both who seems to be vouching, as an eyewitness, to the veracity of the often mythopoetic things he observes. If there is someone important in the vicinity, we feel sure that that person will invite Malaparte to dinner; he always has access to the rulers and dealmakers. The characters in these books will explain their often indefensible beliefs and actions to Malaparte in paragraph after paragraph of highly articulate dialogue. In a handsome bit of intertextuality, Malaparte has French officers discussing in *The Skin* whether one can believe anything in *Kaputt*. They're about to enter and "liberate" Rome; they've just eaten a couscous lunch on the grass prepared by Moroccan soldiers.

> "Do you want to know," said Pierre Lyautey, "what Malaparte will say about this lunch of ours in his next book?" And he proceeds to give an extremely amusing description of a sumptuous banquet, the scene of which was not the woods in Albano but a hall in the Pope's villa at Castel Gandolfo. Seasoning his discourse with a number of witty anachronisms, he described the porcelain crockery of Cesare Borgia, the silverware of Pope Sixtus—the handiwork of Benvenuto Cellini—the golden chalices of Pope Julius II, and the papal footmen busying themselves about our table while a chorus of angel voices at the end of the hall intoned Palestrina's "Super flumina Babylonis" in honor of General Guillaume and his gallant officers.

Malaparte the character has his revenge. While the meal was being prepared, an imprudent Moroccan had stepped on a mine and had his hand neatly severed from his body. Now that the repast is coming to an end, Malaparte claims that he has eaten the hand, which found its way into the dish, but that until now he was too polite to mention it. His French hosts, looking at the bones, are sickened and turn green; only later does Malaparte reveal to a laughing American pal that he made the whole thing up and skillfully arranged a ram's bones on his plate to resemble a hand. What's interesting here is that Malaparte answers the accusation of lying by inventing another deceit.

Malaparte might be a narcissist, but he's certainly not the boring kind. He exists as a presence in these two books but always as an observer in the background who refuses to condemn even the most savage acts. Some of his contemporaries criticized his coolness, but today we are grateful that he presents rather than judges the horrors he encountered. He doesn't try to do our feeling for us.

We've grown accustomed to thuggish politicians, who strut and lie and see everyone else as either an enemy or a friend, who admire autocrats and dismiss democratic leaders, who are loose-lipped narcissists and have no idea what a clownish figure they cut—but we're not used to writers who worship or at least advocate tyrants while maintaining their own dandified coolness. Writers are seldom at the very heart of brute force, but Malaparte understood it well. He is a participant-observer of sadistic power who could pretend after the war that he had just been an innocent bystander. This tension between the insouciance of contemplation and the guilt of complicity lends his work an unparalleled dynamism.

The scenes covered by a single chapter are sometimes joined only by a poetic theme. For instance, in *The Skin* there's a chapter called "The Black Wind" that begins with the narrator dreaming of a black wind while in Naples, though this location is thrown in only because the entire book nominally takes place there during the American occupation of 1943. But soon we're in the Ukraine in 1941 and a real black wind, not a remembered one, is blowing constantly and blackening the landscape and all the animals, including Malaparte's mount. As he rides through the opaque black wind, he hears voices coming from above and eventually he sees that many ragged or naked Jews have been nailed to trees. They are in excruciating pain and scorn him for his pity "as a Christian" and beg him to shoot them through the head. He's psychologically incapable of killing them and rides on in despair. He sinks into a fever, and when, a few days later, he has recovered and retraces his path, he sees that all the Jews crucified by the Nazis have died. Now, instead of moaning, the crucified victims have fallen into a terrible silence. By a bit of legerdemain Mala-parte tells us he recognized that silence, which he experienced much earlier during his Mussolini-imposed exile on Lipari where his only friend was his dog Febo. The animal becomes his best friend and sole comfort during his relegation. Then one day Malaparte and Febo are abruptly transferred to Pisa. Febo goes out for his daily exercise and never returns. Malaparte scours the city for him and eventually discovers that he's been kidnapped and sold to the veterinary clinic at the univer-sity. Poor dying Febo is all trussed up, and his stomach has been exposed for an experiment. Malaparte wonders why none of the dogs is barking, and the vet tells him that the first thing they do is to cut their vocal cords. In the space of a few pages we've moved from Naples to the Ukraine to Lipari and Pisa—and backward in time from 1943 to 1940 to 1933. And these disparate tales have been strung together on the slender threads of the black wind and the deafening silence. And the grotesquely parallel deaths of the Jews and the dogs.

What sort of writing is this? We scarcely believe the crucifixion scene, at least in this highly stylized El Greco version, and Maurizio Serra tells us not to believe the more plausible-sounding details of Malaparte's house arrest in Lipari. In *The Skin* he says he was taken in chains to the island, but in fact he traveled untrammeled with his mother and two policemen. While there he could read, write, listen to the radio, and receive letters from friends—and write an unpublishable collection of invectives against Muss, whom he calls "The Great Imbecile." There is a bit of duplicity even in the publishing history of these two books. Malaparte pretended he'd finished *Kaputt* in the fall of 1943, but in fact he hadn't prepared it for publication till the spring of 1944; by falsifying the dates, he wanted to suggest he'd written the book before the fall of Mussolini and the Allied landing so that he would look like an early, eager antifascist.

What sort of man was Malaparte? He usually had a mistress but never married, even though Mussolini made it clear that unless he did, the dictator would never appoint him an ambassador, Malaparte's fondest wish. He liked men and could be a regular guy with them, but he could not sustain a friendship with a man. He seemed even less capable of becoming close to a woman, though he was famous as a womanizer. His dog was his dearest friend. Calling him a narcissist seems warranted: he wrote a book called *Woman Like Me*, built a spectacular house cantilevered out over a cliff in Capri that he called House Like Me, and spent three hours every day doing his toilette. One critic said of Malaparte that "at every wedding he wanted to be the bride and at every funeral the dear departed." An enemy said, "He loved his mother and luxury hotels," though in fact he was fairly stoic and certainly courageous; he fought some twenty duels and was severely injured in several. He rigorously maintained his figure—he was six feet tall and weighed 162 pounds—though as he grew older he let himself go; a French writer noted that toward the end he had the bloated face of an emperor disgusted by his spaghetti.

Although his fascist allegiances represented a bad career move, nevertheless Malaparte's fame has continued to grow in Europe. Milan Kundera has written about him, as has Dominique Fernandez; Bernard-Henri Lévy carried *Kaputt* with him into the battle of Sarajevo. Margaret Atwood is a major fan in the New World; maybe she is drawn to his combination of high political seriousness and mythology.

It's difficult to pin down precedents for or influences on Malaparte. Serra tells us that Malaparte admired Chateaubriand, and we can see that Chateaubriand's trick of remembering his years as a starving émigré in London while decades later he is the overfed French ambassador to London—this kind of bifocal vision—would have appealed to Malaparte. But there are few models for his blend of autobiographical realism and grotesque fantasy, unless it is Céline's *Journey to the End of the Night*, with its boatload of angry French colonials heading toward the coast of Africa and plotting to kill Céline, or the ghostly corridors of a New York hotel, the Laugh Calvin; from his window Céline watches the men in the rooms opposite shave at night without removing the cigars from their mouths.

But whereas Céline is always as complaining and paranoid as a taxi driver, Malaparte is discreet, urbane. His vision is Baroque, terrifying, unruffled. In *Kaputt*, his book about the war on the eastern front and Finland, there is a grotesque scene worthy of Visconti's *The Damned* in which a German "king" of Poland (appointed by the Nazis) invites all his guests to visit the Kraków ghetto, which he is convinced is far more humane than the Western press would suggest. At a certain point a German soldier fires his gun; he explains to the German king of Poland that he's shooting at a "rat." The rat, it turns out, is a Jewish child.

In *The Skin* the people of Naples are selling black American soldiers (without the soldiers knowing about it) to other Neapolitans. They are valuable because of their PX privileges—and because they are generous with their pay, especially to the Italian girls they're courting. This strange parody of buying and selling black slaves is presented but not commented on.

In another scene a puritanical Mrs. Flat, an officer in the WACS, is being welcomed to Naples with a big banquet. She is longing to partake in a true "Renaissance" repast, so they have added to the usual Spam and powdered milk a fish course. Throughout the meal they keep hearing the fish course will be a "siren." At last, to everyone's horror, a boiled little girl is served up with a fish tail attached to her body. Revulsed, the Americans refuse to eat the child, though they're assured it's a real mermaid from the city's aquarium.

It turns out that even to this day Neapolitans talk about how the occupying American army, which had forbidden Neapolitans to fish lest they trigger mines laid by the Germans, ate all the rare species from the aquarium; I suppose for Malaparte it was just one small poetic leap from the Emperor William II's octopus and Hirohito's dragonfish to a boiled child served up as a siren.

Perhaps the most beautiful (if grotesque and equally implausible) scene occurs in *Kaputt*. The Finnish army pursues the Soviet cavalry though the forest, which they set on fire. A thousand Russian horses, running from the conflagration, plunge into the lake, which in a moment freezes over. The next day only the horses' heads are visible, floating above the water. Later, on a Sunday, locals go down to the water and sit on the horses' heads and play an accordion and sing.

These haunting tableaux (and I've mentioned only a few) occur again and again in these two books. Fantastic though they may be, they are symbols adequate to the horrors of the war; they are in the same league as Francisco Goya's *Saturn Devouring His Son* or his *The Disasters of War*.

Serra gives us a congenial insider's view of Malaparte. As an Italian diplomat, he understands how to do research into the archives of the Fascist years. He understands the complex Italian social realities that Malaparte's life touched on and explored. He has a sophisticated and complicated view of Mussolini, whom he never confuses with the strutting caricature invented by his enemies. He presents the dictator as a micromanager who personally appointed every dogcatcher in Italy, absorbed every crumb of information brought to his huge empty office in the Palazzo Venezia, never forgot a slight and seldom rewarded a service, a man who read everything, feared and disliked Hitler—in short, a fascinating figure who should be the subject of a later Serra biography. Although Malaparte only met Mussolini five or six times face-to-face, the two men were obsessed with each other. Perhaps Malaparte dramatized this obsession best in his friendship with the dictator's glamorous son-in-law, Galeazzo Ciano, and Mussolini's daughter Edda. In *Kaputt* Malaparte devotes a whole long chapter, "Golf Handicaps," to the last idyllic days of the fascist elite, Count Ciano's world right out of the F. Scott Fitzgerald milieu of boating and cocktails and adultery and beautiful clothes.

I like this writing because it is exotic and vivid and oneiric. I've always been fascinated by a mixture of realism and myth, which in my own fashion animates my novels *Nocturnes for the King of Naples* and *Caracole*. There is great imaginative energy in Malaparte, as there is in Gabriel Garcia Marquez; everything is compact, eloquent, and endlessly inventive.

Chapter 16

The greatest novel in all literature is *Anna Karenina*. I've read it ten times, though I'm none the wiser for it. I think I first studied it when I was thirty, living in San Francisco and being mentored by Simon Karlinsky, the head of the Russian department at Berkeley and a friend of Nabokov. Under his guidance I read Chekhov, Gogol, Ivan Goncharov, Pushkin, Tolstoy, Yevgeny Zamyatin, and many others. Simon had grown up in Manchuria; his mother owned a dress shop in Mukden. As a teen he moved with his family to Los Angeles and aspired to be a composer. In the army he brushed up on his Russian. His musical hopes faded after he saw one of his ballets performed and he hated the score. When his car fell apart in Berkeley by chance, he started to teach Russian there as a language instructor. Soon he was head of the department. He wrote a gay biography of Nikolai Gogol and articles about the history of gay lit in Russia for *Gay Sunshine*. He became an expert in pre-Pushkin Russian drama. He wrote books about Marina Tsvetaeva, the woman poet killed by the Soviets. He introduced me to Mikhail Kuzmin's 1906 *Wings*, the first gay Russian novel.

Tolstoy himself said that if he wanted to say what *Anna Karenina* was "about," he'd have to write it all over again. It is full of push and pull, largely between Tolstoy's reluctant allegiance to his social class and his severe criticism of it. According to translator Richard Pevear's introduction, Tolstoy originally intended Anna to be fat and coarse and ugly and her husband Karenin to be a long-suffering saint (Karlinsky told me that in 1970). Tolstoy must have felt there was something unsatisfactory aesthetically about this original plan and tone, and he set the book aside for a long time. When he returned to it, Anna had become beautiful and wonderfully sympathetic, torn between her passion for her lover, Vronsky, and her love for her little son—and repulsed by her husband with his veiny hands, knuckle cracking, protruding ears, and sober rigidity. As Pevear points out, most of the characters in the novel had their counterparts in real life—with the notable exceptions of Anna and Vronsky. They are fully imagined, though each has the distinctive physical reality so difficult to create ex nihilo. Vronsky has his robust red neck, hairy chest, evenly spaced teeth, and bald spot. He weighs 160 pounds. Anna has her quick, firm, and light step and her slightly broad hips. As Lvov sees him, "Vronsky was a sturdily built, dark-haired man of medium height, with a good-naturedly handsome, extremely calm and firm face." He loves his own body. Anna's beautiful hands and quick tread are her hallmarks.

They each have a moral profile as well. Anna's is that love pardons everything if it's true and passionate. Passion-love—not esteem-love or spiritual love or sisterly love or even maternal love—is her guiding principle, and she ends up hating Vronsky and despising everyone else, herself included. Lvov, the character most resembling Tolstoy, is tempted by suicide since he finds life so purposeless, but eventually, after listening to a peasant's wisdom, he ends up embracing God and the good. Just as he is enlightened by an uneducated muzhik, the wisdom he recovers is the unquestioning faith he'd first learned at his mother's knee.

Vronsky has "a code of rules"—a cardsharp must be paid but not a tailor, no one except a husband can be deceived, one may give but not receive insults, he must respect an honorable woman such as Anna and sooner cut off his hand than fail to show her respect. In short, a "gentlemen's code," or rather an aristocrat's. But Tolstoy's characters are also beset by unconscious motives, desires, or impulses they refuse to admit to themselves. Anna's is jealousy; Vronsky's is ambition ("Ambition was the old dream of his childhood and youth, a dream which he did not confess even to himself, but which was so strong that even now this passion struggled with his love"). Encountering an old comrade, once his equal, who has just received two promotions and a decoration, revives Vronsky's ambitions for rank and glory; if he runs off with Anna and abandons the service, he must give up his military commission and dash his career hopes. One of Anna's great faults is that she idealizes Vronsky: "As at every meeting, she was bringing together her imaginary idea of him (an incomparably better one, impossible in reality) with him as he was."

Vronsky's ambition and conformism to his class codes, turned upside down by his passion for Anna, provide him with an inner conflict. She is more resourceful and imaginative, much finer as a sensibility, but for her, too, passion is destructive. We mustn't forget that Tolstoy's 1889 novella *The Kreutzer Sonata* is a somber look at carnal pleasures; when a wife cheats on her husband, he kills her, but jealousy is not the cause of this violence but, more generally, the "swinish connection" of sex. Couples hate each other when they surrender to sexual desire.

Tolstoy's method is to picture different kinds of marital love and approve only of Lvov's for Kitty. Anna's hatred of her husband, though entirely understandable, allows her to flout morality, cheat on her husband, abandon her son, and kill herself; she is the victim of passionate love. Like Emma Bovary, Anna is a great reader of novels, which awaken but never slake the appetites. Anna, one might say, is an Emma who has succeeded. Emma craves luxury and total devotion from a man. Anna has both—and is miserable. Both have imaginations overexcited by literature. The key scene in *Anna Karenina* occurs during a blizzard on the train back to Petersburg; Anna tries to read an English novel, can't concentrate, and then envies all the characters. When the train stops for a moment, she gets off for a breath of fresh air—and runs into Vronsky, who is quite obviously lovesick over her. One could say she's been prepared for this great passion by the longings raised in her by the novel. In the train she reads by the light of a candle clamped to her book. Hundreds of pages later in *Anna Karenina*, the last words about her are: "And the candle by the light of which she had been reading that book filled with anxieties, deceptions, grief and evil, flared up brighter than ever, lit up for her all that had once been in darkness, sputtered, grew dim and went out forever."

The novel opens with Anna's brother, Stiva, who squanders his money, neglects his wife and children, frequents loose women; he is the victim of the love of pleasure. Anna's husband, Karenin, is moralizing, unforgiving, self-righteous, and in love with social position, not human beings. He wants to be "correct," not human—though, being Russian, he has an elated moment in which he acts totally out of character. Anna almost dies of puerperal fever when she gives birth to Vronsky's daughter. Karenin is so overwhelmed and bewildered that he forgives Anna, embraces Vronsky, and takes care of the new baby. This extreme change of heart is only temporary, however. Early on, Tolstoy writes that Karenin "stood face-to-face with life, confronting the possibility of his wife loving someone else besides him, and it was this that seemed so senseless and incomprehensible to him, because it was life itself. All his life Alexey Alexandrovitch had lived and worked in spheres of service that dealt with reflections of life. And each time he had encountered life itself, he had drawn back." Tolstoy compares him to a man walking over an abyss on a bridge that starts to crumble.

———

Just as Tolstoy shows different kinds of married love (there is even a gay pair, an old and young soldier, whom everyone ridicules), in the same way he shows various forms of piety, almost all false. Lydia Ivanovna adheres to that "new, rapturous, mystical mood which had recently spread in Petersburg," a sort of self-satisfied pietism. When Karenin tells her he feels ashamed of the position of cuckold he finds himself in, Lydia ecstatically replies, "It was not you who accomplished that lofty act of forgiveness, which I admire along with everyone, but He, dwelling in your heart . . . and therefore you cannot be ashamed of your action."

But she is a hypocrite, always falling in love with men and women who are distinguished, important. She is governed by a French clairvoyant, who pretends to fall asleep and speak as an oracle. It is he, a thorough fake, who pronounces against a divorce between Anna and Karenin—and thus seals Anna's fate. Anna herself, after living apart in Italy, is struck by how Lydia is consumed by hate though she professes to be a Christian. "In fact, it's ridiculous," Anna thinks, "her goal is virtue, she's a Christian, yet she's angry all the time, and they're all enemies on account of Christianity and virtue."

Possibly the words that occur the most often in this book are *shame* and *shameful*, if it's not *blush*. Was that just a leakage from Tolstoy's own experience onto his characters? Several times it's mentioned how awkward Lvov feels in society and in the city, in general. He constantly feels he's committed a faux pas or broken the rules somehow or offended someone he loves.

That unease is typified by Lvov's attitude toward the custom of paying calls: "How is it? A stranger comes, sits down, stays for no reason, bothers them, upsets himself, and then leaves." This is an example of the technique of defamiliarization at which Tolstoy excels and which the later Russian formalists celebrated. Essentially it's the technique of describing a familiar social rite (a first ball, the opera, social calls) as if one is from Mars and fails to understand the governing conventions.

Could it be that Tolstoy's natural turning to this device sprang from his own social awkwardness, his shyness? Of course there are literary forebears such as *Tristram Shandy* (extremely popular in Russia) or Pushkin himself, but Tolstoy's reliance on this device feels more a matter of his character than his influences.

He returns to this alienated way of looking at things again and again. The death of Lvov's brother in a dirty provincial inn produces feelings akin to those he experienced upon seeing his newborn son: "This beautiful baby inspired only a feeling of squeamishness and pity in him—" until Dmitri suddenly sneezes. "He scarcely noticed the strange feeling of senseless joy and even pride he'd experienced when the baby sneezed." In the same way the unearned tenderness and wonder that Lvov feels during the night before his engagement to Kitty is firmed up is typical of Tolstoy's ability to "excavate" clichéd sites and dig up new treasures.

As I mentioned, Tolstoy started off by conceiving Anna as a she-devil and Karenin as a saint. When he began writing the book three years later, I would contend that there are pentimenti in the finished composition that give glimpses of this original design. As early as the ball in which Anna meets Vronsky, Kitty perceives something "terrible and cruel" about Anna. Toward the end of the book, Anna is possessed by a "demon," her word for jealousy. When she first acknowledges she's in love with Vronsky, she knows feelings that are "joyful, burning and exciting"—a heady mix that can lure an unsuspecting woman to destruction. Anna forgives her brother for cheating on his wife, Dolly, and convinces Dolly to forgive him too—which leads to a life of unhappiness and poverty. Karenin's sudden, short-lived spirit of forgiveness to Anna, Vronsky, and their baby girl is a leftover from the initial sketch of Karenin as a saint, I imagine, just as Lydia Ivanovna's praise of Karenin's saintliness is surely a pentimento.

Tolstoy was dominated by moral ideas, as Pevear says in his excellent introduction. He had always intended Anna's suicide as the punishment for her adultery, but he struggled with himself over this tragic outcome. In the long interval between conception and execution, Anna had become warm, maternal, attractive, and imaginative, and Karenin had become unfeeling, coldly ambitious, physically repulsive, and lacking all human sympathy, concerned only with his reputation and his career. Vronsky's love makes Anna realize Karenin never loved her and simply observed the proprieties. Mikhail Bakhtin, the Soviet-era critic, argued that Tolstoy was constantly in conflict with his own preconceptions and those of the reader. That's what provides the artistic struggle on every page, this restless investigation of every idea and sentiment. Bakhtin calls it "the dialogic imagination," that is, a mind constantly in conflict, in dialogue, with itself.

Just to choose a trifling example, take his shifting attitudes toward Russians speaking French. Tolstoy was a count and subscribed to some of the values of his class, though he always called them into question. Lvov, Tolstoy's stand-in, admires other Russians for their ease and good accents in speaking French, but he becomes irritated with Dolly when she makes her daughter respond in French whenever she is addressed in French. He vows to himself he'll never require his children to speak French. He despises the pastimes of his fellow aristocrats and complains that in Moscow he is so busy being idle he can accomplish nothing.

Only now as an old reader do I recognize how alienated Tolstoy must have felt from his social class, and that this "defamiliarization" is the chief ornament of his writing. As an adolescent I envied Tolstoy's knowledge of all the rites of passage of ordinary life, and I feared that my homosexuality would deprive me of an understanding of "real" people and what they undergo—birth, courtship, marriage, adultery, divorce, and so on. Now I see that these experiences (or their equivalents) touch every life.

In *Anna Karenina* we see both Tolstoy the realistic portrayer of contemporary society and Tolstoy the moralist. Many readers, especially in Europe and America, love the realist and deplore the moralist and consider Tolstoy's late writings with regret. But my position is that, as long as there is a balance between the two approaches, the writing takes on an unrivaled seriousness. So many novelists of our time eschew any "message," as if it's an aesthetic flaw. Maybe critics want to preserve our self-defeatingly clamorous culture by making sure no radical idea actually gets through and can be heard. And yet the morality of Dickens's *Hard Times* and Tolstoy's *Resurrection* is what gives them rigor and animation.

Just two more notes about Tolstoy. First, he does show a range of parent-child relationships. Karenin grew up an underloved orphan. Vronsky despises his mother; Anna loves her son but not her daughter. Lvov dreams not of passion but of family life: "He could not be at peace, because he, who had dreamed of family life for so long, who felt himself so ripe for it, was still not married and was farther than ever from marriage." Lvov loved his mother, who died young.

The other note I want to make is Tolstoy's relationship to Stendhal's ideas about love. Stendhal's favorite of his own books was *On Love*, where he proposes that two people need some outside trigger to make them fall in love. In *Charterhouse* Fabrizio falls in love with his aunt, the duchess, when someone utters the word *love* in their presence, which acts as a wake-up call. In *Anna Karenina* this moment of what Stendhal calls "crystallization" occurs when Anna, all stoked by the novel of "English happiness" she has been reading on the train, runs into Vronsky at the train station during a blizzard. He salutes and bows and asks if he can be of service to her. She takes a long time to answer. "She had no need to ask why he was there. She knew it as certainly as if he had told her that he was there in order to be where she was"—an idea that frightens her and makes her happy. This is the famous "crystallization" of Stendhal. Just as Tolstoy followed Stendhal's manner of depicting war (it's too confusing for the participants to make sense of it), in the same way, I'd contend, he follows Stendhal's theories about how people fall in love.

For instance, just as Anna overrates Vronsky, Stendhal tells us that after crystallization the lover endows the beloved "with a thousand perfections" and tends to "overrate wildly," just as Anna feels intense pleasure in thinking beside the train in a blizzard that Vronsky has followed her: "A woman in love finds so much happiness in the feelings she is experiencing that she is unable to pretend; tired of being prudent, she throws caution to the wind and flings herself blindly into the happiness of loving." Love is different for women and men: "What brings certainty and happiness to one lover [the man] brings danger and almost humiliation to the other [the woman]." Stendhal feels love feeds on "solitude and leisure," both of which Anna has in abundance. "Beauty"—in this case Anna's— "is only the promise of happiness." Stendhal tells us that women most admire force of character in a man—"hence the success of very serious young officers." The fact that Officer Vronsky's passion is boundless and imprudent means (to him and to Anna) it's not just a high-society ritual. Stendhal believes people are ripe for love when they are "bored by living without loving." In other words, Tolstoy could easily have been using Stendhal's book to establish the sequence of pleasures and pains, doubts and exaltation, in love. What is so remarkable about *Anna Karenina* is its classic, inevitable topography of love. To be sure, Tolstoy draws on his own weirdness—all that shame, particularly the shame Anna feels after finally sleeping with Vronsky. But Stendhal's usefulness, sanity, and innocence serve as useful correctives to Tolstoy's puritanical gloom.

Tolstoy also had ideas about art, which he dramatized in *Anna Karenina*. Vronsky, idle and in Italy, decides to become a painter, but he soon becomes bored by it, especially when he meets a real painter of talent, Mikhailov. For an instant Tolstoy gets into Mikhailov's head. As Vronsky and Anna are first looking at his work, Mikhailov becomes utterly dependent on their opinions, even though he despises them as dilettantes: "For those few seconds he believed in advance the highest, the fairest judgment would be pronounced by them, precisely by these visitors whom he had so despised a moment ago. He forgot everything he thought before about his picture during the three years he'd been painting it." When the visitors approve of something, "Mikhailov was delighted . . . That this opinion was one of a million opinions which, as Mikhailov well knew, would all be correct, did not diminish its significance." Every writer (or painter?) knows this irrational power we assign to complete philistines or strangers who sit in judgment of our work.

Vronsky looks down on an aristocratic friend who writes, since gentlemen don't "scribble." Mikhailov looks down on Vronsky's painting, though he knows he can't forbid him to do it. "It was impossible to forbid a man to make a big wax doll and kiss it. But if this man with the doll came and sat in front of a man in love and began to caress his doll the way the man in love caressed his beloved, the man in love would find it unpleasant." Mikhailov finds Vronsky's way of taking his daubs so seriously an insult to true art. Karenin reads all the latest books but is untouched by them; he simply wants to be au courant. Anna reads novels obsessively, especially after society banishes her, and they only further coarsen her sentiments.

We feel in reading Tolstoy that nothing was beyond his powers—the relief a poor peasant woman feels after the death of her baby (one fewer mouth to feed); the amorousness between a horse and his rider (Vronsky); the elation a child feels on seeing his mother (Anna) who he had been told was dead; the irritation an old family retainer experiences when her housekeeping ways are changed by the new mistress (Kitty); the envy Dolly feels temporarily when confronted with Anna's beautiful, perfectly appointed house, until she realizes how miserable Anna is. There is even the suggestion that Karenin lusts after all those healthy, attractive gentlemen of the bedchamber with their fat legs—a mixture of envy, desire, and disapproval. The last few pages describing Anna's thoughts on her way to her death (perhaps the beginning of stream-of-consciousness in literature) convey unforgettably her despair and her hate for everyone and everything.

Tolstoy's worldliness makes him an assured, accurate observer of society—and his spirituality makes him a biting critic of society, just as Proust's bad health and Jewishness and homosexuality turned him into a deeply disabused observer of the society his snobbism had caused him to court. In both Tolstoy and Proust there is a constant dynamic tension between their newfound values and the comfortable habits of their familiar milieus.

Who is our Tolstoy today? Certainly the young Anglo-Indian writer Neel Mukherjee has the requisite breadth of compassionate understanding, nowhere more so than in *A State of Freedom*, his great hymn to India's poor. Everyone from a fierce young female Communist soldier to a miserable peasant who hopes to earn a few pennies from a dancing bear he captures and trains, from a maid who is kept prisoner by her bosses in Mumbai to a cook who must constantly outdo herself to satisfy the anglicized son of her employers—here are the few victories and steep defeats of an entire population of the oppressed, the baseline of human suffering.

Chapter 17

Every year brings new novels that are entirely or largely original. Books about literature, critical works, emphasize continuity, since it's easier to trace influences than to see what is new. A book reviewer will compare everything strange to Kafka or everything romantic and epic to Melville, no matter how distinctive a new work of fiction might be. And yet when I look at the books that were published recently in various languages, I can find many surprises. Real writers prize what is original.

For instance, Daša Drndić's excellent novel *Trieste* is what might be called "docufiction"; that is, it combines large bits of raw information (the names and dates of Holocaust victims from Gorizia) with the tale of a child born to a local woman and a Nazi soldier—a child raised in a nursery for privileged "Aryan" babies.

The border between fiction and nonfiction is getting thinner and thinner. Ben Lerner, a young American, recently brought out a novel titled *10:04* in which he tells what seems an autobiographical story of a successful young Brooklyn writer and places it in the blackout that occurred in New York after Hurricane Sandy. One of the themes of the book is the strange doubling of déjà vu, though the past experiences don't fully coincide with the present; this doubling seems to parallel the close but not exact fit between the author and the protagonist.

Of course the most celebrated example of this erased frontier between novel and memoir is *My Struggle*, the six-volume examination of Karl Ove Knausgaard's life. People incorrectly compare him to Proust. Proust reinvents his life story, whereas Knausgaard remains as faithful to his experiences as possible. Whereas the protagonist of *À la recherche du temps perdu* is a neurasthenic, asthmatic mama's boy, Knausgaard is average to a fascinating, hallucinatory degree—he likes beer, girls, sports, pop music—and where he is abnormal, in his fraught relationship with his father or in his adolescent battle with ejaculation praecox, he remains just as riveting. No one has ever attempted this level of micro-confession before.

In France, Emmanuel Carrère, after writing fiction successfully (*La Moustache, La Classe de neige*), has turned to one masterpiece after another of nonfiction. In some of his books he plays a role, major or minor; in others he is almost entirely absent. For instance, in *L'Adversaire* he tells the real-life story of a man who pretends to be a doctor and to work in Geneva but who actually sits in his car all day in the woods and maintains his false story with his wife and children, his parents, his in-laws, his mistress, living off their retirement savings, pretending he is investing them at advantageous rates—until, when the mistress demands that he immediately reimburse her, his whole world falls apart. He burns his home with his family in it, murders his in-laws—and is captured and sentenced for life to prison. In prison he claims that he has repented and found Christ, though Carrère seriously doubts him.

In a *Paris Review* interview, Carrère gives us a practice he has followed, a piece of advice given by the German Romantic Ludwig Börne: "For three successive days, force yourself to write, without denaturalizing or hypocrisy, everything that crosses your mind. Write what you think of yourself, your wives, Goethe, the Turkish war, the Last Judgment, your superiors, and you will be stupefied to see how many new thoughts have poured forth. That is what constitutes the art of becoming an original writer in three days."

After struggling for several years to write *L'Adversaire* in the third person, from several different points of view, Carrère essentially abandoned the project, having accumulated 100,000 pages of research. At the last moment he decided to write a sort of memo to himself in the first person about what the man and the event had meant to him. He started by comparing his own activities on a particular day with those of the murderer Jean-Claude Romand: "On the Saturday morning of January

9, 1993, while Jean-Claude Romand was killing his wife and children, I was with mine in a parent-teacher meeting at the school attended by Gabriel, our eldest son. He was five years old, the same age as Antoine Romand. Then we went to have lunch with my parents, as Jean-Claude Romand did with his, whom he killed after their meal." The rest of the book followed easily.

Carrère admits that he uses all the techniques he learned as a novelist to make his nonfiction narratives taut and suspenseful. He has gone on to write about post-Soviet Russia, about the devastation of the tsunami that he witnessed in Java, about a semi-pornographic letter he wrote to his girl-friend, about his maternal grandfather's collaboration with the Nazis in occupied Bordeaux, and, most recently, in *Royaume*, about all his struggles with religion and the history of Christianity.

If treading the thin line between fiction and memoir is one innova-tion in literature, then another is represented by Vladimir Sorokin, who writes a sort of fantasist dystopia in *Day of the Oprichnik*. Like Gary Shteyngart—who imagines in *Super Sad True Love Story* what New York would be like under the rule of the Chinese, a world in which everyone's statistics and net worth will be flashed publicly as one walks down the street—Sorokin paints a horrifying picture of the future of a lawless, violent Russia. But with this difference: not all the elements in Sorokin's novel are exact fits or exaggerations of Putin's Russia. Many of the happenings and gadgets are fanciful inventions or reenactments of Russia's imperial past, which lend a fairy-tale atmosphere to this dark tale. Dystopia (logical or fanciful) is proving to be an entertaining or frightening direction for the novel to take.

If dystopia is a grim picture of the future, the modern novel has seri-ously rethought the historical novel, a genre that was often dismissed in the past. *Pure* by the British writer Andrew Miller is a painfully exact reimagining of the reburying of hundreds of bodies in late eighteenth-century Paris. Whereas the historical novel a hundred years ago was often a costume drama, a sword-and-cape melodrama full of romantic wish fulfillment and contemporary sentiments in brocaded gowns, the renewed historical novel points up the strangeness of the past. Penelope

Fitzgerald's *The Blue Flower* forgoes the thick impasto of historical research in favor of the breathing detail; we feel as if we're in the same room as the characters. *Master Georgie* by Beryl Bainbridge takes us by the hand to the Crimean War, just as Hilary Mantel's *Wolf Hall* transports us to the dangerous court of Henry VIII. We can see the mole on a neck, the trembling of a hand as it touches a necklace. Zeroing in on telling details—this is the formula for the new historical novel. It is one I followed in *Hotel de Dream* about the late-nineteenth-century American writer Stephen Crane.

Of course not all the innovations in fiction are formal; in many cases they are the expression of new voices, previously unheard. Chimamanda Ngozi Adichie's *Half of a Yellow Sun* creates the tensions in the Christian half of Nigeria during a conflict with the northern, Muslim half. Neel Mukherjee in *The Lives of Others* offers us a passport into India—several periods, many regions, different castes. It was nominated for the Booker; the book that won that year was *The Narrow Road to the Deep North* by the Tasmanian writer Richard Flanagan, a re-creation of the life of Australian prisoners of war in Burma under Japanese rule. What makes this book remarkable is the compassion and insight it shows toward the Japanese characters during defeat and occupation.

The novel is alive and thriving through various strategies of renovation. The merging of fiction and reality, of memoir and narrative, is one great current source of strength. The reimagining of the historical novel is a second. And the third is the admission of new voices previously unheard or silenced.

Gay subject matter is now very familiar, but there remain many areas to explore. For instance, in *Jack Holmes and His Friend* I wrote about something very common in real life, the nonsexual friendship between a straight man and a gay man over many years, a story I tackled first from the gay guy's point of view and then from the straight man's. John Boyne treats the same subject—friendship between a gay man and a straight man—in his masterful *The Heart's Invisible Furies*. In my recent novel *Our Young Man*, I take up the subject of a male model who never ages—in that way like Dorian Gray, except not evil.

When I began to write *A Boy's Own Story*, nobodies did not write their memoirs. You had to be a famous general or actor or inventor. I called my book a novel, which gave me the freedom to change the chronology and to make my character a bit more representative than I actually was in real life. Now this blend of genres is called autofiction, but then no such term existed.

I ended up by writing a trilogy including *The Beautiful Room Is Empty* and *The Farewell Symphony*, books that took us through the beginning of gay liberation in 1969 and into the AIDS years. I found this subject matter exciting because it was new; most writers are looking for subjects that are both new and universal.

I've never written about the future (perhaps I don't have that kind of imagination), but I have published two historical novels. For me the way into a historical novel is to find a blank page, something unknown, and fill it in. When history gives out, fiction takes over. In the case of Stephen Crane, he was reputedly writing a gay novel about a boy prostitute, but he was forced by friends to tear it up—too scandalous. I decided to write it for him, interweaving it with known details of Crane's own life and early death, at age twenty-eight, from tuberculosis.

When I wrote *Fanny* I knew that Frances Trollope, mother of the novelist, had come to the United States in the 1820s and lived on the Memphis plantation of the Scottish idealist Frances Wright. I wanted to pit a survivor, Mrs. Trollope, against a rich, uncompromising idealist, Miss Wright. Much was known about each woman, but only public acts; it was up to me to invent the unrecorded feelings during this very optimistic period in American history.

I've also written three fantasy novels—not sci-fi fantasy but strange overlayings of different historical periods: ancient Japan and modern New York in *Forgetting Elena*, for instance.

Because I write biographies and essays as well as novels and plays, in my mind there is a clear distinction between truth and invention. Like most readers, I'm offended when writers make things up in what purports to be a memoir. The contract with the reader is very different in a novel and in a real autobiography.

But I've wandered rather far afield. I just wanted to suggest that literature is as rich and fertile as it has ever been, and that writers are finding new ways to make its appeal broader and deeper. The novel remains the one artistic form to explore our thoughts, to get inside our heads, and that is where we live.

Postface

When I was a little child, my sister, who was nearly four years older, was astonished that I couldn't read. We were in my mother's old Ford, driving around the main square of Hyde Park, and my sister pointed to a sign and said, "You honestly can't read that?"

"No," I said sullenly. "What does it say?"

"Graeter's," she announced triumphantly, the name of Cincinnati's premier ice cream maker. "Can't you see that? What does it say to you?" She wasn't being mean; she was genuinely puzzled. Reading was a magical portal—once you passed through it, you couldn't even imagine going back.

I must have been four. Two years later I could read, or at least "sound out" syllables (that was the method then). When I realized that I could interpret these hieroglyphics, I felt so free, as if a whole new world had been opened to me. Now I could hear a chorus of voices, even those coming from other centuries and cultures. I was no longer bound to the squalid here and now, to my mother's web-spinning of agreeable fantasies or my father's sudden eruptions of rage, to the sweating summers of that age before air conditioning.

I remember toddling into my mother's room, where she was taking a perfumed bubble bath in the late afternoon. I announced (or maybe thought), "I'm free. I can read."

Could I really have had such an improbable thought at age six? Or have I just told myself that that thought occurred to me then? And yet I remember my mother's sweetness, the good smell, the afternoon sunlight, and my very real feeling of joyful liberation. And, quite concretely, reading has always struck me as a passport to the world, one in which characters are more real than actual people, where values are more intense than in the dim light of reality, where characters fly up into destinies rather than paddle around in ambiguity.

I felt like a blind person who'd just regained his sight. I was no longer a Cincinnatian but rather an earthling. If things were clearly written in English, there was no text that was off-limits. I never read the standard children's classics. No *Wind in the Willows*. Only recently did I get around to *Treasure Island*.

In my twenties and thirties no book was too ambitious for me; I worked my way through Theodor Adorno and Heinrich von Kleist, Roland Barthes and Michel Foucault, though I was drunk most of the time and often had to hold one eye shut. I suppose I was hanging out with a pretty brainy crowd back then, and I felt I had to keep up. I doubt I retained much, though in my thirties and forties I reviewed several books by Barthes and Foucault.

I was so driven back then, it never would have occurred to me to reread a book! My goal was to have read everything, or at least the major works that appealed to me, that seemed essential. Perhaps because I'd never done any graduate work, I felt inferior. I'd never read *The Faerie Queene*. Worse, I'd been a writer for eight years for Time-Life Books, the ultimate home of the middle-brow. Although I invariably said defensively, "I'm not an intellectual," I wanted to be one—or at least to be able to refuse demurely that title. Sometimes I took comfort in the idea I was an artist, not an intellectual. I even resorted to the ridiculously snobbish notion I was a "gentleman amateur" and not an intellectual. But I've always wanted to have the choice to join any club, especially one that might reject me. For instance, I made a major effort to join the Century Club, for which one had to be sponsored by eleven or twelve current members. Two years after I was accepted, I resigned. Too many lawyers.

Now I do reread at least two books every year—*Anna Karenina* and Henry Green's *Nothing*. Although these two novels are so different one from the other, they both reward closer scrutiny, so much so they scarcely resemble the same book one remembers having read the year before. People complain about the Kitty and Lvov parts of *Anna Karenina*, but that's a frivolous charge. Their love stands in dramatic contrast to Anna's and Vronsky's passion and is the necessary counterweight to that tragic tale. In the same way, some readers treat *Nothing* the way they regard all comedy—as lightweight. Actually it is a profound study of the generations and social classes—and unexpectedly it sides with the older, richer people.

The other book I've reread five times in my life is Proust's. When I was a teenager I read it as the bible of snobbism; it gave me a whole vocabulary to describe this vice that Proust calls "narrow but deep." Now I read it as the definitive condemnation of snobbism.

In this memoir I've reread a few favorites by Colette, Nabokov, and Tolstoy and read for the first time novels by Guyotat, Giono, and Malaparte. Do we prefer to revisit books we love or to explore the unknown? Are we happier to find new things in the old or to detect familiar themes and strategies in the utterly new and startling? The brilliant novelist of modern manners Alison Lurie once explained to me why she was more popular in England than in America. "For the English I'm writing about an unfamiliar subject [American academic and artistic life] in a familiar style of social satire, whereas for Americans I'm writing in an unusual style about familiar subjects." Has she touched on an explanation of why we like certain books and not others?

Joe Brainard reportedly said on his deathbed, "The best thing about dying is that you never have to go to another poetry reading." How many times I've had to sit through poetry readings in a stuffy room with subaqueous light at the end of a long day and fight against falling asleep! The mind loves a narrative, and in my half sleep my poor brain has spun cartoons made up of chance words, my embarrassment, trace memories (what Freudians call dismissively "the daily residue"), and my shipwrecked will to wake up, or at least not snore.

Everyone says poetry is an oral art, and perhaps some of it is meant to be read out loud. Good actors can make us understand passages in Shakespeare that use obsolete language, though I hate it when pedants hope to indicate the line break or the caesura. I could never make sense of *The*

Tempest until I saw it onstage. On the page I could never keep track of all the characters. Charles Lamb argued in an essay that reading Shakespeare is preferable to seeing him produced, and maybe hammy acting and garish sets and thundering exits and entrances do topple certain of Shakespeare's cloud castles, but great performances can dial into sharp focus even the vaguest verse.

But does modern poetry gain from being recited out loud? James Merrill was a smooth, trained reader and the smile in his voice could give the reader permission to laugh at his improbable mixture of metaphysics and gossip. His light social tone so often gives way to the sublime that a reader less civilized than he scarcely knows what is funny and what is serious (sometimes both at once, since he thought wisdom was expressed in puns and that the language itself *is* the collective unconscious).

Percussive poetry like Pound's translation of the Anglo-Saxon *The Seafarer* as read by the author himself to the beat of drums can be riveting; a casual scanning of the page would never render the granitic, prehistoric force of this masterpiece. In his recitation (now on YouTube) Pound rolls his *r*'s, thuds the final *d*'s, and maintains a shaman's monotone. Maybe Paul Verlaine's musical verse (or John Keats's) is improved by being read out loud, but most twentieth- or twenty-first-century verse is too abstract or too dense to be understood on a single hearing. The *mise-en-page*, the line breaks, the Latinate or Anglo-Saxon origins of the words, as in *tomb* and *grave* ("The tomb in Palestine / Is not the porch of spirits lingering. / It is the grave of Jesus, where he lay")—these are all elements that surrender themselves only to close reading.

With prose the problem is the speed. Everyone reads at a different pace, and some texts are not interesting or intricate enough to be dosed out at conversational speed. We get it; we want to scan it. Perhaps some prose is enough like a taut play script that it profits from being read aloud, but almost always a live reading of prose is an exercise in vanity. It may be valuable for the fiction writer to gauge the response of his audience, to listen for contradictions or unintended echoes, to detect where people's attention wanders. But do these practical benefits for the writer outweigh the torture undergone by the public?

Silent, solitary reading (if the book is good) is the best conversation, with all the uhs and ahs edited out, the dead metaphors buried, the dialogue sharpened, the descriptions vivid, the suspense rising, the characters hovering between the unique and the representative. In the great Italian and French guides to good conversation during the Renaissance and seventeenth century, conversation must avoid pedantry and cruelty and seek above all to please and to entertain. Finally it must be natural; affectation is the worst sin, far worse than flattery, which may even be desirable. In her definitive study *The Age of Conversation*, Benedetta Craveri (granddaughter to the philosopher Benedetto Croce) argues that good conversation should not make anyone feel inferior or ill at ease but rather the object of a total consideration. And Simone Weil, the French religious philosopher, thought paying attention was a form of prayer.

The novelist or essayist should never mystify for no good reason. We should know why the marquise goes out at five o'clock (if it's relevant). In an essay we should not be thrown off by academese. An idea may be difficult, but not its expression, as I learned from my beloved Marilyn; the words should be as lucid as possible. The assumption should be that the reader is intelligent but not necessarily informed.

Acknowledgments

I would like to acknowledge the generous and extensive help of my editors, Anton Mueller and Michael Fishwick, in helping me prepare this manuscript for publication. My agent, Amanda Urban, and her very intelligent assistant, Molly Atlas, made wonderful suggestions. My husband, Michael Carroll, went over every word, as did the novelist Neel Mukherjee.

My friend, Richard Bates, typed the manuscript. Warren Platt provided me with bibliographical hints. Carrie Hsieh, the production editor, and Miranda Ottewell, the copy editor, did brilliant jobs.

A NOTE ON THE AUTHOR

Edmund White is the author of many novels, including *A Boy's Own Story*, *The Beautiful Room Is Empty*, *The Farewell Symphony*, and, most recently, *Our Young Man*. His nonfiction includes *City Boy*, *Inside a Pearl*, and other memoirs; *The Flâneur*, about Paris; and literary biographies and essays. He was named the winner of the 2018 PEN/ Saul Bellow Award for Achievement in American Fiction. White lives in New York.